AMERICAN CONNECTIONS

✦ ✦ ✦

The Founding Fathers.

Networked.

JAMES BURKE

SIMON & SCHUSTER PAPERBACKS

NEW YORK   LONDON   TORONTO   SYDNEY

SIMON & SCHUSTER PAPERBACKS
Rockefeller Center
1230 Avenue of the Americas
New York, NY 10020

First Simon & Schuster trade paperback edition 2007

SIMON & SCHUSTER PAPERBACKS and colophon are registered trademarks
of Simon & Schuster, Inc.

For information regarding special discounts for bulk purchases,
please contact Simon & Schuster Special Sales at 1-800-456-6798
or business@simonandschuster.com.

Designed by Dana Sloan

Manufactured in the United States of America

1   3   5   7   9   10   8   3   4   2

Library of Congress Cataloging-in-Publication Data

Burke, James, 1936–
American connections : the founding fathers networked / James Burke.
        p.   cm.
Includes bibliographical references and index.
1. United States. Declaration of Independence—Signers—Biography. 2. States-
men—United States—Biography. 3. Legislators—United States—Biography. 4.
Politicians—United States—Biography. 5. United States—History—Revolution,
1775–1783—Biography. 6. United States—History—1783–1815—Biography. 7.
Biography—Miscellanea. 8. History—Miscellanea. I. Title.
                E221.B95 2007
              973.3'130922—dc22
                   2007003500

ISBN-13: 978-0-7432-8226-0
ISBN-10:   0-7432-8226-4

To Madeline

ACKNOWLEDGMENTS

I should like to express my grateful thanks to Jay Hornsby and Patrick McKercher for their meticulous and rewarding help in research.

Thanks are also due to Jack Kelly for his painstaking care with the artwork.

CONTENTS

FALL 1776 AND LATER

PREFACE

The trouble with iconic heroes like the Signers of the Declaration of Independence (note the reverential uppercase) is that they're like stuffed exhibits in museum cases—passed by thousands of children sleepwalking their way through an educational tour, who never visit the signers again. Most of us don't remember their names.

Heroes also become imbued with virtues we wish on them—such characteristics as honesty, selflessness, and courage in the face of danger. And while it is true that what the signers did was dangerous and could have got them strung up, not all were honest and few if any were self-less. Nearly half of them would much have preferred some kind of compromise with the British. One of them even repudiated his signature. And of course the Brits regarded them all as what would today be called "terrorists."

One reason for this book is to remind readers briefly of the signers' flesh-and-blood characters: Some were crooks, some had dysfunctional families, some were involved in financial shenanigans, some were masters at political backstabbing, many were egomaniacs, and a few were just good people.

The other reason for the book is to connect these men to the reader and the modern world. Historical figures are always a surprisingly short distance away in time. You may have heard your grandfather speak of his grandfather, who talked about his grandfather. That's when the signers lived. They're close. And not so different from us.

The past feels like a foreign country only because of all those wigs and breeches and strange behavior. But think: In the 1960s men had shoulder-length hair and wore flared pants. In the 1950s, before contraceptive pills, unmarried motherhood was a disgrace. Behind their contemporary fashions and social rules the signers were essentially much like us. Of course marvels like electricity and airplanes and computers would be incomprehensible to them. But if you were transported to the eighteenth century, would you know how to send a letter or even how to write it? How to prepare a quill pen and a sheet of parchment? And how would you dry the ink? What was the equivalent of an envelope? It's a mistake to think that people in the past were different or stupid just because we don't think they could handle our modern technology. Given time, even a caveman could learn to use a computer. And, by the way, the Upper Paleolithic was only five hundred grandfathers away.

I've tried to link the signers even more directly to us with an approach I've been using for thirty years, which has recently become known as "six degrees of separation." In this way each signer triggers a chain of events that links him to the modern world through a series of connections: Someone he knew knew someone who knew someone, and so on.

These trails through history show how incredibly diverse are the ties that connect us to each other, back and forward in time and space. The network linking the signers and their modern counterparts is peopled by spies, assassins, cuckolds, fraudsters, murderers, the incestuous, bomb-throwers, pillmakers, inventors, artists, musicians, statesmen, royalty, explorers, infanticides, transvestites, counterfeiters, con men, doctors, lovers, heroes, scientists, clergymen, and a host of others. And if you look far enough, you, too, are linked to this network. You are linked to the signers. We all are. It may be a few more than six connections, but not that many more.

In a medium other than print I might have been able to offer each reader (user?) the means to make his own connections so as to become part of the narrative. Perhaps at some point in the future this book will take that form and you'll be able to make the connections yourself. Meantime, next best (and half-proving the point), I've connected each signer to someone or something bearing his name in the modern world.

Why write a book like this? Well, writing beats real work. And I hope you'll find it diverting. History is where we come from, so it's worth a look. And as navigators say: you don't know where you're going if you don't know where you've been.

And perhaps there's a more serious reason. In a world fast becoming more interdependent and interconnected, where change happens faster than ever because of the way people and ideas connect, we are all on a communications network of some sort and we feel the effects of change much more quickly than even only a decade ago. Innovation comes so frequently now that by the time you understand how some new gizmo works it's already obsolete. We need to learn to handle accelerating rates of change by becoming more aware of how change happens. One way to do this is to think more connectedly than we have been educated to do. Because if an event in Uzbekistan is going to cause the closure of the company we work for in Oshkosh, the sooner we find ways to second-guess that event the better for us.

I hope this book will provide an example of interconnected thinking that will encourage you to try it, too.

One last note: Many people believe the Declaration was signed on July 4. In fact that was the date of the congressional vote agreeing to the wording of the document. On July 5 a version was printed and signed by John Hancock (president of Congress) and Charles Thomson (secretary), and this was distributed to state assembles and other interested groups. On July 19 Congress ordered a formal version (in special formal handwriting) to be printed and when this was ready, on August 2, fifty-one delegates finally signed. Five delegates were absent for reasons of ill health or army duties, and these men signed later on. A few congressional delegates never signed.

London 2007

August 2, 1776

CHAPTER ONE

JohnHancock

JOHN HANCOCK (MA) was thirty-nine. He was an egomaniac and nobody liked him. He signed first because he was presiding officer of the Continental Congress. You can tell from the size and flamboyance of his signature on the Declaration (biggest by far) why he was unpopular. When he left Congress to the automatic vote of thanks, none of his Massachusetts colleagues would sign it. Somebody called him "pompous, vain and self-important."

Hancock got what he wanted because everybody owed him money. Thanks to whale oil trade, real estate, and most of all, government contracts he was a mover and shaker, so in 1785 he became seventh "President of the United States in Congress Assembled" (of the ten presidents under the Articles of Confederation). Illness caused Hancock to step aside for the eighth POTUSICA (as the Secret Service might have termed it), Nathaniel Gorham.

Gorham had spent some time on the wild side as a privateer attacking British shipping. What he lacked in public speaking he more than made up for in political smarts, even going so far (in 1786 during a brief, armed insurrection against the Massachusetts government) as to suggest the need for an American constitutional monarch to provide political stability. Gorham approached Prince Henry of Prussia with the offer. No, thanks. Others had the same idea and even major players like

Monroe and Hamilton (and some say Washington himself) sent a delegation to discuss an American royalty with the claimant to the British throne, Prince Charles Edward Stuart (aka "Bonnie Prince Charlie").

However, long before things came to a regal pass the insurrection in Massachusetts subsided and republicanism looked as if it would survive. Besides, Prince Charlie felt obliged to decline on grounds of poor health—a euphemism for being permanently crocked and beating his wife. At this time Charlie (a legend in his own lunchtime) was living in Florence on overextended credit, playing bad cello, calling himself "Charles III of England" and being regularly visited by you-never-know aristos and various hangers-on with an eye to the main Stuart-comeback chance.

One such visitor was florid, bushy-eyebrows John Moore, ex-Glasgow doctor turned tutor and culture-vulture-tour-of-Europe companion to the umpteenth Duke of Hamilton. The duke dropped in on such eminences as Empress Maria Theresa of Austria, Emperor Frederick the Great of Prussia, and (inevitably) Voltaire. All of which went into Moore's little notebook and ended up as a multivolume work ("A View of Society and Manners in . . .") about what-was-hot-and-what-was-not in demimonde Italy, Switzerland, Germany, and France. Everything a traveling Brit wannabe had to know. The work flew off the shelves and gave Moore overnight literary cred even with such real writers as Dr. Samuel Johnson. And Johnson's ménage à trois (some say sado-maso) lady friend Mrs. Hester Thrale.

Hester was a tiny, plump, witty Welsh twenty-five-year-old when Johnson met her. Minutes later he had moved in and was great pals with Eton-and-Oxford Mr. Thrale (with whom Hester had a platonic marriage). The lady herself (who had coarse hands but delicate writing) hosted dinner parties for Johnson and his literary cronies, made jokes in Latin, French, Spanish, and Italian, and generally enlivened the otherwise less-than-glamorous house in Deadman's Place from which Thrale ran his brewery. Until the stroke that killed him and turned Hester into what the papers called an "amorous widow."

The Anchor Brewery (still going strong today) boasted that it sold ale "from Russia to Sumatra" thanks to Henry Thrale's business acumen.

Which failed him only once, when he tried making beer without hops or malt and lost so much money Hester's family had to bail him out. But he was canny enough to recognize the value of new technology when he saw it and was the first to use the new hydrometer (introduced by the Excise to measure the alcoholic strength of booze so they could tax it appropriately—initially, to pay for the war against the American rebels; and then for some other excuse).

Hydrometers floated more or less deeply in a more or less alcoholic liquid, and in 1803 the hydrometer developed by Bartholomew Sikes was designated official. A year later, after Sikes had turned up his toes, his widow found that "official" meant an order for two thousand instruments. So she made sure her daughter's husband, Robert Bate, got the contract. Everybody lived happily ever after. With that kind of backing, Bate was able to branch out and make telescopes, barometers, spectacles, theodolites, the official Troy pound for the U.S. Mint, and anything else required in a world crazy about measurement. Including one gizmo that measured nothing. A toy, really. In 1819 Bate built the kaleidoscope for its inventor, eminent Scottish science buff David Brewster.

Brewster's little multimedia-before-multimedia was an instant rave. And then was pirated right and left. Story of the ingenious Brewster's life, really. At a time when there was everything still to discover, Brewster discovered. He also set up the British Association for the Advancement of Science, became an honorary something everywhere, and wrote 299 scientific papers on arcana ranging from spectroscopy to refraction to polarization to crystals to photography. And 1,240 other articles (for the general public) on God, life on other planets, philosophy, railroads, physics, and whatever else was required by the editors of the slew of mags from which Brewster tried to make a living. Alas, all he's remembered for today is the no-profit kaleidoscope.

On which in 1817 a serious dissertation was penned. "In the memory of man, no invention . . . ever produced such an effect," enthused writer and physician Mark Roget, whose feelings of inadequacy drove him to wider interests, in one case, foreshadowing Hollywood. In 1825 Roget wrote that if you saw a moving carriage wheel through a window with a vertical Venetian blind the slats didn't stop you seeing the wheel rotate (persistence of vision being what the eye does to fill the gaps in between the frames of a movie). Roget also filled other gaps. His great *Thesaurus*, produced in 1852, answered the scribbler's "tip-of-the-tongue" problem with an exhaustive list of synonyms (similar expressions) useful for every occasion (event).

Similarly useful was Roget's Library of Useful Knowledge, which included an article on optics by Henry Kater. Who started life measuring large bits of India and was best known for his amazingly accurate pendulum. Gravity affects pendulum swing, and Kater showed that a one-second swing in London required a pendulum 39.13929 inches long. Kater also asked the classic question: "If the universe is infinite then everywhere you look you should see a star. So why is much of the sky dark?"

One answer came from the pen of a man better known for his grisly tales of murder. First thriller writer, poet, critic, and drunk (it killed him) Edgar Allan Poe's last work, "Eureka," suggested that if the universe were infinite then the darkness was where stars would be, if they weren't so infinitely far away that their light never reached us. This was all part of Poe's Big Bang theory (a hundred years before the Big Bang theory). Poe's gee-whiz imagining was described by Poe's editor Evert Duyckinck as "a mountainous piece of absurdity." Poe wasn't the only insultee. It was Duyckinck who also called Melville's *Moby-Dick* "intellectual chowder."

For over thirty years Duyckinck ruled the editorial roost in New York, publishing anybody who was anybody (Hawthorne, Melville, Longfellow, Cooper, Irving, et al.) and frightening the rest. And helping to move American literature out from under Eng. Lit. In 1860 Duyckinck produced an anthology of poetry illustrated in England by the Dalziel family of engravers. Back in 1840 they'd done the first edition of *Punch* magazine and then in 1841 that of the *Illustrated London News*. The Dalziels kicked off the Victorian mania for the pictorial press and their gilt-embossed Fine Art Gift Books (the original coffee-table adornments) were deemed collectibles while the the Dalziels were still alive.

The Dalziels also reproduced the work of the Pre-Raphaelite Brotherhood, who aimed to go back to the simplicity of art-before-Raphael with painting that was so detailed it was photographic, none more so than the work of Holman Hunt, who even dressed up in Arab costume (in his studio) to paint when he was working in Cairo. He and his fellow traveler Thomas Seddon, both devout Christians, then moved on to Palestine and were so blown away by their first view of Jerusalem on June 3, 1854, that they spent months on works about Jesus that made them both a fortune.

Seddon had arrived in Egypt ahead of Hunt and bumped into (and painted) another great cross-dresser, Richard Burton (on the way to his third Forbidden City, in disguise as an Arab sheikh). Explorer Burton (who claimed to speak forty-six languages and dialects) wrote more travel books than the Blue Guide and his Great Idea was to find the lake that was the source of the Nile. He found the wrong lake but made the front page anyway. After which, in 1861, he became consul in Fernando Po (small dot off West Africa) and then hit the big time with Santos (smaller dot, deepest Brazil).

On cabin-fever escape trips out of Santos to Rio Burton met and conversed in Arabic with Brazilian emperor Pedro II, aka Dom Pedro de Alcantara João Carlos Leopoldo Salvador Bibiano Francisco Xavier de Paula Leocadio Miguel Gabriel Rafael Gonzaga de Bragança e Borbón. A plump bookworm with a dumpy wife (and enjoying the occasional side affair), Pedro aimed to modernize Brazil. To which end he spent years elsewhere looking at police precincts, city waterworks, trains, schools, and (in 1876) the U.S. Centennial Exhibition in Philadelphia. Where he was transfixed by Bell's telephone ("My God! It talks!") and spent four hours a day for two weeks looking at every exhibit with Brazilian potential. He missed the lecture by Brit surgeon and antiseptic freak Joseph Lister (of "Listerine"), who was visiting Philadelphia to publicize operating-theater use of his new carbolic antiseptic spray.

In Lister's audience (as much transfixed by carbolic as Pedro was by telephones) sat Robert Wood Johnson, apprentice pharmacist, who realized there might be a market for a more individualized application of Lister's idea. Within ten years Robert and his brothers were Johnson & Johnson. Within a century they were a multi-billion-dollar international company. And "Band-Aid" was in the dictionary.

By the 1990s the company was a major supporter of the new National Marrow Donor Program. In 1991, with the aim of increasing public involvement in the program, retired U.S. admiral Elmo Zumwalt established the Marrow Foundation. In 1996 the Zumwalt Community Award went to a Charlotte, North Carolina, radio talk-show host for above-and-beyond work on the bone-marrow drive.

The name of the radio host was JOHN HANCOCK.

CHAPTER TWO

Josiah Bartlett

JOSIAH BARTLETT (NH) was forty-six. A redhead, doctor, judge, and a fine figure of a man who dressed posh (ruffles, silver buckles), Bartlett threw himself into revolutionary matters by stealing Brit gunpowder, after which his militia rank was removed by the royal governor. A year later the governor was out and Bartlett was in. And on every major congressional committee.

Between doctoring (great bedside manner), soldiering (field surgeon), fathering (twelve), administrating (president, New Hampshire), having his house burned down, and losing his wife (most of which he dealt with on horseback or by guttering candle), small wonder he died worn out. But not before his Marine Committee had commissioned the American navy's first vessel.

Captain of the good ship USS *Ranger* was John Paul, a sexually hyperactive Scots pirate on the run from a Caribbean murder charge and calling himself Jones. In 1778 Jones took *Ranger* across the Atlantic to attack Scotland. There followed much hit-and-run stuff up and down the British coastline that included the famous encounter when in response to, "Give up?" Jones did *not* say, "I have not yet begun to fight," but something (in French) more like, "Not me. How about you?"

By this time Jones's exploits (ably puffed by Jones) had made him the darling of French pro-American aristos, and their wives, most notably that of Jacques Donatien le Ray de Chaumont, who held open house for Americans in Paris. Le Ray gave Jones a bigger ship and persuaded the French king to support the American rebels (by doing so Louis XVI bankrupted France and lost his throne). *Après la révolution* with writing on the wall for the nobility, Le Ray's son James hightailed it to American citizenship and ditto wife.

In his adopted land he bought large bits of New York state around Otsego (not to be confused with Oswego), became pals with the great and the good (not difficult with a family friend named Ben Franklin), and introduced the locals to French essentials such as merino wool, vines, and silkworms. Key facilitator in all this agribusiness was Judge William Cooper, Le Ray's land agent and wrestler extraordinaire. For whom Le Ray's business affairs were a mere bagatelle. Over the years Cooper bought more than 750,000 acres and then sold them to more than forty thousand settlers. Cooper died one of the richest men in America, leaving behind a son (Fenimore) who would become one of the country's first major novelists by writing about his father's lifestyle.

Judge Cooper's sidekick had been fur trader George Croghan (obscure beginnings in Ireland), who used his Native American languages to relieve the natives of their land at knockdown prices even when he was superintendent of Indians under the colonial Brits. Croghan's technique was remarkably modern: borrow scads of money so as to buy millions of acres, then do the absolute minimum to develop them and sell off the land in highly profitable small bits. So long as the game went your way this was a license to print money. Alas for Croghan, the game in question was the short-lived Brit plan to establish the new colony of Vandalia (see elsewhere) on the banks of the Ohio. When the plug was pulled on the scheme just before the War of Independence, in a flush of foreclosures Croghan went out with the water.

Early on, Croghan's boss had been commander of U.K. forces in North America General Jeffrey Amherst, who had taken Canada from the French in 1760 and then hired Croghan to deal with the Native Americans. After germ-warfare attempts (giving the tribes smallpox-infected blankets) had failed, the French and Indian War followed and Amherst went home to glory he expected but didn't get ("a man of inca-

pacity," it was said). After being made governor of this and that he bum-
bled his way up to field marshal and sir, stopping only to put down
("bungle," it was said) the 1780 Gordon Riots in London.

Riot cheerleader Lord George Gordon was a rabid anti-Catholic
who led sixty thousand Protestant rioters on an orgy of burning, loot-
ing, and prison-breaking in opposition to a new act outlawing discrimi-
nation against Catholics. Five days of turmoil saw the mob breaking
into distilleries and torching Catholic chapels. Then they headed for
the Bank of England. It was time for Amherst to bring in ten thousand
troops, who shot and bayoneted the crowd into rapid submission.

Just before the fun and games, the sight of troops bivouacking in
Hyde Park was so mind-boggling as to warrant recording by watercolor
whiz Paul Sandby. Who had turned the genre into a must-have with his
early pix of bucolic Scotland. Returning to London in the 1760s his career went: Royal Academy, views of Windsor Castle, meteoric rise to
fame and fortune with "Select Views" of places as unfashionable as
Wales. And some (like Ireland) he hadn't even visited. No matter. Nor
had the buyers.

Chief of whom was John Stuart, third earl of Bute, who also got
Sandby to immortalize his new stately home, Luton Hoo House (designed by latest-rave architect Robert Adam). Bute retired to books and
botany at Luton after a brief and acrimonious career in politics. With
more titles and money than you could shake a coronet at, Bute's job as
tutor to the future King George III (and possible affair with George's
mother, and then George's wife) brought him the prime ministership.
Totally out of his political depth, after two turbulent years of backstabbing and tax raises he returned to the backwoods and oblivion. Where
he supported intellectuals and writers, organized Kew Botanic Gardens,
wrote nine volumes on plants, and visited his brother James in Italy.

James was U.K. minister to the Turin Court. His *chargé d'affaires* was
an enigma named Louis Dutens. For somebody with humble (and
worse, French) beginnings, Dutens lived such a charmed life he must
have known where bodies were buried. Apart from servicing the Bute
family, Dutens was also hanger-on to other nobs and spent years either
as traveling companion or house guest to anybody who'd have him. He

was almost certainly a government spy and rumor mill. His 1805 memoirs exposed the secret American offer of the U.S. throne to Bonnie Prince Charlie. Dutens also wrote now totally forgotten stuff on history, geography, poetry, and philosophy, produced a study on fire prevention, and was a big fan of Thomas Jones, instrument maker.

In an era of nonstop exploration the secret of navigational success was "gradation," the little marks on your theodolites that swiveled the gizmos by a specifically teeny amount and made the difference between accuracy and being lost. Such marks were Thomas Jones's forte, so he was flavor of the month. Especially with his invariable (i.e., bet-the-farm) pendulum, accurate to within splits of second and vital for astronomers.

One such Jones client was Sir Thomas Brisbane, soldier friend of the duke of Wellington and therefore successful. On his return from a job in the Caribbean a near-shipwreck got him interested in better navigation, i.e. more accurate astronomy about the stars you aimed instruments at to work out where you were at sea. In 1820 Brisbane became governor of New South Wales, a place where (because Australia faces toward the center of the galaxy) there were more stars than you could count. So he counted them. By 1825 when he was encouraged to go home ("too pro-convicts" or "too prosettlers," take your pick), Brisbane had logged no fewer than 7,385 southern-sky stars at the observatory he built in Paramatta outside Sydney. His return to the United Kingdom was followed by the usual gold medals, baronetcies, honorary degrees, and a quiet harrumph retirement.

Meanwhile his *Paramatta Catalogue* was published by Greenwich Observatory Assistant and major criminal William Richardson. In 1846 the Greenwich astronomical calm was rocked by Richardson's indictment for having had sex with his daughter Anna Maria and then poisoning the resulting infant, whose tiny body was discovered by workmen clearing Richardson's cesspit. The newspapers loved it.

Richardson's boss, Britain's astronomer royal George Airy, who was having a really bad day for other reasons, fired him. Airy needed a scandal like a hole in the head, being up to his ears in how wide railroad tracks should be, what to do about smoke abatement and gas sales, the design of Big Ben, gravity in coal mines, and all the other things Victorian intellectuals did. Plus a ton of paperwork, the entire reorganization of British astronomy, and the imminent arrival of his ninth child. All this, and on October 21, 1845, a shy young Cambridge astronomer arrived uninvited at Airy's door with some nonsense about the existence of "something new in the night sky." A servant accepted the scribble and sent him packing. Airy eventually wrote asking for more details. Too little, too late.

Shy John Couch Adams had done the sums that showed that the orbit of Uranus was being affected by a force that could only be the gravitational field of Another Planet Nobody Had Yet Discovered. Alas for Adams, the same idea had struck a Frenchman, Urbain LeVerrier, who wasn't so shy and persuaded the people at Berlin Observatory (fancy equipment) to go looking. They found Neptune just where Adams had predicted. Egg remains on Airy's face to this day.

Adams went far, ending up director of the Cambridge Observatory. In 1864 one of his college pals, Charles Bromby, went farther, i.e., to Tasmania. As bishop there he built Hobart Cathedral. Charles's older brother John took much the same route. In his case, to Melbourne, Australia, where in 1858 he was the first headmaster of the Church of England Grammar School and hired a passing Yale graduate to teach math. A little earlier back in the States Erastus De Forest had disappeared just before he was due to leave on a trip with his aunt. The *New York Times* suspected foul play. Two years later his family tracked him down, down under. In 1861 De Forest headed home via India and (wild oats sown) settled down to a quiet and incomprehensible life of statistics.

Twenty-five years later he established a Yale prize in mathematics and seven years after that (in 1893) math-physics undergraduate Lee De Forest didn't win it, in spite of being a distant family connection. No matter. Lee made his mark with a connection of a different kind. In 1905 he invented the Audion, which boosted feeble electrical signals. So AT&T inserted one of these gizmos every so many miles along the phone line and in 1915 started its long-distance cross-country service. Now you could hear coast to coast.

In 1928 Lee De Forest hired young electronics whiz Allen Dumont.

Who at age ten had contracted polio, then read a lot, then became an engineer. By 1939 Dumont was manufacturing the first TV set. In 1945 he set up America's fourth TV channel, the Dumont Network. Dumont was yet another inventor lacking in business acumen and was eventually bought out by Hollywood. But not before he had garnered an astonishing number of stations across the country (215 in all) that tuned in to his (and the nation's) number one TV show: Bishop Fulton Sheen's *Life Is Worth Living*.

When the series started in 1952 philosopher and theologian Sheen was auxiliary bishop of New York. On the show all he did was give sermons (with the aid of a blackboard, chalk, patriotism, and piety) attacking Godless Communism. The public couldn't get enough of it. Sheen made the cover of *Time* and won an Emmy. And he changed the life of a young actor named Ramon Gerard Antonio Estevez.

Who in honor of the bishop took the stage name of Sheen. Beginning in 1999 Martin Sheen starred in the acclaimed TV drama series *The West Wing*, playing the role of President JOSIAH BARTLET.

CHAPTER THREE

WILLIAM WHIPPLE (NH) was forty-six. With a life of seafaring and commerce behind him, he was already a man of some financial standing when the time came to take a stand. Whipple was an easygoing, unassuming type and might have left history without a mark other than his signature had he not been chosen in 1777 as general of militia to negotiate the terms of surrender by the British after Saratoga. That Brit defeat would bring the French in on the side of the Americans and make independence virtually certain.

Saratoga was the military swan song of experienced British general "Gentleman Johnny" Burgoyne. Heading down from Canada to hit the American rebels (and traveling with thirty carts of personal effects including champagne and a mistress), Burgoyne's supply line stretched too thin. And his New York reinforcements never materialized. And there were twenty thousand against his six thousand. And it was raining. And the Americans weren't fighting in a gentlemanly manner. And all the other excuses. So he never stood a chance. Went home to England, recriminations, and a successful playwright career.

Years earlier, before leaving England for America, Burgoyne had already written his first stage piece, a comedy titled *Maid of the Oaks*, celebrating the marriage of his nephew the earl of Derby. The bash took place at Epsom, just outside London, at the house ("The Oaks") Burgoyne had leased to the earl. Like Burgoyne, the earl was an inveterate gambler, horse fancier, and steward of the local races. On May 4, 1780, he started a new annual race over a mile and three quarters for three-year-old colts and fillies (prize money in modern terms of about seventy thousand). The name of the race depended on the flip of a coin. Which is why the Derby's not called the "Bunbury" (as it would have been if the other guy had won the toss).

But Sir Thomas Charles Bunbury's horse Diomed won that first Derby so he got his own back. Bunbury was the grand panjandrum of English racing, a boozer and (because he spent more time with mare than wife) cuckold. The best thing about Bunbury was his brother, Henry William. By all accounts a charmer. After the obligatory cultural Grand Tour of Europe Henry settled down to the unexacting life of the super-rich, indulging in his hobby, drawing caricatures. His work became instantly collectible because, unlike his acerbic contemporary Hogarth, Bunbury's drawings never went for the jugular. In 1787 Henry produced *The Long Minuet as Danced at Bath*, poking fun at dancers in a drawing eighty-four inches long. The first strip cartoon.

Bunbury was also groom of the bedchamber to George III's second son, and in 1787 at Windsor Castle he met a sad second mistress of the queen's wardrobe, an unmarried lady in her midthirties with two rave-success novels (*Evelina* and *Camilla*) under her belt. And being chased round the garden by the mad king. Fanny Burney resigned the royal job in 1791 and two years later was sad no more. Lightning struck in the form of a dashing Royalist French army officer in exile. Fanny married him and as Mrs. D'Arblay lived happily ever after. Until 1811 when, in Paris, she was diagnosed with breast cancer. Her account of the twenty-minute mastectomy conducted without anesthetic (it didn't exist and she fainted twice) makes some of the most chilling reading of all time ("I then felt the Knife tackling against the breast bone—scraping it!").

Holding the scalpel was General Dominique-Jean Larrey, the already legendary favorite surgeon of Napoleon famous for having done two hundred successful amputations in one day during the Russian campaign. Larrey had also invented the battlefield "flying ambulance" in 1797, so he was the soldier's friend. Good thing, as it turned out, when at Waterloo he was captured by the Germans. About to be shot, he was recognized, taken to Prussian field marshal Gebhard von Blücher, and then sent home with an escort because two years earlier he'd saved the marshal's son.

Seventy-two-year-old Blücher was an old soldier in every sense. A fanatical leader of cavalry charges, he loved war, drink, women, and gambling. He retired and staged a comeback three times. And toward the end went ga-ga, convinced he was pregnant with an elephant. By 1814 he was so famous an English engineer named a new locomotive after him. Mispronounced by the locals as "Blusher," it was the first engine to use flanged wheels. When its steam escape valve frightened the horses, engineer George Stephenson sent the steam up the smokestack, thereby boosting the draft, fanning the flames under the boiler, and doubling the power of his engine.

This was one of the reasons Stephenson's "Rocket" won the 1829 Rainhill locomotive competition. First prize was the contract to haul the first-ever passenger trains running on the new Manchester-to-Liverpool track. Coming second at Rainhill (by a smidgen) was "Novelty," a loco built by Swede John Ericsson. Who went off in a huff to America and in 1862 would become world-famous for building the semisub USS *Monitor*.

Ericsson's first idea for the U.S. Navy had been a propellered frigate. They jumped at it. On February 28, 1844, all seven hundred tons of the screw-driven USS *Princeton* were floating down the Potomac. On board, the newly invented linoleum flooring and a glitzy champagne get-together featuring President Tyler, Dolley Madison, and the whole Washington in-crowd. The secretary of the navy called for one last shot from the ship's giant twelve-inch Peacemaker gun. Which exploded. The secretary and five others were killed.

Temporary SecNav replacement Lewis Warrington looked around for safer artillery and found it in the form of John Dahlgren. By 1862 the Dahlgren gun was standard equipment (thick breech, less likely to explode), and Warrington was the Navy's ordnance maven with the ear of Lincoln. In 1865, now rear admiral and widower, Warrington married forty-year-old Madeleine Vinton, who wrote anonymous novels of a tastefully Catholic kind and was known as the queen of social etiquette. A leading light in the anti-women's-vote movement (she said for women to be allowed the ballot box would be "immodest" and bad for marriages), in 1878 Madeleine's name was on the bill that made sure the women's vote didn't happen.

Madeleine also spoke several languages, and her translations included a piece by French aristo Charles Forbes de Montalembert. The count was a devout Catholic who spent all his life trying to square several circles: total obedience to Rome but the need for church reform, separation of French Church from State, no religious influence in French education, left-wing politics but respect for the aristocracy. Naturally, he made enemies of everybody. Including the pope, who shut down his newspaper. Montalembert also founded the help-the-poor Society of St. Vincent de Paul and proposed an Ancient Monument Department to save places like Notre Dame cathedral from falling down from decay and neglect.

In 1836 Montalembert married a descendant of St. Elizabeth of Hungary. His wife had breathing problems, so in 1844 Montalembert took her to the healthful climate of Madeira. Where an English clergyman, on the island for similar reasons since the year before, lodged with his wife in a room opposite the cathedral in Funchal. So the two couples met. Like Montalembert, John Mason Neale was Gothic-Revival and social-conscience so they got on like a church on fire. Neale (twenty languages, a believer in head-bump-reading) was so High Anglican he was almost Roman. He also wrote ninety-nine hymns, including "Good King Wenceslas," as well as several Anglo-Catholic novels, not one of which is remembered.

In 1854 (eight years before death from overwork) Neale founded the Order of St. Margaret for nuns with nursing in mind. By 1870 there were fifty members of the order. By 1887 they had a colonial outpost in Colombo, Ceylon. Where in 1892 one Sister Angela was principal of Bishopsgate School for Christian girls (French, drawing, piano), built on cinnamon-gardens land bought for the diocese by Reg Copleston, "boy" bishop of Colombo (aged twenty-seven).

Reg was keen to involve locals in the church and also became an instant expert on the ancient native language: Pali. The vexed question of whether Pali was Indo-European was settled in 1895 (it was) by the vexed, recently arrived Wilhelm Geiger, German professor who up to this point had only been expert on ancient Persian and the dialect of Baluchistan. So Pali was a snip. Geiger spent six months in Colombo, then translated the ancient Pali chronicle *Mahavamsa* and wrote the definitive Pali grammar. Not a great read.

Geiger's son Hans made more of a name by inventing the Geiger counter. He developed the prototype at Manchester U. (in England) so as to be able to count the alpha particles his colleague physicist Ernest Rutherford had found coming off radioactive materials. This led him to investigate how the alpha particles behaved when they hit something. This showed Rutherford (take his word) that there was a ton of power locked up in an atomic nucleus if you could release it. In 1905 Einstein showed how you could do that with $e = mc^2$ (take his word). Seven years later Einstein was a Nobel and had moved on to the relatively more complex matter of general relativity and how gravity affected space (take his word). Einstein was at Zurich Polytechnic at the time.

Where a faculty colleague was Croat organic chemist Leopold Ruzicka (1939 Nobel; hobbies Dutch painters and Alpine plants). Ruzicka was an archnoodler who lived at his workbench and helped to give the world artificial flavors and sex hormones. Which was why in 1931 he was grabbed as director of research and development by the Swiss company Firmenich, for whom he produced the first artificial raspberry taste. And you read it first here.

By 2003 Firmenich was worldwide and flavor of every month with food manufacturers. That year one of their new non–exec. directors was Heinz Imhof (global experience in agribusiness), who in 2002 had resigned from the honorary position of president of the International Food and Agribusiness Management Association (IAMA), a fifty-country organization set up to handle "food-chain" issues.

Imhof's successor as IAMA president in 2002 came from the Harris Nesbitt Food Group in the United States. His name was WILLIAM WHIPPLE.

CHAPTER FOUR

Sam Adams

SAM ADAMS (MA) was fifty-three. And no fool. They said of him: "Eats little, drinks little, sleeps little, thinks much." By all accounts a tough guy to go up against on the floor of any House. "Austere" is the word often used in biographies.

Adams was a gamekeeper turned poacher. After starting out as Boston tax collector for the king, he went to the opposite extreme, becoming chief republican agitator and organizer of the Tea Party in Boston harbor. This in spite of the fact that as late as 1774 he was still trying to get the Brits to come up with a Bill of Rights that might save the situation and urging argument in newspapers rather than mobs in streets. The Continental Congress was his idea.

One of Sam's many admirers was the Marquis de Chastellux. Who came over in 1781 with General Rochambeau in time for the fun and games at Yorktown, when loser Cornwallis and his troops marched out as the band played "The World Turned Upside Down." Never a truer phrase.

Chastellux was fluent in English and was already a member of the Académie Française for a philosophical thing he'd written. And a version of *Romeo and Juliet* with a happy ending. The Chastellux *chef d'oeuvre* was an account of his travels in the United States, 1780–82. Highlights: revolutionary places and people, how American youth was promiscuous and ill-mannered, how American animals were all smaller than European ones, and a suggestion that Hebrew become the official U.S. language. All this translated in 1787 by George Grieve.

After early radical politics in England, by 1781 George had to skip the country for the United States, where he met George Washington, then headed for Paris. Where he became infatuated with (and sexually obsessed by) the recently dead Louis XV's mistress, Madame du Barry. Whose jewels were stolen during an absence with yet another lover, and in 1792 while du Barry was in London looking for her sparklers, Grieve got the French revolutionaries to seal her house and confiscate her papers (so he could read them) and to make her number one Most Wanted.

On du Barry's return, the two had a wrestling match in her bedroom and he hauled her off for interrogation. On the way he's said to have propositioned her, been spurned, and exacted revenge as chief prosecution witness in the case that took her to the guillotine. Like any superstar, Madame du Barry (born Jeanne Becu) had for years lived a life of ups and downs: ex-hooker turned love machine (you name it, she'd do it), royal pillow talk with Louis XV, ambidextrous sexual proclivities, and a plan to establish a chivalrous order for all women who'd had more than ten lovers. Her private papers were dynamite.

Back in 1771 a notorious blackmailer, pimp, and cheap French crook named Morande, living in London at the time, had threatened to publish an exposé of du Barry's whorehouse beginnings (*The Secret Memoirs of a Woman of the Town*). King Louis went ballistic. The French police had a private word with their English counterparts, who said awfully sorry they couldn't stop Morande. But if certain visiting French persons tried to drown, kidnap, or otherwise murder him, the Brits might not notice. Kidnapping failed so Morande was given a very large bribe and a job spying on the Brits. An offer he couldn't refuse. By 1774 he was helping launder French money and guns over to Boston. By 1781 he was delivering the lowdown on British military secrets and had persuaded James Watt across the Channel to Paris with his (top-secret, "Brit-eyes-only") steam engine.

The chap who had engineered Morande's turn-around (and who

passed the money over, so Morande would burn the du Barry papers) was himself a turn-around of sorts. The Chevalier d'Eon was small, shapely, and squeaky-voiced and the word passed that he was a woman in male drag. D'Eon was a French diplomat in London and even his boss didn't know he was working back-channel directly to Louis XV. When XV died and XVI learned of the secret network of XV's spies (called "The Secret"), he disbanded the network except for d'Eon. Who was by now (confusingly) dressing as a woman (for espionage reasons). XVI said d'Eon could come back to Paris, but only if he stayed in skirts and handed over all his papers (it was suspected he was a double agent, but what cross-dressing had to do with the matter is not clear).

Only after d'Eon's death did they find out he was, after all, a man. And to prove it there was a testicle in the museum of Dr. John Heaviside, who had been present at the removal. Heaviside, a surgeon at St. Bartholemew's Hospital in London, was an unoffical collector of bits of his patients, dried, pickled, or injected with wax. He also kept the skeleton of a two-foot-three-inch woman and that of a man with one too many ribs. Heaviside's anatomical museum was the greatest of the day, even if (as was said) some of his exhibition-case description cards were "bordering on the miraculous."

Royal surgeon by 1790, at the Eumalian Club Heaviside mixed with the artistic and literary elite: Boswell, Johnson, Reynolds. And Richard Payne Knight. Who spent his life erecting a fake medieval castle-home complete with grounds landscaped to look like a painting (Knight was last-word authority on this "picturesque" art style). Knight blotted his chattering-classes copybook by claiming Homer didn't write Homer and that the Elgin marbles weren't really Greek. Worst of all, in his history of priapism he suggested the Holy Cross was a phallic symbol.

As befitted a rich antiquarian-about-town, Knight collected things and people. Including young history-painter Richard Westall (the king was potty about his stuff), who produced 384 major works, achieved membership of the snobby Royal Academy, was revered by continental engravers of his work, and illustrated the books of such as Sir Walter Scott, Robert Burns, and the poisonous Byron.

Westall also knew a real poisoner, name of Thomas Griffiths

Wainewright. Art critic and history buff, the bejeweled Wainewright was a self-confessed lover of beauty, cats, and the color green. Also a minor dauber (his paintings of women verged on the pornographic). Wainewright wrote art criticism for the *London* magazine in such purple prose that even Oscar Wilde called it "a style so gorgeous it conceals the subject." After an excessive lifestyle had emptied his bank balance, in 1829 Wainewright poisoned his uncle to get the family property. Then in quick succession in 1830 he slipped a fatal drop to his mother-in-law and sister-in-law Helen. Wilde claimed Wainewright confessed to him that murdering Helen was indeed a dreadful thing to do "but she had very thick ankles."

Finally arrested for the insurance fraud that followed these strychnine efforts, Wainewright was transported to Tasmania, where he died. Relieving the unfortunate Tasman governor John Eardley Eardley-Wilmot (sic) of only one of his many problems. During his term the island received thirty thousand convicts but no money to handle them. It was said that homosexuality was rife. Sixty-year-old Eardley-Wilmot (too liberal for the settlers) was also rumored to hug young girls on sofas and to bring women convicts to Government House for "lewd entertainment." There were even suggestions of an affair with his son's fiancée.

The fiancée was not affianced for long. In 1850 the beautiful Julia Sorrel married another (the local education inspector, Thomas Arnold) and headed back to England. Where her new brother-in-law Matthew was on his way from being a minor Victorian poet ("Scholar-Gypsy," "Sohrab and Rustum") to being (another) school inspector and then social critic. Matthew Arnold spent thirty-five years on trains to small towns, inspecting schools and marking exams. This humdrum lifestyle was interspersed with trips to the Continent to report on foreign education. Arnold came back from these escapades to attack English stodginess and divide the English into Barbarians (aristos), Philistines (middle class), and Populace (workers).

In Paris Arnold met his hero Charles-Augustin Sainte Beuve. Who had an affair with Victor Hugo's wife and wrote a novel about it. Sainte Beuve (the first professional literary critic) wrote the kind of beautifully overpolished prose-about-prose that only undergraduates have to read today. Sainte Beuve's thing: "to understand the work-of you have to know the life-of." Academician, university teacher, essayist, and senator, he inevitably attended Princess Mathilde Bonaparte's salon.

The princess was Napoleon's niece, with a monster Russian husband from whom she was separated (woman-of-character Mathilde left him with his mistress, whom she relieved of her jewels). Mathilde's salon was filled with talent: Gounod, Delacroix, Flaubert, Pasteur, Berlioz, as well as others then famous, now not so. Now-forgotten stars like Venezuelan Raymondo Hahn, six-year-old child prodigy who played for Mathilde's guests. Hahn wrote his first and most famous song (now forgotten) at age thirteen. Then went on to write 120 piano works (now forgotten) as well as innumerable "art songs" (now etc.). And, as somebody said, never left the nineteenth century.

In 1894 Hahn met and fell for Marcel Proust, who used him as a character in *Remembrance of Things Past*, the thirty-two-hundred-page stream-of-consciousness meganovel Proust never finished over his last ten years and which began with the thoughts triggered by the sight of a pastry. Great if you can handle three-page sentences. Homosexual social climber and snob Proust was referred to by a contemporary critic as: "One of those small-time fops in literary heat." But his powerful expression of a sense of universal decay influenced novelists everywhere.

Apart from inspirational cakes, another of Proust's literary triggers was a "small mediocre phrase" in a sonata by his pal and fellow homosexual Camille Saint-Saens. Prodigy Saint-Saens played piano at age two, wrote his first song at age five, and spent twenty years as organist in the ultrachic Madeleine church in Paris wowing the crowd with weekly improv on the organ. He loved Roman theater decoration, geology, butterflies, and the occult. And hated the music of Richard Strauss, who in 1919 started the Salzburg Festival with Max Reinhardt.

Born Max Goldmann, the Austrian Jewish actor-producer was known for his great crowd-scene work, led the renaissance of German theater after World War I, and was prolific (452 productions on 23,374 occasions, according to one American academic). Things were going gangbusters for Reinhardt until 1933 when enter stage right the Nazis. After they began removing his assets, including a castle, Reinhardt lit out for Hollywood.

Where he met his old protégé from Berlin days, Ernst Lubitsch. Who by 1922 was making his cinematic name for witty, sarcastic dialogue and zany humor with such stars as Garbo and, later, Jimmy Stewart. And in his 1931 hit: *The Smiling Lieutenant*, with Claudette Colbert. Who went on to stardom playing opposite Clark Gable in the 1934 Frank Capra classic *It Happened One Night*.

Originally written as a story for *Cosmopolitan* magazine by journalist-novelist SAM ADAMS.

CHAPTER FIVE

John Adams

JOHN ADAMS (MA) was forty. Known as "His Rotundity." A shoe-maker's son turned lawyer, Adams was also known variously as vain, irritable, and cantankerous. The Declaration of Independence was his idea, though he later complained that Jefferson got all the glory. From the outset Adams said he wanted power and "reputation." In 1797 he got it as the country's second president, even though back in revolutionary days he had lobbied against the left-wingers in favor of royalist trappings like a lifetime presidency, a hereditary Senate, and personal-fortune requirements for representatives (£100), senators (£300), and governors (£1,000). The idea being to reduce the likelihood of corruption. Hope springs eternal.

In 1798 bribery came back to haunt him during negotiations with the French revolutionaries over their likely help against the Brits (again!), when the negotiators for zee foreign minister demanded a quarter-million back-hander for the man himself and twelve million for *la France*. Adams said stick it and told Congress about the scam. He referred to the blackmailers as: "X, Y, and Z." Congress went ape. Things were about to go totally pear-shaped when Napoleon took over in France. Whereupon sweetness and light supervened.

The mysterious X, Y, and Z turned out to be an American banker living in Hamburg and two Swiss. One of whom was J. Conrad Hottinguer. Who in 1816 was witness to a contract signed by thirty-one-year-old Laurent Clerc, a teacher in Paris. The contract (with an American in Europe on a head-hunting visit) was for Clerc to go to Hartford, Connecticut, and teach for three years. Clerc's career to this point had been remarkably successful, and this contract required him to teach geography, history, Bible studies, arithmetic, and grammar. And sign language, since his pupils would be deaf (and in some cases, dumb).

No problem. Clerc himself was deaf and had been trained at the Paris Institute for those similarly challenged. He had happened to be on a visit to London when he met his future employer, Thomas Gallaudet (whose son later set up what eventually became the modern-day Gallaudet University for the deaf in Washington, D.C.). Gallaudet was in the United Kingdom to check out the Braidwood family schools for the deaf. The Braidwoods (who'd started out in Edinburgh) taught deaf pupils to make sounds by feeling their teacher's larynx so as to recognize a correct sound when they made it themselves, and by using a small instrument to position their lips, jaw, and tongue. Unfortunately for Gallaudet, Braidwood required nondisclosure, lots of money, and several years' training for any would-be teacher.

Braidwood's methods worked remarkably well. In a famous test the famous Dr. Johnson provided a word one and a half feet long long and a deaf Braidwood pupil spoke it perfectly. Another of Braidwood's Edinburgh pupils, John Philip Wood, was so good he ended up as a qualified accountant in charge of auditing the Excise Office. Where he revealed corruption, incompetence, and expenses fraud on a massive scale.

In 1813 Wood got married, marking another triumph for the Braidwood system and its aim of giving pupils a normal life. Wood's new wife was the sister of Scotland's best-known publisher, Robert Cadell, close friend and business partner of Sir Walter Scott. Scott was very big business. As the first successful historical novelist (twenty of his twenty-three books), Scott's work burst upon an English public fascinated by the Gaelic past it had recently tried so hard to wipe out with the Highland Clearances (a "sheep in, people out" policy that emptied Scotland and filled Canada, and that was carried out in savage retribution for Scotsman Bonnie Prince Charlie and his clans' having nearly made it to London and the throne). Walter Scott's novels and their tartan Disneyfication of Scotland sold like hot bannocks, and everybody involved got very rich.

One of the very few times Scott put a foot wrong was in 1818 with *Provincial Antiquities and Picturesque Scenary* (sic) *of Scotland*. Which failed in spite of the illustrations by up-and-coming young painter J. M. W. Turner. Who in 1792 had started walking all over the country, doing twenty-five miles a day with his possessions and food in a bag on the end of a stick, producing landcape sketches and watercolors for a magazine. The year after Scott's book came out, Turner left England (as every painter tried to) for Rome and the Great Experience. After a few weeks of the usual Old Masters copying, Turner developed his own style and changed the world of painting. His scrapings, blottings, wipings, and scratchings of the wet paint created dreamlike visions of light and color unlike anything that had gone before (take a look at *The Fighting Temeraire*).

During another trip to Rome, in 1819, Turner also made the obligatory visit to the new excavations at Herculaneum, where he met and dined with Sir Humphry Davy, big science cheese and the darling of London beauties, who flocked to his lectures at the Royal Institution. Davy isolated potassium and sodium, invented a miner's lamp, won a Napoleonic prize (even though there was a war with Napoleon at the time), and wrote the definitive *Agricultural Chemistry*. And wasn't boring. Davy was in Herculaneum trying to unroll Roman papyrus documents stuck together by the Vesuvius eruption and seventeen-hundred-plus years in the ground. After six months' effort, in the face of Italian obstructiveness and a chemical solution that wasn't the solution, Davy was the only thing to come unglued and left.

So did his sidekick Peter Elmsley. At 240 pounds, Elmsley was known as the fattest undergraduate of his day. As genial as he was obese, Elmsley (rich, Oxford, sinecure vicarage) indulged in two pleasures: food and ancient Greek. Years of digging in Italian libraries for manuscripts by Sophocles and Euripides turned Elmsley into the leading Greek scholar in Britain. In 1822 he applied for the chair of divinity at Oxford. He didn't get it. Second prize was the offer of the bishopric of Calcutta. No thanks.

This left the job to Reginald Heber. An altogether more qualified man since he was a full-time divine, was married to a cathedral dean's daughter, had traveled widely, and was gung-ho to get the word out to the idol-worshipping heathens. Heber ended up spending only three hectic years in India involved with the poor and needy as well as dealing with the "predicaments of Indian Princes" (caused by the gradual removal, by the Brits, of their princely authority and valuables) and generally overdoing it until he expired in a bath. But not before writing fifty-seven hymns. One of which, "Greenland's Icy Mountains," would be set to music by the man who wrote twelve hundred hymns of his own and singlehand-edly created a musical culture in American schools. Or (depending on your view) singlehandedly destroyed a flourishing indigenous musical tradition ("backwoods" and "unscientific," he called it).

Lowell Mason's "Better Music" movement started in Boston (where he founded the Academy of Music), then spread to every school curriculum throughout the country. It earned him America's first doctor of music degree. Mason's approach to music teaching (based on European classical music) was influenced by an 1837 European visit to an obscure Swiss named Johann Naegeli (Mason arranged two of his hymns). Naegeli was the inventor of the Swiss choir and wrote dozens of tunes for the Swiss Reformed Church. And inspired Mason by his classroom methods. Which were inspired in turn by another Swiss, Heinrich Pestalozzi. Who inspired everybody.

Pestalozzi believed in teaching children through direct experience of life. Observation led to awareness led to measurement led to description led to writing. No books, no timetables, no punishment, no teachers (except other kids). It seemed to work. His school at Yverdon in Switzerland became the radical-chic must-see after it opened in 1805. Glitzy visitors included the Russian ambassador. Confusingly, a Greek. John Capodistria's meteoric rise took him (in only eighteen years) from obscure Corfu doctor to Russian foreign minister to first republican Greek head of state. After which (in 1831) he was assassinated for insulting somebody's family honor. Whereupon the Brits, Russians, and French opted for a (less-precarious, they thought) monarchy and installed Otto I. Confusingly, a German.

Seventeen-year-old Otto was the son of King Ludwig I of Bavaria and spoke about as much Greek as he did Sanskrit. Accompanying him were three regents: two nonentities and Count von Armansperg. Who'd made enemies cleaning up Bavarian government finances and would soon do the same for Otto. Once Otto reached the age of throneship he spent more time thinking up regulations for chimneysweeps than running cabinet meetings. The London *Morning Chronicle* described his reign as "incompetence and imbecility." Crime levels rose and carriage-jacking happened right outside the Royal Palace, where nonstop full-dress balls were held. Athens University was opened with thirty-three professors and fifty-two students. And the medieval city was indiscriminately destroyed by German archeologists so as to leave the Greek ruins looking like museum pieces. Eventually the exasperated Greeks ran Otto and von Armansperg out of town.

In 1853 Armansperg's daughter Princess Caroline arrived in Hoboken, New Jersey, where she met and married Julius Froebel, himself on the run from a death sentence in Germany for his involvement in the 1848 revolution. Froebel (mineralogist, educator, and revolutionary) spent several years in Central America becoming the authority on Mayan architecture and linguistics. He and Caroline ended up in Algeria.

Julius's brother Karl went further, becoming a fervent supporter of Karl Marx, an educator setting up kindergartens in Prussia (the schools were banned), and finally a political exile in Edinburgh, Scotland. Where in 1875 he opened a school. In 1898 one of his little pupils was Clementine Hozier (she remembered the school as "a strong smell of haddock"). Hozier was the granddaughter of the tenth earl of Ainslie and known for her beauty. In 1908 after a classic whirlwind romance she married a young politico on his way up, then down, then up again.

The second up took him all the way, and in 1940 Winston Churchill was prime minister just in time to lead Britain through World War II. Churchill's director of atomic energy research was physicist John Cockcroft, who after the war ran the U.K. Atomic Energy Research Establishment. In 1953 Cockroft sent a young man to Geneva to help design and build CERN's first proton synchrotron, in which atomic particles were (and still are) smashed into each other at high speed.

In 1975 Cockcroft's young protégé became CERN's director general. His name was JOHN ADAMS.

CHAPTER SIX

Rob Treat Paine

ROBERT TREAT PAINE (MA) was forty-five. And the only signer who'd been to Greenland (back in the 1750s). He'd then given up whaling for the law (no fool). After which, as a circuit judge, he rode the back trails to other remote spots in Massachusetts. According to Benjamin Rush, in Congress Paine "rarely proposed anything and opposed nearly everything anybody else proposed." Paine was cautious, pragmatic, blimpish, and not entirely certain that an all-out revolution was the right way to go. In 1775 he signed the "Olive Branch Petition" to George III, looking for a way to "avoid the impending calamities that threaten the British Empire." His Majesty binned the petition. So calamities happened.

Well before the independence dust had settled, Paine (with Washington, Franklin, Jefferson, and Hamilton) was thinking ahead to a world in which the country would have to earn a living. So in 1780 in Boston they all set up the American Academy of Arts and Sciences to kick-start the economy (i.e., agriculture). In 1784 the academy offered membership to a passing Italian, Count Luigi Castiglione. Who then disappeared for three years and came back with a giant diary of his trip through the mid-Atlantic states. The work featured plants, animals, and topography as well as Native Americans and their languages. It also included the prediction that America would one day be a superpower.

Of course, Castiglione was then granted membership in the eggheads' think tank, the American Philosophical society in Philadelphia. The society founder's son, William Bartram, had already done Castiglione's trip years before. Between 1773 and 1776 he had gone as far west as Baton Rouge, fought alligators and hostile locals, and returned to open a Botanical Garden that's still open today. He reported that things were changing fast. In the Southeast where there had once been 1.3 million Native Americans, by the time of Bartram's visit the native population was dropping below forty thousand. While not exactly using terms like "noble savage," Bartram's romantic description of Native Americans and their pristine wilderness home influenced the ideas of such as Wordsworth and Coleridge.

By 1785 Bartram's Botanical Garden in Philadelphia was attracting the great and the good. And the foreign, in the personage of André Michaux. Whose mission to America in 1786 (for Louis XVI) was to find and ship back to France lots of small saplings that would one day be big oaks that would one day be the French navy. To which end Michaux set up a plant nursery in downtown Hackensack, New Jersey. Ho-hum stuff for a guy who'd already done Turkey, Syria, Iran, and Afghanistan.

Soon Michaux was off again (as they all were) south and west, shipping back to France such esoteric amazements as cranberries and sweet potatoes. Alas just as Michaux was beginning to enjoy things, Louis XVI lost his head and the revolutionaries stopped Michaux's paycheck. By 1800 his savings had run out and he was back in Paris. No slouch: A quick change of clothes and he was off again, this time for Australia. He never made it. On the island of Mauritius, after a row with the boss, he jumped ship.

Good news for Captain Nicholas Baudin, whose expedition into the unknown (back then, the excitement equivalent of the Apollo missions) had even attracted intellectual stowaways, and for Baudin, Michaux's disappearance just meant one fewer mouth. Baudin had cut his naval teeth in the Caribbean during the War of Independence, then brought back ostriches and zebras from South Africa for the Austrians, then returned on a French expedition to the Caribbean. From there, the homeward-bound cargo had included 450 stuffed birds, 4,000 butterflies and insects, and 8,000 plants. So Baudin's present trip to Australia was a mere exploratory jaunt.

One of Baudin's key Australian aims was to see if Tasmania was an island and anyway claim it for France. Alas, on April 9, 1802, in Encounter Bay, South Australia, Baudin encountered HMS *Investigator* coming round the other way. With bad news. *Investigator* had just sailed round Tasmania, called it an island, and claimed it for the Brits. *Investigator's* captain, Matthew Flinders, was one of those "been there, done that" types. He had taken breadfruit trees from Tahiti to Jamaica with the infamous Bligh (*Mutiny on the Bounty*) and done five years circumnavigating Australia (the name was his idea) so he was laid-back enough to lower a cutter, row over to Baudin's *Géographie*, and chew the fat for a while.

Meanwhile, back on *Investigator*, young William Westall was busy drying out his paper and applying wet paint to the latest lot of sketches. Westall was the ship's landscape artist (necessary in a time without cameras) and was later said to be lazy because his natural history colleague Ferdinand Bauer painted a thousand plants and two hundred animals but Westall only managed 120 views, including the first of aborigines. On his return to London in 1804 (via China and India), these pieces got him into the Royal Academy. After which Westall went northeast to paint the Lake District and impress Wordsworth. After that a nervous breakdown. After that in 1820 marriage to a young woman who, fortunately for a disorganized noodler like Westall, was to be his rock.

No surprise. Her brother was Adam Sedgwick, professor of geology at Cambridge, general science bigwig (friend of Queen Victoria, Royal Commission on University Reform). And leading light in the great strata row. If rock strata were the-older-the-deeper then how about strata on mountaintops? And the fossils in them? Sedgwick (who is said to have uttered the phrase, "I shall leave no stone unturned") thought history was one long series of catastrophic events that reshaped the Earth's surface and threw up mountains. And sometimes if some species got wiped out God had to start them off again. Or replace them. So when Sedgwick's pupil Darwin came up with evolution, Sedgwick didn't like it.

In 1819 Sedgwick set up the Cambridge Philosophical Society with math colleague George Peacock. George was another one of those do-everything Victorian nerds (weights, measures, education reform, coinage, Gothic cathedral restoration). George's big moment came when he read a French math book and realized (and said so, loudly) that the French way of writing calculus (dx/dy) was better than Newton's. You could hear the appalled silence as far away as Oxford. George persisted. He finally got his professorship and gave lectures on astronomy (standing room only) and on dx/dy (not a soul).

Small wonder, then, when French boffin Jean-Baptiste Biot (inventor of the saccharimeter for measuring the sweetness of molasses, who calculated the speed of sound through air and sewage pipes and who thought Newton was the bee's knees) turned up in Cambridge, he and George had a bit of a calculus contretemps. Such rows were nothing new for Biot, who had recently been enjoying more of the same in the Shetland Islands with a bunch of Brit surveyors who were there to cooperate with Biot's French survey team on the same set of geodesic observations (to see how different their results would be). The boss of the Brit team, Thomas Colby, argued with Biot so much that Colby did his observing on a different island, thus confounding the entire purpose.

In 1824 Colby (one hand, but dexterous, they said) went off to measure the topography around Belfast. Or tried to. Looking though the murk at some distant hilltop, all they were seeing was murk. Until Colby's young sidekick Thomas Drummond produced a gizmo that burned magnesium and lime in front of a parabolic mirror, producing a light of such amazing brightness you could see it even through Irish weather. In next to no time Drummond's light was in lighthouses, saving ships from sinking without trace. And, from the same fate in theaters, actors. Who took to limelight with all the abandon of an alcoholic in a brewery.

None more so than C. W. Macready, king of Shakespearean tragedy, who in 1837 during a brief two-year stint as manager of Covent Garden introduced Drummond's new light and changed the nature of acting. First because the limelight was used only on the leading actors (so from then on stars were "in the limelight"). And second because with that much light there was no need to go on overacting and waving your arms about. So the whole business became more naturalistic. Macready had a long and distinguished career (except for one episode in New York where missiles included rotten eggs, tomatoes, and half a sheep), and when he finally retired in 1851 his London farewell dinner was attended by many great and good, including Dickens and Thackeray. Tennyson's poem "Farewell, Macready!" was read. The Prussian ambassador also turned up.

Baron von Bunsen (who had a Welsh wife) gave parties at the Prussian legation to which even Queen Victoria came. And he had the biggest address book in Europe. One of Bunsen's correspondents was Christian Ehrenberg, German expert on the teeny-weeny. After travels all over the Middle East and Siberia collecting forty thousand samples of plants and animals, Ehrenberg spent the rest of his life peering down a microscope, labeling the invisible. And discovering that many rocks were really made up of zillions of minute plant and animal fossils. Which is why he was able to take a look at some red earth from South America and write to Charles Darwin saying important things about date and content.

Ehrenberg wrote a thousand letters. Nothing, compared with Darwin's epistolary efforts. One of which, in 1875, was to congratulate Anton Dohrn on having just opened the world's first marine-studies lab in Naples, Italy (where opening anything was not easy, bureaucracy-wise). Dohrn, godson of Mendelssohn, was nuts for crustaceans and had the brilliant idea of getting governments and universities to sponsor fully equipped work tables at his lab. He soon had eighty tables and the place was jammed with would-be snorkelers from all over.

Including one American researcher, William Ritter, associate professor at Berkeley, who turned up at Dohrn's in 1894 and then went home fired with the idea of doing something similar on the California coast. By 1912 he had persuaded a newspaper magnate to fund a research station at La Jolla, California. It became known (after the magnate) as the Scripps Institution of Oceanography.

In 1962 a young postdoc was there on a fellowship. After which he went away to become a world authority on the rocky-intertidal-shore communities of organisms such as barnacles, limpets, surf-grass, and kelp. And especially: what happens to these little critters when pollution strikes.

This rock-pool whiz was ROBERT TREAT PAINE.

CHAPTER SEVEN

Step. Hopkins

STEPHEN HOPKINS (RI) was seventy. And partially paralyzed. So he had to use his left hand to steady his right. So his is the only medically shaky signature on the document. As opposed to nerves. By this time Hopkins was an experienced local government man (Rhode Island governor for nine consecutive years until 1768) and was probably the first person to make a public fuss about "taxation without representation."

With a lot of expertise in the shipping trade, Hopkins was a natural for the Secret Committee set up to create the U.S. Navy. He also introduced the first Rhode Island bill to outlaw the import of slaves. And facilitated the start-up of Rhode Island College, later known (after Hopkins's pal and fellow abolitionist Moses Brown) as Brown University.

Moses Brown was a power in the land thanks to the family businesses in whale oil and metal founding. From 1787 he sent ships to China with iron, rum, ginseng, and tar in exchange for silk, tea, and lacquered goods. He was also a Quaker and big on education. And he knew the new country wasn't going to do well if it didn't keep up in science and technology. So in 1789 when an illegal Brit emigrant, recently arrived in New York, contacted Brown out of the blue with a providential textile-machinery tech-transfer proposal, Moses had him in Providence, Rhode Island, within days.

Samuel Slater was illegal because that's what you were if you left England for America with anything industrial in your bags. In fact Slater's bags were technologically empty, but his textile-industry apprenticeship papers were sewn into his clothing, and the plans for the latest textile-making gizmos were in his head. Within weeks of arriving in Rhode Island, Slater was doing just what the Brits didn't want: calling on his photographic memory to build the bits of Industrial Revolution that America could use to manufacture cotton goods instead of having to send the raw stuff to Britain.

Slater had learned it all from Jedidiah Strutt, who was known as a particularly enlightened mill owner because he employed seven-year-olds but really preferred to wait until the kids were ten. Strutt made stockings and in 1769 was very open to suggestion when approached by geek Richard Arkwright, who was looking for finance to build his new water-powered spinning frame that automatically twisted yarn onto bobbins and dramatically upped production. They built it and Strutt went into textiles, big-time.

Strutt mixed with movers and shakers like lame, pockmarked bigwig (he wore a big wig) Erasmus Darwin. Erasmus (grandfather of you-know-who) was the polymath's polymath: meteorology, geology, chemistry, mechanical birds, pumps, textile technology, and (his profession) doctoring. And botany, about which he produced reams of somniferous poetry titled *The Loves of Plants* (all about the sex life of eighty-three species of vegetation).

Loves was critically shredded by the right-wing "Anti-Jacobin" mag produced to counter the pro-French-Revolution-speak being peddled by crazies such as Darwin, Coleridge, and Wordsworth, which was stirring up mutiny in the navy, mobs in the streets, trouble at the Bank of England, and the end of civilization as they knew it. One of the mag's writers was George Ellis, an amiable diplomat and antiquary, whose major contribution to culture was to delve into medieval Eng. Lit. His friend the novelist Sir Walter Scott called him the "Tressan of England."

In 1797 the real Tressan had come out with a study of European and Middle Eastern myths that included a lengthy disquisition on the ancient Druids (already a bandwagon topic among British pseuds). In keeping with things Druidical, most of Tressan's stuff was invented and included quotations from the third-century Scottish epic folk-poem "Ossian." Itself a forgery. So Dressan was fake, citing fake.

In Britain the Druid revival was masterminded by Edward Williams, counterfeiter and drug addict. Williams had left the building trade to make better money and began producing "ancient" Welsh manuscripts that were supposed to reveal the secrets of the ancient Druids and Bards (of whom Williams said he was one of the two survivors). In 1792 Williams held the first Druid Bardic Meeting in London, conducted according to a ceremony based on yet another "original" manuscript. Williams called himself "Iolo Morganwg" and also promoted the idea that America had been discovered by the twelfth-century Welsh Prince Madoc.

In 1797 in common with other freethinkers Williams-Morganwg became a Unitarian (a sect whose adherents regarded Jesus as human and promoted rationalist democratic principles and were therefore on the government's "extremely dangerous" list). Unitarian views were most publicly expressed by leader (and discoverer of oxygen) Joseph Priestley, in no time the object of governmental rent-a-mob violence. Result: In 1794 he headed for safety in Northumberland, Pennsylvania. Where among other things he wrote a letter lacerating the atheistic work of Frenchman Constantin Volney and accusing him of "hottentotism" (Volney said humans had originated in Africa).

Volney's historical survey of ancient empires (titled *Ruins*) was published in 1791 and defined social progress as the gradual relinquishing of ancient beliefs. The book went over big with the Romantics, who were deeply into the old. Especially the fashionable new study of the long-gone Indo-European language of Sanskrit, which Volney had learned in Paris. Where a fellow student was Friedrich Schlegel, historian, philosopher, and one of those prolix German Romantics whose aim was to understand the mind of the past so as to understand its culture. The only German past readily available was Gothic, so Schlegel expounded on it. Often, it was said, in language incomprehensible even to his friends.

One of whom, Klemens Brentano (pal of Herder, Goethe, and other Romantic biggies), did his literary bit by producing a series of old Germanic folk tales (some of which he made up). He spent much of his life wandering all over Germany falling for women and writing them erotic verses. Except for the six years (1818-24) he spent at the bedside of nun Anne Catherine Emmerich while she dictated her visions to him and bled from her various stigmata (palms, head, breast, side). Brentano's poems and dramas were unknown in his lifetime (and forgotten after he died), but his *Passions of the Christ* (the transcription of Emmerich's visions) was a best seller in several languages and much later inspired a Hollywood movie.

In 1813 one of Emmerich's bedside visitors was young Princess Mimi Gallitzin, who went on to marry the penniless Prince Salm and then watch her fortune get squandered. The squander was particularly bad news for Augustine Smith of Loretto, Pennsylvania. Smith was the name imaginatively used in the application for U.S. citizenship by Mimi's émigré brother and missionary, Prince Demetrius Gallitzin. Who was the first Catholic priest ordained in the United States and by this time had spent $150,000 of his own (and borrowed) money to buy land, which he then sold to settlers on easy terms (Gallitzin bought at four dollars and sold at one dollar). He also established a church at Loretto (back then, in the Allegheny wild lands).

In 1827, saddled with debts his sister couldn't now help him to pay off, Galltzin appealed for charity from the public. One of the givers (two hundred dollars) was Italian cardinal Capellari. Who changed his own name four years later to Pope Gregory XVI. And then had a rough ride. Italian revolutionaries wanted the church out of the Papal States (a large bit of central Italy), and in order to make their point took over Papal-State cities like Bologna. Gregory cracked down hard with spies on every corner, snatch squads, and then foreign troops. This upped the ante, and by 1832 the new (instantly proscribed, death-penalty-for-membership) "Young Italy" movement was calling for nothing less than a republican government, a united country, and a church that kept out of politics.

Leading this bunch of hooligans, a young Genoese lawyer called

Giuseppe Mazzini was soon caught and offered exile or exile. By 1836 he was in the home-from-home for political runaways, London: destitute, living on potatoes, and planning his return home. In the end his compatriots went for a constitutional monarchy, so Mazzini didn't live happily ever after. In spite of all the support he got from British liberals.

Especially John Macadam, who'd started out as a shoemaker then turned revolutionary, then lost his customers, then spent fourteen years in North America, where he agitated for Mazzini's cause. Back in the United Kingdom, by 1847 he was big in the "Friends of Italy" movement and raising money for Garibaldi. In 1858 he was on the Glasgow welcoming committee for visiting fellow Garibaldi fan and M.P. John Bright.

In Parliament for over twenty-five years, Bright's greatest triumph was the repeal of the Corn Laws, which (to keep U.K. farmers happy) blocked the import of corn unless the price of the local British stuff was astronomically high. Result: starvation among the poor, riots, and massacres in the streets. Bright also promoted such insanity as separation of church and state, no slavery, universal ballot, no Crimean war, no colonialism, and worst of all, education for the working classes. In spite of which by 1878 he had made it into the cabinet. That same year he persuaded a cookie-making friend to stand for Parliament.

From a tender age George Palmer had had a curious ambition: to develop the world's first continuous-process cookie-manufacturing process. By 1846 at the age of twenty-eight he had done so. When Bright met him, Palmer (in the shape of Huntley and Palmer Ltd.) was well on the way to becoming the world's biggest cookie maker, selling such delights as Digestives, Ginger Nuts, Wafers, Osbornes (named after Queen Victoria's summer residence), and 150 other mouth-watering varieties. Whatever sweet thing you might want with your cup of tea, coffee, or cocoa, George made it.

Fittingly, the man Huntley and Palmer Ltd. chose as chief chemist in 1906 (Edward Armstrong) was an expert on all things carbohydrate. A specialty he'd picked up while working on his Ph.D. in Berlin under 1902 Nobel German chemist Emil Fischer. Who (fittingly) knew everything there was to know about the molecular behavior of tea, coffee, or cocoa. One of Fischer's pals was Gustav Krupp Bohlen und Halbach, who married Bertha Krupp in 1906 and took on the Krupp family name, becoming managing director of the giant steel and armaments firm. And then building a monster gun named "Big Bertha" for use in World War I.

In 1936 one of the Krupp shipyards built a freighter, the *Cairo*, later named the *Stier* and in 1942 converted into a "raider." In May that year the *Stier* sailed into the South Atlantic, where she sank three Allied cargo ships. On September 27, in fog and rain squalls, she encountered a U.S. merchant ship that unexpectedly opened up with machine guns and a four-inch cannon, hitting the *Stier* in the rudder and the engine room. The superior firepower of the *Stier* sank this opponent within an hour. However, the *Stier* was now also on the way down to a watery grave, so her crew went over the side.

Leaving the *Stier* to become the first German warship in World War II to be sunk by an American Liberty ship: the STEPHEN HOPKINS.

CHAPTER EIGHT

William Ellery

WILLIAM ELLERY (RI) was forty-eight. Well-heeled son of Rhode Island's deputy governor, after Harvard and business he went into politics, then law, then entered Congress just in time for the Great Continental Loan Office shambles.

Congress had decided to pay for the war by raising $5 million from the public. In return for which the public would get government bonds at a 4 percent annual interest rate over three years. Congress then borrowed enough money from French investors to be able to pay back the public. However, what bondholders finally received turned out to be not money but French exchange notes. No problem, as these were cashable in Paris. Except it took forever to get your cash. And because by 1781 the U.S. currency had inflated out of sight, what you got was peanuts.

All of which made U.S. bondholders extremely unhappy and also discouraged foreigners from investing in the U.S. economy. In consequence of which things financial were getting decidedly problematic. But for a while, before all this happened and things went from bad to bankruptcy, the original government bonds were almost as good as money and were spread around, where needed, by the Continental Loan Office.

Rather a lot of the bonds went to John Brown of Rhode Island (via his friend William Ellery, at the time state commissioner in charge of issuing the bonds) for "services rendered." This included Brown's building navy ships in his shipyard and making armaments in his foundry. Brown ended up wealthy enough to be president of the new Providence Bank. The other major source of Brown's income was his distillery, which did so well because he was also a slaver. He and close shipping associates the four D'Wolf brothers made a ton of money by shipping rum to Africa, where they exchanged it for slaves, then shipping the slaves to the Caribbean, where they exchanged them for sugar and molasses, then shipping this back to Rhode Island where they distilled it into rum. Which they then shipped back to Africa, etc.

This little trick was known as the "triangle trade" and nice work if you could get it. And soon it was also against the law. So the D'Wolfs branched out. In 1806 one of them, John (later uncle-by-marriage of Herman Melville) was sailing the Northwest Pacific coast picking up pelts from the local Native Americans. His plan: take the skins to Russia and trade them. In Sitka D'Wolf bumped into the boss of the Russian-American Company (the Russians owned Alaska at the time) Nicholas Rezanov. To whom John sold his ship the *Juno* so Rezanov could go off to San Francisco, set up Californian colonies, and buy food for his starving Alaskan colonists.

Rezanov himself had just arrived in Sitka on board the first Russian round-the-world expedition. Which then shoved off to continue round the world, carrying teenage explorer Otto von Kotzebue. Nine years later Kotzebue was in command of the brig *Rurik* and set off for another round-the-world itinerary: June 1815 leave St. Petersburg and go Cape Horn, Chile, Kamchatka, California, Hawaii, Guam, Philippines, South Africa, London, arrive back St. Petersburg August 1818. During the trip Kotzebue discovered nearly four hundred Pacific islands, atolls, and assorted specks of land and wrote a best-selling account of the voyage.

But not as best-selling as the piece written by his on-board naturalist Adalbert von Chamisso (French aristo family, ran away from guillotine, settled in Berlin, hence the "von"). Soldier-turned-botanist with an interest in the creepy, in 1811 Chamisso spent time at the Swiss villa of Romantic maven Madame De Stael. By the time of his voyage with Kotzebue (during which he identified floating fruits as Pacific island vegetation colonizers), Chamisso had written poetry set to music by Schumann as well as his own internationally acclaimed *Peter Schliemihl, the Man Who Sold his Shadow* (to the Devil, in return for a bottomless purse, but finds happiness only wearing magic boots and botanizing—weird or what?).

The story resonated with Robert MacNish, doctor in utmost northern Scottish nowhere (Caithness) where, apart from nothing else, the solitude got to him. Go there and you'll see what he meant. On his return to big-city Glasgow in 1824 MacNish's hair fell out, he became paranoid and wrote: *The Metempsychosis* (two drunks agree to exchange bodies and can swap back again only by selling their souls), *The Anatomy of Drunkenness* (a study of the shakes, slurred speech, feeling no pain, etc.), and *Philosophy of Sleep* (a study of nightmares, trances, and sleepwalking). The kind of stuff that would today get MacNish's head examined.

Which is what MacNish himself did, depositing a plaster cast of his own skull with the secretary of the Edinburgh Phrenological Society, Robert Cox, who analyzed bumps on the head to see what was wrong with you. When he wasn't feeling skulls Cox was a lawyer. In 1847 he was hired to represent a bunch of botanizers who'd had a "heated exchange" with the sixth duke of Atholl and his gamekeeper goons, who had prevented the botanizers from walking up Glen Tilt.

Tilt is in the middle of the Highlands, an as-advertised picture-perfect Scottish Glen. And back then it was, like large bits of Scotland, the exclusive property of the Duke of Atholl. Whose message to the plant-picking ramblers heading onto his land was: No Way. A red rag to the Right of Way Society to which these veggie enthusiasts belonged. Amazingly they won their court case and today you, too, have the right to walk up Glen Tilt (so long as you stay on the road).

Leader of the ROW group was Professor John Hutton Balfour of Glasgow and Edinburgh universities. One of the first true ecologists, Balfour taught botany in context (how the plant and its location related to the local geology, meteorology, topography, etc). Balfour lived, ate, and slept botany after starting as a doctor (as so many did, when there were so few specialist subjects to study). He was big in the local Botanical Society, the Botanical Club, professor of medicine and botany, keeper of the Royal Botanical Gardens, and the Queen's botanist for

Scotland. And wrote a book about the links between botany and the Bible. And had a blackberry plant named after him.

Balfour learned a lot about the countryside from senior academic pal Archibald Geikie,who was as nuts about geology as was Balfour about botany. Geikie did the classic thing: picking up fossils as a kid and becoming an obsessive rockhound thereafter. His life was one long climb up the academic cliff face from assistant on Scottish geological surveys to professor and sir. Geikie's real passion was reserved for volcanoes (major opus in 1897: *The Ancient Volcanoes of Great Britain*), and he traveled France and the United States peering into these dangerous hot spots. His major geo-thought was that the landscape looked the way it did because hard rocks weathered less than soft rocks. Made sense.

Geikie also wrote the biography of his mentor, the arrogant, self-opinionated, and aggressively irascible Sir Roderick Impey Murchison. Who was (rightly) convinced that strata didn't tell you diddly about history because strata could go up and down and be interrupted, folded, and other stuff that made it untrustworthy, sequence-wise. Fossils were the only true guide. Once you found a reliable and uninterrupted baseline stratum. Murchison's UBS was Silurian, and he made enemies because he kept on expanding it and snitching fossils from other people's strata. This was Victorian England and the whole of knowledge was up for grabs.

One of Murchison's (very few) friends was Andrew Ramsay, who thought glaciers were so exciting he took his honeymoon among them. Discovered that glaciers scooped out holes that were now lakes. Spoke French at breakfast once a week for life. Said field work beat lab work and that he wouldn't "look at a mountain with a microscope." And fortunately for this chapter (enough geology, already!) had a nephew who was a chemist.

William Ramsay was the chemistry noodler of all time. Most of his life was spent boiling cold stuff. He started by investigating vapor, liquids, and evaporation. Then, what else, moved on to gases. In 1894 he removed everything from liquid air and found something left behind, which he named argon. In 1895 he did the same thing with something else and got helium. Then decided there must be something more to these new gases. He boiled more cold stuff and in 1898 found krypton, neon, and xenon. Got a Nobel for them in 1904. In 1907 (dedication to duty) he boiled off, fractionated, separated, etc. one hundred tons of liquid air. And found nothing he hadn't found before.

This jolly, witty, multilingual, single-minded geek had started out at the Tubingen lab of one Rudolf Fittig, German chemist whose work included all you might have hated about chemistry at school. Words like mesitylene, alkybenzenes, piperine naphthalene, and pinacol coupling reaction (the last *not* what it sounds like).

Alongside Ramsay in this test-tube heaven was a young American, Ira Remsen, who stayed on for two years as lab assistant to Fittig after getting a Ph.D. In 1872 Remsen went home to the United States, taught for a while at Williams College, and then set up the first chemistry department at the new Johns Hopkins University. Where in 1879 he made the great discovery (or didn't).

One night at dinner after a hard day in the office toiling over coal tar derivatives his bread rolls tasted sweet. Then bitter. But not to his wife. So back in the lab next day he licked everything he'd touched (or didn't) and bingo there was the same taste. In a chemical called o-toluenesulfonamide. Which he renamed "saccharin" (or didn't). The doubts expressed here (in parentheses) relate to the fact that exactly the same story was told later by Remsen's assistant Constantine Fahlberg, who patented saccharine and made a fortune. Remsen got upset not about the money but about who'd done the discovering.

In 1891 Fahlberg started earning serious money when R. J. Reynolds used saccharine to sweeten their chewing tobacco. Reynolds put his first factory next to the railroad in Winston, North Carolina. Which was next to the tobacco-growing belt. He also foresaw that cigarettes would soon replace plug tobacco and in 1911 produced the Camel brand. The rest, as they say, is respiratory-medicine history.

Reynolds was born on an estate near Critz, Virginia, just outside the town of Martinsville. Where in 2005 the American Standard Building Systems company was producing homes. One of their models (two floors, three bedrooms, 2,606 sq.ft.) was named the WILLIAM ELLERY.

CHAPTER NINE

Roger Sherman

ROGER SHERMAN (CT) was fifty-five. By this time he'd had years of experience in business (small farm, surveyor, general store) and public service (justice of the peace). Down-to-earth, a talented politico, good at agreement rather than confrontation, Sherman was a key figure in the Great Compromise that resolved the problem of small states' voting rights by going for the two-house system (in one house the number of representatives reflected the population of a state while the other had two senators for each state).

Six feet tall and blue-eyed, Sherman impressed people with his pithy views (sample: "Minorities talk, majorities vote"). He signed more documents than any other member of Congress: Declaration & Resolve 1774, Declaration of Independence, Articles of Confederation, and Constitution. He was also on the Committee for Postponed Matters that set up the Electoral College and defined the president's powers.

Fellow Postponed Matters committeeman was Rufus King, Harvard graduate and lawyer who in 1795 was sent as U.S. minister to London, where he got the Brits to settle for six hundred thousand pounds war reparations (cheap at the price). In 1799, with Federalism back home not rock solid (and definitely not in need of a sudden influx of unstable "republican" radicals) King also got London to agree to prevent certain Irishmen from emigrating to the States after their recent (failed) uprising.

The 1798 Irish rebellion (imitating similar efforts in France) had put the wind right up the English. Even though the "United Irishmen" movement had been infiltrated and all their plans revealed (so that on May 23, when the secret republican army turned up at the secret rallying points in Dublin they found themselves in a hands-up situation with government troops already there), one bunch managed to take the town of Wexford. There followed three months of fighting and very nasty mutual atrocities all over Ireland, abetted but not aided by French support (the first arrivals didn't land thanks to bad weather and incompetence; the second arrivals landed and failed thanks to good weather and incompetence).

The Irish rebellion was finally put down: thirty thousand people died and countless properties were gutted. Windows were smashed, including those of the rather plain Maria Edgeworth, in Edgeworthstown, County Longford, where her (English) family had owned the town for two hundred years. Ironically, the damage was done by pro-Brits who suspected her father of Irish sympathies. Maria painted a vivid picture of the rebellion in her novel *Patronage*, the first of fifteen books that established her as Ireland's leading woman writer. Her greatest success, *Castle Rackrent*, was a Gothic novel all about the downtrodden position of women. The book (as one critic said) was like Ireland: full of "whiskey, decay, rot, guttering candles, tobacco, damp, horse-dung and dust."

In 1802 when the Edgeworths were on a visit to Paris, one morning at breakfast the door opened and Maria's father shoved into the room a middle-aged and rather pompous Swede, who thereupon proposed marriage. Maria refused, ostensibly because he wouldn't come to Ireland and she wouldn't go to Sweden. It must have been a fast exchange of views. Abraham Niclas Clewberg-Edelcrantz took it on the chin and left to complete his tour of Europe inspecting theaters and picking up new industrial ideas for Sweden's king Gustav IV. Niclas was an odd bird: earlier private secretary to Gustav III, after which director of the Royal Swedish Theaters, in 1794 he invented (copied?) a semaphore system remarkably like that of Frenchman Claude Chappe of earlier the same year. By 1803 Niclas was in Birmingham, England, buying steam engines from James Watt.

One of Watt's lesser-known pals was William Playfair, inventor of the line chart, the bar chart, and the pie chart. Since he lived in an age obsessed by trade and economics it's hard-to-believe-but-true that Playfair's charts never made it to the boardroom until modern times. Back in 1777 Playfair had spent three years drawing engines for Watt, then tried and failed to sell Watt's copier (write document in mix of wet ink and gum arabic, press against tissue paper while wet, read copy through tissue), then tried and failed to run a silver-plating business (typically, Playfair's businesses went: overambitious ideas, followed by fights with partners, major debts, bankruptcy). In 1785 Playfair started writing about economics and critiqued Adam Smith. Some nerve.

In 1789 Playfair was in Paris associating with Joel Barlow in the American Scioto scam. The Scioto Associates' cunning plan was to sell options on 5 million acres in Ohio to Frenchmen who thought they were buying title to their land. Two shiploads of unfortunates even went there and discovered the small-print truth. By which time Playfair was long gone. Another Scioto associate got out from under, too.

Andrew Craigie had been the first (and only) U.S. chief apothecary during the War of Independence. Then (surprise) went into the pharmaceutical business (failed), then financial speculation (failed), then the Scioto enterprise (failed). Accused of little more than "not doing anything to stop Scioto," he avoided prison and carried on with his speculative life. This included a grand (failed) plan to put together an international consortium to buy the U.S. debt to France. After being ruined by speculation in a bridge in Cambridge, Massachusetts, and the purchase of Washington's old headquarters, Craigie sank into penury and in 1819 died. Leaving his wife in the headquarters to take in lodgers.

One of whom, in 1837, was Henry Wadsworth Longfellow (who would later own the building). At the time Longfellow was still only an academic. He'd done six years teaching modern languages at Bowdoin (after they made him go to Europe for three years to learn French, Spanish, Italian, and German) and in 1834 had become a Harvard French and Spanish tutor, although his favorite language was Italian and he spent years on a translation of Dante's *Divina Commedia*.

Around 1838 Longfellow and a colleague tried (and failed) to help a young Italian visitor to get a job at the university. Antonio Gallenga had been teaching Italian at Harvard Young Ladies' School for two years. Finally, when nothing better turned up he returned to England. Where as a young Italian freedom fighter (the reason he had been on the run in the United States as "Luigi Mariotti") he was greeted with open arms and immediately welcomed into salon life. Which in 1839 London meant being taken up (if that's all it was) by Marguerite Countess of Blessington, man-eater, writer of "silver-fork" novels of upper-class manners, and the toast of the town. Admirers included Dickens, Disraeli, et al.

Blessington's up-and-down career had to this point included a forced child-bride marriage (he died drunk), a liaison with an army man (who charged ten thousand pounds to walk away), marriage to rich Irish landowner Earl Blessington (he died of a stroke), and finally a long relationship with handsome Count d'Orsay (twenty years younger and married to the countess's stepdaughter). Blessington, best known for her *Conversations with Lord Byron,* was already living and loving well beyond her means when the 1845 Irish Potato Famine struck and suddenly she had to leave London for lower-cost-of-everything France once the bottom had dropped out of the Irish agricultural market and the income arriving from her Irish estates vanished.

As did the hopes of a man hoping to head the other way. The potato famine delayed the opening of the Queen's College in Cork, Ireland, so it wasn't until 1849 that things over there picked up again and math genius George Boole finally had an Irish job to go to. Up to this point Boole had had the least interesting life of any intellectual giant in history. For the first fifteen years he ran schools in nondescript places like Lincoln, while starting to write math papers, published in various nondescript mags. Then in 1847 he wrote the amazing, world-changing *Mathematical Analysis of Logic.* Generally ignored (even by nondescript mags), the article said that logic could be handled by algebra, e.g., using 0 and 1 to mean "no" or "yes" (or "off"/"on," or "none"/"all", etc.). Added to which, if, say, x represented "dog" and y represented "brown," then using 0 1 as "none/all": $(1-x)(1-y)$ would mean "all objects that are

neither brown nor dogs" (are you still here?). Sixty years later this gob-
bledygook electrified Claude Shannon, American inventor of information theory, when he realized that electrical circuits (on/off) could solve
Boolean algebra logic equations. We call the result "digital."

In 1864 Boole's wife, Mary, killed him when he caught a chill and she,
thinking that "like cured like," threw buckets of cold water over him
and he died. Mary was an eccentric lady who joined fringe groups like
the antivivisectionists and next-world communicators. Her belief in
homeopathic remedies like the one that put paid to her husband had
taken root when she was a child in France, where her father had gone to
be treated by Samuel Hahnemann, founder of homeopathy and bane of
pharmacists.

Hahnemann (his maxim: "Doctors . . . can change a minor illness into
a serious one") expressed opposition to the contemporary fashion for
bloodletting and purges. His evident success during the cholera epidemic of 1830 made him popular with the British royal family, so in
1850 a Hahnemann Hospital was opened in London. A year later one of
the founder members, Hungarian Matthias Roth (another runaway agitator), opened the Institute for the Cure of Diseases by Swedish Gym-
nastics. This technique included slow leg movement and structured
coughing. Models of gymnastic positions were shown to enraptured
crowds at the Paris Expositions of 1867 and 1878.

On the latter occasion (the Franco-Prussian War now over and paid
for) the financially extravagant Exposition attracted 13 million visitors
to fifty-three thousand exhibits lit by forty-three hundred gas jets. Star
attraction: the Trocadéro Palace, a Byzantine-Moorish affair described
by one eminent critic as looking like "a bath-house of ill repute." In
which top of the bill was the monster organ, played by many, including
Liszt, Franck, and Saint-Saens and built by Aristide Cavaille-Coll,
who'd erected over five hundred such instrumental extravagances, including the one in Notre Dame cathedral. The organs Aristide built
were unusual in that they were capable of making very gradual transi-
tions from pp to ff. This influenced the writing of composers of the time
such as Saint-Saens (whose work is full of pp to ff).

When the Trocadero Palace was torn down in 1936, Aristide's organ was refurbished and electrified by Victor Gonzalez. Who passed on his know-how to German organ builder Rudolf von Beckerath. Who (after World War II) passed on his know-how to an American, John Brombaugh.

In 1980 Brombaugh built an organ for the Christ Episcopal Church in Tacoma, Washington. In February 1996 the church hosted an organ recital of composers known to Bach: Brunckhorst, Praetorius, Buxtehude, Pachelbel, C. P. E. Bach, and the old man himself.

The organist was ROGER SHERMAN.

CHAPTER TEN

Sam^d Huntington

SAMUEL HUNTINGTON (CT) was forty-five. And first President of the United States (in Congress Assembled) for four months in 1781. He was also one of the early examples of rags-to-riches America, starting as a self-taught plowboy and ending honorary doctor, chief justice of Connecticut, and state governor.

A consummate politico, while in office he did nifty work dealing with rebellions, mutinies, land grabs, and foreign territorial claims. He also drafted the first U.S. copyright law (thank you). He put a foot wrong only once, when he caused matters to hit the Protestant fan after he took holy water at the Catholic funeral of a Spanish grandee.

Don Juan de Mirelles, a merchant from Havana, was also a bosom pal of Washington and on April 24, 1780, visited the American army camp in Philadelphia, where he got a thirteen-gun salute and was due for a parade and maneuvers followed by fireworks but then suddenly went down with a fever and died four days later. Washington was a chief mourner. The reason this overdressed Hispanic person got the treatment was that he represented Spanish king Carlos III. Who was rooting for an American win and the eventual return of ex-Spanish, now-British real estate including Gibraltar, Jamaica, Bermuda, and Honduras. So Carlos was helping things American along with a fortune in weapons and cash sneaked across the pond via the French after closed-door meetings with B. Franklin. To this day the Spanish money-laundering exercise remains the war's best-kept secret.

Back home Carlos played the benevolent despot, persuading Madrid residents to stop throwing their slops out of the window, generally (if chaotically) helping the Spanish economy, toning down the Inquisition, chucking out the Jesuits, building the Prado, and (in 1789) hiring Francisco Goya as court painter. Goya had hung around Madrid for five years designing tapestries and schmoozing anybody who might offer a leg up. Finally, through a royal favorite, he got an invite to the palace and was in like Flynn, enjoying bed and board at the crown prince's house. In next to no time Goya was becoming an international fave and being friendly ("very," it was said) with the duchess of Alba. When he painted a nude (the *Maja Desnuda*) and then repainted the head it was rumored that the body in question was guess who.

Almost from the start Goya's work caught the eye of a man whose art collection was growing so fast it needed bigger and bigger palaces to hang it in. No problem if you were an Esterhazy prince like Miklos II of Hungary and "money" wasn't a word you knew. Miklos's collection finally hit over one thousand, including works by Da Vinci, Canova, Lorrain, Raphael, Rembrandt, Correggio, Poussin, and others too ordinary to list. Miklos was also pretty cool on the baryton (a kind of cello). So, being insanely rich, he got his in-house composer to dash off 125 little numbers to play.

This workload didn't seem to cramp the style of Franz Joseph Haydn, who somehow also found time to teach Beethoven, encourage Mozart, and scribble 108 symphonies, 150 trios, 445 arrangements of Scottish songs (yes!), and the rest. Starting in 1791 came a couple of visits to London (where he pulled off a mere twelve symphonies), during which Haydn became a superstar with the British royals and had many little flirtations. Back in Vienna after 1792 he produced "Deutschland Uber Alles" and, some say, his greatest opus: *The Creation* oratorio. With words by a Scot, translated for Haydn by the Austrian court librarian, Baron Gottfried van Swieten.

The baron wrote ten forgotten symphonies and is remembered because he was fired in 1791 for being part of a world conspiracy run by a bunch of weirdos based in Bavaria and known as the Illuminati, a subset of the Masonic Order. Those who believe in such guff maintain that these guys caused the French Revolution, the American War of Independence, the Bolshevik Russian Revolution, and many other world-changing events you'd know about if these guys hadn't covered their tracks so well throughout history. And (if you look carefully and watch your back) They Are Still At It Today.

In 1797 the whistle was blown on these "plotters" by an Edinburgh professor of science, John Robison, with his modestly titled: *Proof of a Conspiracy Against All the Religions and Governments.* Instantly into four editions, it was eaten up by churches and governments at a time when (thanks to crazy left-wingers ushering in Armageddon with stuff like voting rights and freedom of speech and secular humanism) the world was clearly going to hell in a handbasket. Robison got extra space to express his views when offered the editorship of the third edition of the *Encyclopedia Britannica.* Apart from including over three hundred articles on theology, Robison also introduced the idea of specialist articles and set the form of all future encyclopedias.

As an Episcopal bishop with Anglican unity in mind (not easy in Scotland), Robison was also part of his own little conspiratorial group: the "Hackney Phalanx." Among several stop-the-rot aims, this high-church Anglican coven committed everything including slander to counter the democratizing effects of the kind of schools being introduced by Joseph Lancaster, who taught poor street children by the simple method of doing without teachers and paper.

Each class was taught to read (using big cards with words on them) by children who could already read. And everybody wrote in sand because paper cost money. Toys rewarded success and punishment for misbehavior was washing. Children took to the system with the enthusiam of pigs in manure. So did royalty. Alas, Lancaster peaked early, then lost the plot (it was claimed he flogged for fun). In 1818 he went bankrupt, was run out of town, headed for Canada, and ended up in Caracas, where Venezuelan head of state Simón Bolívar (who'd visited Lancaster's London school) came to his wedding.

Bolívar was variously president or dictator with "limitless powers" of various South American countries and in the process extracted from Spanish clutches Bolivia, Peru, Ecuador, Colombia, Venezuela, and Panama. And for this reason was known as the Liberator. When he met Lancaster he'd been in England to raise support for his revolutionary adventures. He had some success, attracting to his side more than two thousand Irish disaffected (given the English treatment of the Irish at the time, "disaffection" was the natural condition of the Irish).

One of these, Daniel Florence O'Leary, briefly became Bolívar's aide de camp, leaving behind a precarious Irish existence on potatoes and dreams to become one of the heroes of South America and ending up general in Bolívar's army. When Bolívar left for exile in 1831, O'Leary shipped out for Europe, where he failed to get diplomatic recognition for Venezuela. He then moved back to Caracas, and in 1841 the outgoing Brit consul-general recommended him as temporary replacement.

Consul Robert Ker Porter intended to return to Venezuela after a quick trip to Russia but died there. Earlier on he'd made his mark as the painter of giant canvases (first and most spectacular the 120-foot, 700-people, 2,500-square-foot *Battle of Seringapatam*). By 1803 Ker was internationally known for such big military set pieces, so the tsar of Russia ordered several dozen yards for the St. Petersburg Naval Academy. While working on this job Porter married a Russian princess and traveled extensively in Russia. Then got the Caracas consulship.

Porter's sister Jane (who brought back his body) wrote romantic but inaccurate historical novels (best: *The Scottish Chiefs*), all of which were slaughtered by the critics. When she tried her hand at drama (*Switzerland*), the play opened at Drury Lane and closed the same night. Late in life she had a (motherly?) thing with a young American writer, Nathaniel Willis, visiting Europe as social correspondent for the New York *Mirror*. Nathaniel was Yale and poetry and did best with light pieces about social glitz, which went over like a lead balloon with the British upper-crust elite whose parties he crashed in search of material.

In 1833 Willis went on a junket around the Mediterranean on board the USS *Delaware*, showing the flag to various potentates in Egypt and Syria and taking in the sights of Jerusalem. Running the trip was Commodore Todd Patterson, who'd spent twenty years in New Orleans after doing good work in the 1812 war (and at one particularly scary moment saving the life of Andrew Jackson). Patterson's chaplain was George Jones. After the trip was over he went back to the United States and agitated successfully for the establishment of a naval academy so that more flag-showing could be accomplished. In 1851 the U.S. Naval Academy at Annapolis opened with Jones as chaplain.

In 1853 Jones was on Commodore Perry's historic voyage to open up Japan and spent much of the two-year trip making 328 drawings of the mysterious zodiacal light: the glow in the sky seen just after dusk or before dawn, which is caused by light from the hidden sun reflecting off tiny dust particles in space. A few years later Jones's work came to the attention of a major Italian astronomer at the Milan Observatory, Giovanni Schiaparelli. Who would become famous for the greatest piece of misinterpretation in astronomical history. In 1877 Schiaparelli described lines he had discovered on Mars as *canali* ("channels"). Decades later these lines turned out to be an optical illusion, but not before Schiaparelli's word had been translated wrongly into English as "canals." Front-page stuff when the papers decided this meant there were people on the Red Planet.

Which gladdened the heart of those who published books by H. G. Wells and especially Jules Verne, who'd almost invented the science-fiction genre with his *Journey to the Center of the Earth*. Many great novels later in 1885 he (or perhaps his son Michel) was commissioned to do a piece on the life of an American journalist living in A.D. 2889. The piece was full of predictions like video phones, color photography, lasers, and the internet and was set in a world where the United Kingdom was a U.S. colony. Verne (or son) got the commission from a flamboyant playboy millionaire American newspaper proprietor living in France.

James Gordon Bennett was nuts about women, parties, and sport in that order and sponsored any event involving high tech and high speed. In 1911 at a Paris banquet following the latest Gordon Bennett balloon and airplane race, French industrialist Jacques Schneider announced the Schneider Trophy for seaplane races. In 1935 the trophy was won by an American, Lieutenant Jimmy Doolittle. Who progressed to greater fame on April 18, 1942, when he led the daring raid by sixteen B-25 bombers flying eight hundred miles off a carrier to hit Tokyo, Osaka, Nagoya, and Kobe.

All the more daring because as the planes arrived over target the business of opening the hydraulically operated bomb-bay doors, dropping the bombs, and then closing the doors involved slowing to 250 miles per hour and taking nearly three minutes to do it all. During which time, the phrase "sitting duck" took on urgent new meaning. Not long after this the problem was solved by using high-pressure air to operate the doors, thus reducing the time to twenty seconds.

Cheers all round for the guys who provided the air pump: the Weatherhead Company. In 1993 the Weatherhead Foundation endowed the Albert J. Weatherhead III Professorship at Harvard's Faculty of Arts and Sciences.

In 2005 the holder of the chair was political scientist SAMUEL HUNTINGTON.

CHAPTER ELEVEN

WILLIAM WILLIAMS (CT) was forty-five. And full of fire and brimstone. A little too much so for some of his contemporaries. In modern terms he might be described as Christian Socialist. Many of his colleagues in Congress said he was parochial, small-minded, and driven by self-interest. Williams had spent much of his life before the Big Day on mind-numbing points-of-order-Mr.-Chairman minutiae at local government committee meetings all the way from parish to state level. So he was dull. But no dummy: Marrying Governor Trumbull's daughter was a good move. He was also antisouthern, anti-Philadelphia, anti-commerce, anti–New York, and anti-French. From the beginning he'd bombarded the public with tub-thumping articles on independence written under pseudonyms that fooled nobody: "A Friend of His Country," "An American," etc.

Because of his pettifogging and earnestness, Williams was known as "William Wimble" by the local satirists, a group of young writers who produced poems, essays, and scatological cartoons (of Williams with his trousers down) and who were known as the "Connecticut Wits." Their (otherwise fairly indifferent) work is remembered only because in 1793 it was edited into the first *Anthology of American Poetry* by one of the lesser Wits: Elihu Hubbard Smith.

Smith (medical studies, no degree, in spite of which he later practiced in New York) failed at both writing and doctoring. In 1795 he wrote an opera that closed the theater. In 1797 he published the first U.S. national medical journal. His own contributions to the mag included such cutting-edge stuff as the plagues of Athens since ancient times and the natural history of the elk. Smith also indulged in some of the first ether-sniffing, as did many of the New York medical community.

These included Archibald Bruce, who had qualified as a physician in Edinburgh, Scotland (the best medical school of the day), and then left for three years in rocky parts all over Europe indulging in his grand passion: mineral-collecting. Mineralogy geeks back then were like collectors of vinyl phonograph records today. All they ever did was show each other their collections and ask you not to touch. In 1812 Bruce went a little further, identifying a new mineral. A native magnesia of New Jersey, it was named after him: "brucite."

While in Europe Bruce bumped into the Honorable Charles Greville, holder of the minerals-freak record with what was regarded as the greatest collection of stones in the world. When the collection was sold to the British Museum there were 14,800 samples, including 5,200 faceted gems. Alas, by that time Greville was no longer around to enjoy the proceeds. By 1784 his collecting habits and rakish fun and games had already left him broke. Temporary financial reprieve came in the form of a deal he struck with an elderly uncle, who agreed to make Greville his heir (so now Greville could borrow against expectations) in return for Greville's mistress, the lovely Emma Lyon, known for not wearing underwear.

Emma was shipped off to the Kingdom of Naples, where the old buffer (Sir William Hamilton) was U.K. minister to the Neapolitan crown. After a while she took the easy way out and in 1791 became Lady Hamilton. Two years later the heroic Brit admiral Horatio Nelson turned up, was smitten, and began a torrid affair as Emma's only true love. Or so he thought. Too many rumors exist that she was playing both sides of the street and having a lesbian relationship with the Neapolitan queen Caroline. This may be why Caroline was able to get Emma to get Nelson to provide ships and protection when a temporary revolution in 1798 forced the royals to flee Naples to Sicily for a year.

Along with Prime Minister Acton (with whom the omnivorous Caroline was also having an affair).

Sir William Acton had started life as an officer in the Tuscan navy, where his introduction of shallow-draft boats (good idea for a coastal force) got him recommended to Caroline, who wanted the Neapolitan fleet beefed up. Acton did so and by 1779 was minister of war and heading rapidly for the top job (and marriage with his thirteen-year-old niece). Acton's only serious rival for power was Francesco d'Aquino, prince of Caramanico. So in 1786 Acton promoted Caramanico sideways to become viceroy of Sicily. Where in 1795 Acton probably had him poisoned. Before which the prince managed to be the best Sicilian governor ever: fixing land reforms, curbing the power of the barons, opening schools. And giving a job in Palermo to a mediocre northern Italian teacher of theology and mathematics.

In spite of the fact that Giuseppe Piazzi had never looked through an eyepiece, he became director of the Palermo Observatory. No building. No equipment. This was Sicily. In 1787 Piazzi spent three years in London and Paris learning the trade and ordering equipment. In 1791 he was finally able to take his first look at the Palermo night sky and decided to produce an updated, more accurate star catalogue. This involved checking the individual positions of 6,784 heavenly bodies. The romance of science.

On January 1, 1801, Piazzi found Ceres in the gap between Mars and Jupiter (where people had said there ought to be another planet). Alas, the grand old man of astronomy Sir William Herschel sniffily decreed it was only an "asteroid." Herschel (who had started as oboist in a German military band, moved to England, graduated to organist and composer, then got the telescope bug) called the shots in astronomy because he'd discovered Uranus and several moons, identified nebulae as the place where stars condensed, and (as he said) had looked deeper into space than anybody. And had seen stars whose light "must take two million years to reach the Earth."

This last remark knocked the socks off Herschel's strange friend Thomas Campbell, already a depressive alcoholic syphilitic (it would kill his wife) trying unsuccessfully to make a career as a poet. Campbell enjoys the dubious distinction of being the first Brit to write a poem with an American theme. Catchy title: "Gertrude of Wyoming." Like all of his work it left not a mark. Campbell did, however, manage single-handedly to kick-start the project for what would become University College, London. And ran a literary mag, with quality contributors like essayist William Hazlitt. In 1822 Campbell gave a rave review on a piece by Hew Ainslie, Scottish brewer, poet, and expat.

Ainslie (seeing the writing on the wall for his writing) had just left for the United States. After a couple of years in New York state discovering he was also not meant for farming, in 1825 Ainslie arrived at the newly founded utopian commune of New Harmony, Indiana. A year later Ainslie left when "harmony" turned out to be a misnomer. Rows, back-stabbing, and incompetence characterized the social experiment, and it shut down soon after. Back in brewing, Ainslie finally did well and settled in Kentucky.

Meanwhile, New Harmony's CEO, British libertarian mill owner Robert Owen, had gone home in a huff, leaving his son Robert Dale to become an American citizen. After a more-senses-than-one flirtation with the ideas of another reformer, Frances Wright (at her Nashoba commune for freed black slaves in Tennessee), Robert ended up in the Indiana legislature and then the U.S. Congress. Where he pushed through the Smithsonian bill as well as speaking and publishing on divorce, education, birth control, and other such op-ed stuff, including the abolition of slavery. This may be why proslavery president Franklin Pierce got Owen out of the way in 1853 by sending him as U.S. representative to Naples, Italy.

No place for liberal views like Owen's, the place was being run by King Ferdinand II (known as "Bomba" after he bombarded Sicily's main cities in 1848, the year of Europe-wide revolution). Some of Bomba's character references give a flavor of the man: treacherous, corrupt, superstitious, egocentric, bigoted, dictatorial, and badly educated. By 1851 it is reckoned he had forty thousand political prisoners. By the time he died in 1859 Bomba had made it virtually certain that his son and heir wouldn't be around for long.

Francis II didn't help things by being a weak, vacillating namby-pamby keen on persecutions and massacres, whose own palace guard mutinied. When he had the ringleaders shot, the guard disbanded and left him. So in 1860 one shove from the advancing Garibaldi and Francis was out of there with wife and all the loot he could carry.

A year later Garibaldi was in control. And a return-from-exile thirty-four-year-old chemist was back in his lab. Stanislao Cannizzaro knew more about atoms and molecules than most people, at a time when nobody was even sure if atoms were indeed the smallest bits of molecules. In 1860 this small matter was top of the agenda at the first-ever chemistry conference (in Karlsruhe, Germany). Cannizzaro turned up and solved the puzzle by showing how you could use the behavior of molecules to tell things about the atoms inside them.

Nine years later a Russian named Dmitri Mendeleev used Cannizzaro's ideas to arrive at the most fundamentally important concept in the history of chemistry. He designed the Periodic Table, in which the chemical elements are arranged in columns according to their atomic weight and their tendency to interact with other molecules. This periodic arrangement suddenly made possible the prediction of chemical behavior. Strangely enough, when the fourteenth edition of the *Encyclopedia Britannica* came out in 1929 Mendeleev got a write-up but only for his teaching techniques.

By 1937 the fourteenth edition was still going (though not strong) when it came to the attention of University of Chicago veep William Benton, who discovered that the encyclopedia was reluctantly owned by Sears Roebuck. Benton's offer to chip in a hundred thousand dollars of his own money helped persuade Sears to give the *Britannica* to the University of Chicago, where under Benton's able administration sales increased fiftyfold and the university made millions.

Benton had begun as an advertising executive partnered with Chester Bowles in Benton and Bowles, inventors of soap opera, pioneers of consumer research, and in 1936 the sixth-biggest ad agency in the world. During World War II Bowles left the agency and went into price-administration work for the government. In 1944 the Advertising Club of Western Massachusetts gave him their Pynchon medal for excellence in public service.

In 1962 the medal winner was Edward Breck, promoter of the shampoo hysteria created by his "Breck Girls" ad campaign, featuring an image (sensuous yet chaste, seductive yet girl-next-door, sexy yet apple-pie) that shaped American womanhood's self-perception for fifty years.

The artist responsible for the campaign from the late 1950s until his death in 1976 was WILLIAM WILLIAMS.

CHAPTER TWELVE

WILLIAM FLOYD (NY) was forty-one. The word that comes to mind for Floyd is "harrumph." Reported to be pretentious and opinionated, he was well connected (host to Jefferson and Madison when they visited Long Island on a botany trip) in spite of the fact that he came from a family with (it was rumored) pro-British tendencies. Floyd spent much time in Congress saying little. Brief official biographies of him do the same. In 1777 he was voted onto the New York Council of Safety set up to look under stones for loyalists.

A fellow councilman was John Morin Scott, Yale lawyer, a leading figure in New York politics, who became New York secretary of state and was so outspoken in his revolutionary speeches that he was considered too much of a firebrand even for the first Constitutional Congress. Scott made his mark on history, in a manner of speaking, when he was one of the three-man committee (the second committee out of four to attempt the job) mandated to design the Great Seal of the United States. Scott's committee added the thirteen red-and-white stripes, the olive branch, and the stars.

In 1778 Scott was courted by the British Carlisle Commission, at the time in disarrayed retreat after four months in Philadelphia, where their offer of everything but independence had turned out to be too little, too late. And they'd compounded any felony by trying (and failing) to sow dissension in American ranks with "you-can-be-members-of-Parliament" offers to individuals and states. Individually delivered and behind con-gressional backs.

This devious trick was the brainchild of a Carlisle Commission member, Adam Ferguson, already professor of pneumatics (philosophy of mind), major Scottish thinker (biggest thought: "Money is not the root of all evil") and leading member of the Edinburgh chattering classes. Ferguson established the right of the individual to lead a private life without government interference, met the retired Voltaire, and was good mates with such senior brains as Adam Smith. Late in life Ferguson was stricken with a paralysis and after being cured became a vegetarian.

As was his physician, Joseph Black, known for his frugal habits, skeletal appearance, pallor, and green umbrella. When Ferguson knew him Black was professor of medicine at Edinburgh University and an expert on indigestion and gallstones. Place-in-history-wise, it was Black's spare-time work for the Scottish whisky distillers (how much fuel boiled how much liquid to steam and then how much water condensed the steam into how much whisky) that led him to discover that steam stored massive amounts of heat (latent), which was why it took so much cold water to condense it.

Black told James Watt about this and suggested how to solve the steam engine problem. Standard procedure was to inject hot steam into a piston cylinder, then splash the cylinder with cold water, cooling it down and causing the steam inside to condense. This produced a vacuum in the cylinder so the outside atmospheric pressure pushed the cylinder piston down. Problem was, the hot steam gradually warmed the cylinder, so less and less condensation, so less and less vacuum, so less and less piston movement. Leading to eventual slow-down and stop. Black said that condensing the steam in a separate box submerged in icy water and linked to the cylinder by a tube would do the vacuum-creating job efficiently and save the cylinder from cooling down and spoiling the piston stroke. Or words to that effect. The rest (the "separate condenser") is steam-power history.

One of Black's pupils was pompous Matthew Guthrie, who went off to Russia and never came back. Which gave him no choice but to become a prolific letter writer. His correspondence (with nearly everybody in Europe's science community) discussed you-name-it from scurvy to fossils, buckwheat, gout, steel-making, insects, textiles, geography, birds, rheumatism, Russian cough drops, and other such esoterica. He traveled the length of Russia and even had time to translate Empress Catherine the Great's opera *Oleg* and to offer it to London publishers. No takers.

One of Guthrie's acquaintances (who wrote even more letters than Guthrie) was Jean Hyacinthe de Magellan. A Portuguese who had started out as a priest, went secular and settled in England, where he became one of the first industrial spies (for the French). By this time (late 1700s) Magellan knew all the Industrial Revolution players and had set himself up as a corresponding go-between for scientists and engineers all over Europe, passing on information and instruments. So it was easy for him to give the French top-secret intel on stuff like Watt's steam engine, Black's heat research, and the latest loom designs. Late in life when he'd made his pile he lost a lot by investing in one of history's greater liars and then incredibly helped publish the liar's memoirs.

In 1771 great liar Count Moritz Benyowsky had escaped from Russian exile in Kamchatka, then traveled to Alaska, Japan, Taiwan, Macao, China, and Madagascar (or not, since everything he wrote about the trip was unbelievable exaggeration). Madagascar gave him his Great Idea: make the island a French colony. Back in Paris, Louis XV seemed keen, so Benyowsky headed once more to Madagascar and made himself king. Louis cooled, so Benyowsky tried Austria. Mixed reactions, so he headed for the United States, where (according to his memoirs) he fought at Savannah (or not), met Washington (or not), and reached the rank of general (or not). Finally, with money from Baltimore businessmen he took off yet again for Madagascar. Where in 1786 he died fighting the French.

That was the bare-bones version. The full account made such a splash that a play (one of 250 written by German August von Kotzebue) based on Benyowsky's adventures enjoyed its U.S. premier at the Holiday Street Theater, Baltimore, on October 19, 1814, a special night in

American history because it was also the night and location of the first public performance of "The Star-Spangled Banner."

Two years later author Francis Scott Key was a founding member (together with such as Andrew Jackson and Daniel Webster) of the American Colonization Society. Whose aim was to solve the problem of trouble-making freed black slaves by removing them to Africa "so as to make slave property safe." In spite of (surprise, surprise) opposition from blacks, the scheme went ahead with the support of President Monroe. On April 25, 1822 the first African Americans stepped ashore in Liberia (capital, Monrovia, named after the president). Only a year earlier the Liberian real estate had been bought from the natives (with the help of a persuasive pistol) for goods worth three hundred dollars. Holding the gun was Monroe's envoy, U.S. Navy lieutenant Richard Stockton, grandson of the signer.

Seventeen years later, in 1838, Stockton took shore leave and set up the Delaware and Raritan Canal and then the Camden and Amboy Railroad (free tickets to politicos). One of his partners in this venture was the seventy-four-year-old John Jacob Astor, once a poor immigrant, who had done well in fur trade and land deals, so he now owned 7 percent of all the private wealth in the United States and was the country's first multimillionaire. At this time Astor was just back from fifteen years in Europe where, among other things, he had tried in vain to represent the case (for child support) of Betsy Patterson, deserted by her husband, Napoleon's brother Jerome. Astor's appeals to Jerome's sister Princess Pauline Borghese went unread while the lady in question was busy furthering her reputation as the inventor of one-night stands.

Nymphomaniac, hefting more jewels than Tiffany's, the beautiful Pauline shocked Europe by commissioning a nude statue of herself (by Canova) holding a hand over her ear because it was her only imperfection. Pauline bathed in milk, was crazy about rum, and canoodled for four years with a young Italian composer, Giovanni Pacini, who wrote over eighty operas as well as oratorios, songs, and symphonies. And confessed that he "frequently slighted the string section." Pacini had the sheer bad luck to arrive on the scene between Rossini and Verdi so nobody remembers him (fyi, his masterpiece was *Saffo*).

Forgotten, too, was Pacini's librettist, Francesco Maria Piave, who also wrote for Verdi. For whom he penned such greats as *Rigoletto*, *La Traviata*, and *The Masked Ball*. This last starred two conspirators with the unlikely names of Tom and Sam because of a major rewrite required by Verdi's censor, who (in politically dangerous times, with democracy erupting all over Italy) objected to an opera about regicide. So what was planned as an opera about the assassination of Gustav III of Sweden became an opera about the killing of a British governor of Boston, U.S.A. These minor changes were demanded because just as the original opera was about to go on stage in Naples (1858) somebody threw a bomb at French emperor Napoleon III and the word "copycat" was in the air.

Four years earlier the emperor, who had plans to make France ("once again") great with overseas expansion and colonies and suchlike, lunched with Brit industrialist Henry Bessemer. Who sold him on the idea that France would get more bang for the imperial buck with more accurate artillery shells that would spin in flight after venting gas tangentially as they went up the cannon barrel. Only problem: cannon barrels strong enough to take this malarkey. Bessemer's answer: Blow air through molten iron, add carbon, and make fast, cheap steel for cannon barrels.

Music to the ears of another metal-bashing Brit, John Brown, who went on to use the Bessemer process to build dreadnoughts for the Royal Navy and in 1899 bought a Scottish shipyard to launch them. In 1920 the John Brown company floated the last-word Cunard luxury liner *Aquitania* with its Egyptian swimming pool, Elizabethan grill room, Louis XVI restaurant, Carolingian smoking room, Greek lounge, and the first Sperry gyrocompass on a nonmilitary ship.

American self-made Elmer Sperry invented a variety of stuff: electric streetcar, mining equipment, monorail, aerial torpedo, and nearly four hundred other patented gizmos. His gun-mounted gyrostabilizer made fire control possible on battleships. Even in a rolling sea their shells would hit the spot twenty amazing miles away. And Sperry's gyro-controlled turn-and-bank indicator went into every airplane.

In 1923 the Sperry company helped a one-legged Russian immigrant, Alexander Seversky, to develop a gyroscopically stabilized bombsight.

Seversky's firm eventually became Republic Aviation and was responsible for producing over fifteen thousand World War II P-47 fighter-bombers. Which were famous for taking massive damage in battle without crashing. Turned out that the really easy way to crash a P-47 (it was too soon discovered) was by landing it with the wheels up. This occurred all too frequently because the cockpit switches for landing gear and flap actuation were next to each other. And identical.

Naturally enough the study of such human-factor design problems was quickly the subject of intense military interest and eventually spawned the new discipline of "ergonomics." In 1952 the first Ergonomic Society was formed by a number of British academics working in psychology, physiology, biology, and design.

The Society's first secretary was WILLIAM FLOYD.

CHAPTER THIRTEEN

Phil. Livingston

PHILIP LIVINGSTON (NY) was sixty. And the nearest thing America had to an aristo. He faced the fight for independence with serious reservations, expecting it would lead America to civil war when left-wing extremists tried to take over. Livingston thought this because he was a leading member of the New York elite, owner of extensive estates, fashionably married, and rich from his activities in privateering and trade.

But he pitched in with the ordinary revolutionaries (and did his best to keep things from going too far to the left). In 1775 Livingston was a member of the Committee for Secret Correspondence and met the mysterious Julian de Bonvouloir. Black sheep of minor French nobility, lame, and broke, de Bonvouloir had spent some time in America, so when Louis XVI started looking for somebody to check out how serious the American rebels really were, he asked the French ambassador in London for a name and de Bonvouloir was it.

His operational orders were to go into deep cover, put nothing on paper, be deniable if discovered, and sound out the possibility of French support for the revolutionaries. De Bonvouloir reported that the Americans were ready, willing, and able to revolt. And they would win. But, he added, the Americans, too, were pussy-footing: Would French money and arms be forthcoming? Would the French stay out of Canada? Could they have some French engineers?

De Bonvouloir's report clinched matters and France was in to the tune of millions in guns, ships, men, and money. Alas, the report arrived back in London too late to reach the Duc de Guines, the ambassador who'd fingered de Bonvouloir in the first place. Guines had already been repatriated for scandalous behavior with Lady Elizabeth Craven. Wasn't really his fault. Lady Craven's open infidelities were noteworthy even in an age that tolerated such peccadilloes. So what she and de Guines got up to must have been something extraordinary (one mag, leaving much to the imagination, said: "criminal intercourse").

Beautiful and witty, Lady Craven wrote light farces and knew all the literary lions. After one infidelity too many, in 1783 her husband left. Then so did she. On a fun-and-sex tour of Europe and then Istanbul before returning to marriage with a Prussian royal. While in Istanbul she was squired around by the French ambassador, Count de Choiseul-Gouffier, who later tried (and failed) to get permission to chip the marble frieze off the Parthenon (at the time, Turkish) before Elgin thought of it. And then, with Homer in hand, the count had headed south looking for a historically real Troy. Then back home in 1789 the French Revolution happened and suddenly the count was out of a job.

So he took off for St. Petersburg, where he found work as Catherine the Great's librarian. And met the lovely Elisabeth Vigée-Lebrun, the most famous lady painter in France and on the run from the French revolutionaries because she'd done a slew of royal portraits, including no fewer than thirty of Queen Marie-Antoinette. Who was by now headless. Vigée-Lebrun's forte was her delicate touch and the way she dressed her sitters in ornate costumes and headdresses to make them look even more refined than they were. She did the same for the Russian elite.

On her way out of Paris just ahead of the mob Vigée-Lebrun had hidden in the house of an architect pal, Alexandre-Théodore Brongniart, who then left town for the anonymity of the French Deep South, aka Bordeaux, where he hid out till the dust settled and Napoleon was firmly in the saddle. Whereupon Brongniart's earlier experience building palaces for princes and their mistresses got him the job of chief of public works. Brongniart's best effort: the Paris Bourse. Second best:

the layout of the Père Lachaise Cemetery, which had recently been opened to provide space for the massive increase in dead bodies thanks to the revolution. Shortly after Lachaise went into business in 1804 it became clear that people thought it was too far out of town to be much of a dead center.

So the Paris prefect Nicholas Frochot hit upon a great promotional wheeze. He collected bits of fancy statuary, sepulchers, etc., from local museums and scattered them around Lachaise. He then exhumed the bones of Molière and LaFontaine and moved them to the cemetery. In 1817 he did the same with national-hero medieval lovers Héloïse and Abélard. Soon *le tout Paris* was dying to be buried in Lachaise. These corpses-to-be included Balzac, Chopin, Gertrude Stein, Oscar Wilde, and (in 1825) Adam Seybert.

Seybert was a U.S. congressman who had risen without trace, settled in Paris a year before his death, and whose single claim to fame was (in 1818) his unreadable *Statistical Annals of the United States 1789-1818*. In which he tried to disprove Malthus's idea that the American population would double every twenty-five years. Unfortunately, he got his data wrong and the book was slaughtered by Sydney Smith's devastating piece in the *Edinburgh Review*. The article included the immortal line: "Who reads an American book? Or goes to an American play?"

Smith was the master of the one-liner: "I never read a book before re-viewing; it prejudices a man"; "Correspondences are like smallclothes [undershorts] before the invention of suspenders: it is impossible to keep them up." He was a great ladies' man and wonderful with children and everybody loved "dear Sydney." After starting the *Edinburgh Review* in 1802 Smith moved to London and the Holland House set (Lord and Lady Holland, whose son married Smith's daughter, ran a left-leaning salon for the city wits). Smith espoused causes: save chimney sweeps, provide legal aid, give women equality. And his lectures were so popular they caused carriage jams.

In 1803 Smith's mag slanged a new set of plays, attacking the concept behind them (different treatments of the violent emotions). "Plays on the Passions," by Joanna Baillie (her plan was for three sets of trilogies on love and hatred) was a first attempt at subtle psychological drama in an age of big productions and overblown acting, so the work received a mixed welcome. Baillie was probably the greatest woman writer of her generation. Introduced to the literary set by her aunt, the well-known poet Anne Hunter, Baillie was innovative, a shrewd observer of character, and wrote plays and poetry, which finally achieved their just due around 1836. Just after Baillie had visited Ealing Grove agricultural school, in London.

The school (carpentry, masonry, and market gardening) was set up for the "vagrant classes" by Baillie's confidante Lady Annabella Byron. Who back in 1815 had fallen for and married the lame and lunatic Lord B. One year and a daughter later they split and she never saw him again. Which for Annabella would have been too soon, given what she'd gone through with him. Byron was (as one of his many mistresses said) "mad, bad and dangerous to know." There were stories of violence and "much worse." Not long after the separation from Annabella, Byron left for foreign adventures and more women, and never came back.

One day Annabella found a sympathetic American ear and told it what the "much worse" had been: Byron's incestuous relationship with his stepsister Augusta and a resultant baby. Her confidante waited till Annabella was well dead before the 1870 publication of a book on the subject. Harriet Beecher Stowe's aim, apart from revealing what a skunk Byron had been, was to raise the whole matter of behavior such as incest in the context of women's rights. Much too outspoken for her readers, the book failed.

Unlike her earlier piece of ground-breaking social commentary, *Uncle Tom's Cabin*, in which blacks were portrayed for the first time as real human beings. *Cabin* made Stowe an instant international star and a ton of money. Much of which went into trying to save her son Fred from booze. By sixteen he was an alcoholic. Treatments like the water cure (drink a lot of it, sleep in sheets soaked with it) failed. The Civil War took him to Gettysburg and enforced sobriety. On the second day of the battle he got shrapnel in the head and an invalid's discharge. Back to drink.

One of his fellow sufferers (from the artillery barrage) was Wesley Merritt, fast-tracked cavalryman who had a good war and ended up commanding one cavalry wing of the Army of the Shenandoah. The other wing got George Custer. In 1882 (by this time known as the "boy general") Merritt was named superintendent of the U.S. Military Academy and arrived at West Point, New York. So, too (as a cadet) did the man later to become known as General of the Armies "Black Jack" Pershing. Whose only failure in a golden career came in 1916 when he was sent to Mexico to catch Pancho Villa after a group of Villistas had attacked, pillaged, and burned Columbus, New Mexico. Bandit, revolutionary, and national hero Villa ran off into the mountains, where the locals hid him. In the end Pershing was obliged to give up and cable Washington headquarters: "Villa is everywhere and Villa is nowhere."

Villa himself had other fish to fry. Mexico was, as usual, in the "my-turn-to-be-president" mode and the name of the game was to change sides when it suited the career. So Villa's ex–dearest friend and revolutionary Vesustiano Carranza was now his enemy, antirevolutionary, and president. And making Villa's life difficult with his Carranza Air Force. One plane. Maintained by an itinerant American, Malcolm Loughead, a car mechanic down from California, where being a gold prospector had not panned out. Nor had a plane built by him and his brother Allen. By 1919 the brothers were back in the United States trying to sell Malcolm's hydraulic brake in Detroit. In order to make life easier they also changed their name to the more-pronounceable "Lockheed."

Eventually the brothers gave up on hydraulics and went back to plane-making and from then on it was onward and upward. Except for one nasty moment in 1973 when the Dutch government was looking for a new antisubmarine aircraft. Lockheed's Orion was one of the alternatives that would fit the bill and to help the decision the Lockheed Company slipped Prince Bernhardt (Queen Juliana's consort) just over one million dollars in return for his "good offices."

When the story broke in 1976 Bernhardt was forced to resign most of his high-profile (and often lucrative) directorships. One of these was the nonprofit presidency of the World Wildlife Fund, which Bernhardt now turned over to Britain's Prince Philip. In 2000 the WWF went to law to protect its initials, requiring the World Wrestling Federation to become World Wrestling Entertainment in 2002.

In March 2003 WWE announced the appointment of its new chief financial officer.

His name was PHILIP LIVINGSTON.

CHAPTER FOURTEEN

FRANCIS LEWIS (NY) was sixty-three. His signature on the Declaration surprised some people because there was a rumor that as late as 1776 he'd applied for the contract to supply the British army in Boston. And his daughter had married a British navy captain. By this time Lewis had a lot of commercial experience in the United Kingdom, Europe, Russia (he'd started the first American company there), and Africa. Lewis wasn't much of a speaker. Somebody, damning with faint praise, called him "steady." But he put in good committee work, especially dealing with munitions and shipbuilding. He also helped to save George Washington from oblivion.

As early as 1777 Washington's far-from-hot military performance had triggered a whisper campaign that he wasn't the right man to command the army. The "right man" was one of the whisperers, General Horatio Gates, victor of Saratoga. Gates's sidekick General Thomas Conway, a self-seeking, hot-tempered Irish-born Frenchman (whose talent Washington described as existing "more in his imagination than in reality") threw himself enthusiastically into what became known as the "Conway cabal" with a spate of anonymous letters to members of Congress, as well as within-earshot slanderous remarks and muttered complaints about Washington's "mismanagement."

When General Washington passed him over for promotion Conway tried bluffing Congress with the threat of resignation. To his chagrin they called his bluff. He then made some insulting public remarks about Washington, so General John Cadwallader called him out. They duelled and Cadwallader shot Conway in the mouth. When the wound had healed Conway apologized to Washington and in 1778 left for France. Where he did well in battle, was given command of France's "Pondicherry" regiment, and in 1781 arrived in Cape Town (French at the time).

A few months later life was complicated by the arrival of the prickly and argumentative Daniel De Meuron with his mercenary Swiss Regiment (half of whom, thanks to unexpected regimental deaths from smallpox, were raw recruits pulled out of the Paris jails). De Meuron complained incessantly about food, accommodation, pay, discipline, and would-be deserters (some, it was said, he tortured into confession). He also collected a hippopotamus, a large number of stuffed birds and snakes, a leopard, and several zebra skins, as well as assorted other bits of natural history. And 2,375 bottles of local wine.

In 1786, after the umpteenth row with everybody, De Meuron grumped off back to his native Switzerland. Two years later his regiment got a new mercenary contract from the Dutch and left for Ceylon (Dutch at the time). De Meuron stayed at home in Neuchatel complaining as usual (about Dutch pay) to anybody who'd listen. In one case a Scotsman called Hugh Cleghorn. Who had other plans for De Meuron.

For some reason seemingly-dull-as-ditchwater ex–history prof. Cleghorn (sixteen boring years in St. Andrews University, Scotland and, by the time of the De Meuron meeting, on his way through Switzerland being Grand Tour–companion to the usual half-witted English earl) caught the attention of the British government with his proposal that British rule in India would be bolstered if the Brits also ruled Ceylon. De Meuron was easily persuaded (by money) to make it happen and the two left for Colombo, soon, thanks to the help of De Meuron's disreputable jailbird crew, to become yet another bit of the British Empire.

Cleghorn's own career took a dive after this because he was cordially disliked by the new British governor of Ceylon, Frederick North. By 1800 Cleghorn was on the boat home, accused (wrongly) of some questionable business relating to the government pearl-fishing industry (he had been in charge of it and some had gone missing). Meanwhile, North made a success of Ceylon (rooted out corruption, set up civil service, was popular, acted benevolent) and by 1805, now ex-governor, was living in Athens, Greece, known around town for his "ramshackle" appearance and agitating for a Greek university (there wasn't one). In the end he had his way and in 1823 North became chancellor of Corfu U. (aka "The Ionian Academy," with academic togas and headbands designed by North).

In 1810 North had met the usual culture-vulture Athenian tourists, including Byron, his pal Hobhouse, and a young architect named Charles Cockerell. One night after drinking too much with Byron and the rest Cockerell took them all off to the nearby island of Aegina to poke around the temple of Aphaia. Where they discovered that (shock horror!) the bits of temple they dug up weren't pristine white as contemporary experts said all marble buildings had once been in ancient Greece. Color residue on the columns suggested that in classical times the place had looked not unlike modern-day Disney World.

Cockerell didn't publish his findings, so it was left to a visiting Frenchman, Guillaume-Abel Blouet, to astonish the world with the polychromatic news. After which Blouet returned to Paris and was given the Arc de Triomphe to finish (no color, please). After which in 1837 he was sent off to the United States to do a quick study on the latest in prison design so he could return to Paris well-prepared to become inspector-general of French prisons.

Blouet took as his model the model prison built in Philadelphia by architect John Haviland and known as "Cherry Hill." Haviland had created a radial-plan design with seven cell blocks set like spokes around an administrative hub from which guards could look down the central corridor of each spoke and monitor prisoners' movements. Not that prisoners moved much. The regime was primarily designed to prevent one prisoner from corrupting another. So everybody was in solitary confinement, working (alone) in-cell, interspersed with two (alone) exercise periods a day. With flush toilets before the White House had them.

Europeans went for this enlightened approach to penology with great enthusiasm. One of the better-known proselytizers was Alexis de Tocqueville, who visited Cherry Hill eight times in 1831 during a visit to the United States (ostensibly for prison-design research but in fact to see if America was doing anything that France ought to be doing, government-wise). Two years were spent wandering from the East Coast to Wisconsin to Louisiana, talking to people and watching what went on. After which de Tocqueville produced a *Study on American Prisons* (forgotten) and two volumes on American democracy (not forgotten).

De Tocqueville's great exposition of the unique American political balance of equality with personal liberty and individualism with com-munity spirit took his book into the best-seller lists in Europe when it was translated in 1840 by the twenty-two-year-old Henry Reeve. Reeve was a networker, particularly after 1840 when he became lead writer for *The Times* of London. He knew everybody who was anybody, including Carlyle, Thackeray, Balzac, Liszt, Sir Walter Scott, and Lamartine. And the arch-schmoozer of all time, Count D'Orsay.

Famous as the shopaholic par exellence. His outfits were must-have for every fashionista: outrageous waistcoats, big hats, and six pairs of gloves a day. And matching footmen in gold and green. Charming, witty, artistic D'Orsay spent time in London as number three in a strange *ménage à quatre* relationship (with Lord and Lady Blessington and their fifteen-year-old daughter, D'Orsay's wife) and possibly father-ing a child by a ballet dancer. Although malicious gossip said anybody who dressed like that had to be at least impotent.

D'Orsay's dancer was Fanny Elssler, beautiful and extraordinarily tal-ented and by this time on the way to New York (child left in care), under contract to the Park Theater. When the theater impresario died and his partner broke Elssler's contract, an international smoothie named Henry Wikoff stepped in. Since Henry was a pal of James Gordon Ben-nett, owner of the New York *Herald*, Fanny got all the publicity she needed. After a hectic two years of performance and a row with Henry she left for Vienna. And Henry went about his abnormal life.

Rich, witty, been-there-done-that raconteur, semidiplomat, semi-journalist, and scandalous womanizer, Henry could charm the pants off anybody (maybe, it was rumored, a First Lady). Mary Todd Lincoln certainly treated Henry as part of the family, giving him free range of the White House and raising every eyebrow in Washington (as Mrs. Lincoln had already done with other of her men friends). She also enjoyed spiritualist table-rapping sessions, low-cut gowns, and conspicuous consumption. In 1861 Henry was discovered to be leaking White House data to his newspaper magnate friend. Whereupon Lincoln personally escorted him off the property.

One of the men who had helped put Lincoln on the property in the first place was John Stallo, German immigrant to Cincinnati turned professor of physics and math turned philosopher turned Republican stalwart, thus bringing Lincoln the sizeable German vote. Stallo was annoyed at what he saw as failure of Reconstruction after the Civil War and switched sides. Result: In 1885 Democratic president Grover Cleveland expressed his appreciation of Stallo's work by making him U.S. minister to Italy.

Stallo arrived just in time to handle (by looking the other way) the delicate matter of Italian colonialist expansion into Africa when Rome invaded Eritrea and set up Italian Abyssinia. One effect of this bit of adventurism was to open the door for the return (after centuries) of Catholic missionaries to the Abyssinian Catholic dioceses, defunct in some cases since the fourth century but kept on the books by popes who had turned them into "titular" (in-name-only) sees. This papal trick retained the option that one day the Church might come back, while at the same time providing bishoprics for people who were ready for the rank but for whom there were no vacant posts.

In 1926 one of these empty Abyssinian seats went to Father Maurice McAuliffe of Hartford, Connecticut, when he was ordained titular bishop of Dercos. Eight years later McAuliffe got the real thing and was made bishop of Hartford. This gave him the authority to approve a request from the Jesuits to set up a local school. After some discussion the town of Fairfield was chosen, and in 1942 the first classes took place. Over the next three years the place grew and raised its academic sights. In 1945 the state of Connecticut chartered Fairfield as a university.

In 1998 the university's professor of philosophy was FRANCIS LEWIS.

CHAPTER FIFTEEN

LEWIS MORRIS (NY) was fifty. Although he probably didn't say, "Damn the consequences, give me the pen," when he signed, Morris risked more than did most of his colleagues. Upper-crust lord of the manor of Morrisania, rich, charismatic, Yale, son of the New Jersey governor, Morris could have stayed at home and sat it out. He chose not to and in consequence suffered the consequences. Morrisania was looted (by both sides) and most of his one thousand acres of woodland were destroyed.

Morris's successful career in the militia was mirrored by that of his eldest son, Lewis Jr., who did so well in the Carolinas campaign that he made bird colonel and became aide-de-camp to General Nathaniel Greene. Whose wife, Catherine, went everywhere with the general (living in tents, on battlefields) and tickled everybody's fancy with her flirty ways (she even wore pants to go riding). Good-looking and witty, she was very friendly with Washington, Lafayette, and Hamilton, to name but the cream.

Alas, her husband had used all his own money to buy army supplies, so after the war straitened circumstances obliged the couple to settle down on the Savannah rice plantation provided by a grateful Georgia. By 1795 the general was dead, Catherine's lodger Eli Whitney had invented his cotton gin, and the two of them were in business. Things went wrong: patent infringement, lawsuits, and workshop fires. Looking for funds to back the gin, Catherine put up the plantation as collateral for shares in the Great Yazoo Land Scam, one of the greatest in American history.

In 1795 the Georgia legislature sold 35 million acres of western Georgia to the Yazoo Company for one-and-a-half cents an acre. When it was discovered that all but one of the Georgia legislators (and a few newspaper editors) had had their palms greased to keep matters quiet, all hell broke loose and the legislation was repealed—as always in these things, too late for the investors.

The basic Yazoo idea had been kick-started back in 1789 by the governor of Georgia, Edward Telfair, when he illegally gave away millions of western acres to friends and colleagues. Telfair (who, no surprise, was instrumental in pushing through the Eleventh Amendment, limiting the extent of the federal judiciary) did well enough over the years to commission a fancy Greek Revival mansion, built in 1819 by itinerant Brit architect William Jay.

Jay had worked in London till the previous year and now introduced Savannah to what was known as the Regency Style: large square house, curving staircases, Doric column porticoes, and cast-iron balconies. Just this side of vulgar. And just the style for Julia Scarbrough, multilingual, sophisticated wife of hubby William, who, because of the couple's extravagant lifestyle, was known in Savannah as the "Merchant Prince." Julia's dinners (or, as she referred to them, "blowouts") were famous all-night affairs.

On May 12 the Scarbrough house hosted a blowout for President Monroe, in town for a joyride on Scarbrough's new toy, the SS *Savannah*. Soon to be forgotten as the first-ever transatlantic steamship. Too far ahead of her time. On May 22 she headed off (not full) for New York and then onward to Liverpool, St. Petersburg, Kronstadt, and Stockholm. Then, disconsolately (and still almost empty), back home. Then to Washington, D.C. By which time Scarbrough's company was being wound up and the *Savannah* was in the hands of a buyer, who took the engines out and ran her on sail. But at least the *Savannah* made the reputation of her engine-maker, Stephen Vail of the Speedwell Works in Morristown, New Jersey.

One day in 1836 Stephen's son Alfred came back from college in New York enthusing about crazy experiments by an art professor named Sam Morse, who needed technical know-how and money to develop a gizmo that would send instant messages along a wire. Stephen Vail provided two thousand dollars and the top floor of the Speedwell factory. Where Alfred and an apprentice made Morse's machine. There were peremptory letters (and rare visits) from the self-important Morse himself.

Alfred Vail is one of communication technology's great unknowns, because it was almost certainly he who invented the telegraph finger-key and what is now called the "Morse" Code. In 1838 at Speedwell the first message flashed along the wire. Not the dramatic 1844 "What hath God Wrought" Morse would use to amaze Congress but something a little more humdrum that Alfred thought up: "A patient waiter is no loser." Later on, Morse's family made sure Alfred was written out of the official history.

Vail's apprentice William Baxter went on to become the inventor of the Baxter portable steam engine. The regular, two-horsepower version was the size of a stove and weighed 1,280 pounds. Linked by a system of belts, wheels, cranks, and gears, it'd turn any machinery. By 1874 thousands were in use all over the country. If a bit of the engine broke it was interchangeable with an identical replacement part. Just like a Colt revolver, which in 1868 was manufactured (as was Baxter's stove) at the Colt Armory in Hartford, Connecticut. Where the same year Colt also began turning out large numbers of the new terror weapon invented by a doctor from North Carolina. Who thought it would reduce the number of soldiers needed in battle and cut down on the number of casualties. The doc was right, but only in a manner of speaking, since the Gatling gun killed more men than had ever been possible before. When its crank-operated, six-rotating-barrel, automatic firing and reloading mechanism went into action, the Gatling spat out between 200 and 350 rounds a minute. To devastating effect.

The gun was immortalized in Henry Newbolt's stiff-upper-lip poem about British troops in the Sudan, outnumbered by a horde of natives ("the Gatling's jammed, chaps!") but bravely rallying to their old-school cricket call: "Play up, play up, and play the game." Newbolt had earlier achieved instant fame with every Victorian patriot's fave: "Drake's Drum" (about how Sir Francis D. would return from the grave if ever needed to save the country from invasion). Newbolt became a major do-gooder, serving on committees, getting a knighthood and a heap of honorary degrees. In spite of the fact that he ran a ménage à trois with his wife and her cousin (Newbolt kept a diary: twelve nights a month with each woman). Then he upped the ante to *quatre* by adding Lady Glenconnor to the group. People knew, but kept it quiet. Victorian morals.

In 1914 Newbolt found himself summoned to a government meeting run by Charles Masterman. Who had had a nondescript career as a bureaucrat, then a brief period in the cabinet, and was now the new chief of the War Propaganda Bureau tasked with "getting the world in accord with British policy" (aka persuading the United States into World War I). Masterman's meeting was like a roll call of Eng. Lit.: Rudyard Kipling, John Galsworthy, H. G. Wells, Conan Doyle, Thomas Hardy, G. K. Chesterton, John Masefield, Arnold Bennett, Ford Madox Ford, and John Buchan. The name of the game was, as Masterman explained, to write books and pamphlets about how Britain would win the war and how dreadful the beastly Germans were. By June 1915 there were over 2 million texts in fifteen languages and a movie: *Britain Prepared*.

One other member of the group had (according to the London *Times*) made "astonishingly accurate prophecies" of the war. This was Hilaire Belloc: French navy, Oxford, farming, walking across America following (and in Napa, California, marrying) his sweetheart, Elodie, made his literary name with *The Bad Child's Book of Beasts*. Belloc's output was prolific and varied: history, satire, criticism, and above all travel books about his walks (e.g., northern France to Rome). Belloc also had a sly sense of humor. ("When I am dead I hope it's said, 'His sins were scarlet, but his books were read.'") His early life in left-wing politics was colored by the outrage he journalistically expressed about crooked share-dealing between cabinet ministers and especially by future prime minister Lloyd George.

In 1911 the British government had decided to open a chain of state-owned radio stations throughout the British Empire and the postmaster general awarded the deal to the Marconi Company. So far, no problem. But later Belloc discovered that the contract had been kept secret until March 1912, during which time the share price mysteriously jumped four times. Belloc revealed (in his mag *Eye Witness*) that the British attorney general had bought shares just after the secret contract was signed and then immediately sold them to Lloyd George. Other members of the cabinet had made similarly sneaky buys and sells.

Guglielmo Marconi himself was entirely unconnected with all this. By now he was an international science star and Nobel. In 1923 he joined the Italian Fascist Party, married an aristo, and was made an Italian marquis. In 1930 he became first president and founder-member of Mussolini's Italian Academy, with its sixty selected intellectuals chosen to give the Fascists spurious respectability. One reluctant (and politically inactive) founding member was a promising young prof. of physics, Enrico Fermi.

In the early 1930s Fermi shot neutrons at the entire Periodic Table of Elements and succeeded in splitting the uranium atom. For this he got the Nobel and in 1938 (with some relief) left Fascist Italy for a job in the United States. On December 2, 1942, in the squash courts under the University of Chicago's Stagg Field, Fermi took his neutron-shooting work an astounding step further. As described on the plaque, in his "atomic pile" Fermi achieved "the first self-sustaining chain reaction and . . . the controlled release of nuclear power."

From Chicago Fermi went to Los Alamos, New Mexico, as chief of the advanced physics department. In 1945 the end product of his work was dropped on Hiroshima. In 1974 as recognition of Fermi's work the U.S. National Accelerator Laboratory was renamed "Fermilab."

In 2004 Fermilab's list of twenty-year service award recipients included LEWIS MORRIS.

CHAPTER SIXTEEN

RICHARD STOCKTON (NJ) was forty-five. And the only signer to change his mind. That November, caught and imprisoned by the Brits (the only signer to be captured), Stockton was treated badly and kept on bread and water. He then also became the only signer to repudiate his signature and swear allegiance to the king. So the Brits released him. Then he died of cancer.

Tall, gray-eyed, and imposing, Stockton was landed gentry, Princeton, law, had spent time in London, and had met George III. He was friendly with Ben Franklin and had only just entered Congress when he signed the Declaration. In 1776 his other major moment came when his apple-of-eye seventeen-year-old daughter, Julia, married thirty-year-old signer Dr. Benjamin Rush, who had qualified in medicine at Edinburgh University, Scotland.

In 1793 Rush got his chance for real fame when a yellow fever epidemic hit Philadelphia and people began dying by the hundreds. Rush came across a book that said "the worse the disease, the more aggressive the treatment." So he started purging and bloodletting like there was no tomorrow (which, if he failed, there wasn't). The generous administration of "evacuants" (as the purges were politely called) plus the loss of three pints of blood a day plus cold-water baths and cold drinks either killed or cured. More lived than died and Rush, saving nine out of ten, was the hero of the hour.

In 1806 Rush was awarded a gold medal by the king of Spain's daughter, now Queen Maria Luisa of Etruria, for his advice on yellow fever during an outbreak there. Etruria was a rinky-dink country invented by Napoleon, who was running Europe at the time. Maria Luisa's father had asked Napoleon for Maria Luisa's husband, Luigi, to be made into something more than just Duke of Somewhere. And Luigi wanted at least a million subjects. So Napoleon obliged. In return for Louisiana.

Which, confusingly, had until 1762 been French. Then became Spanish. In 1800, France got Louisiana back again (in return for Luigi's Kingdom of Somewhere-now-called-Etruria). The deal being that if France then wanted to sell Louisiana, Spain would get first refusal. Three years later Napoleon's plans to set up a French state in America were scuppered by defeats in the Caribbean and in the end (without consulting Spain) he offloaded Louisiana for fifteen million dollars to the United States.

The Americans had initially wanted to buy only Florida and New Orleans. And for only two million dollars. Suddenly Talleyrand (the negotiator in Paris) said: "How much for the lot?" When the Americans asked for an exact description of the eastern boundary of Louisiana Talleyrand said he didn't know but the United States would get whatever France had recently received from Spain. So the Louisiana deal was done and they all repaired to Talleyrand's place for one of his famous dinner parties and the witty conversation for which he was famous.

Charles Maurice de Talleyrand (limping, elegant, aristo) was an excommunicated bishop, ex-revolutionary, ex-émigré (to the United Kingdom and United States) and now Napoleon's foreign minister. His middle name was intrigue, he was not above a bribe or three, and he womanized nonstop (eventually marrying an upper-class hooker).

Above all Talleyrand loved food and wine. Which is why his lucky guests that day were fed by a man known as the "chef of kings and king of chefs," Antoine Carême. Who almost singlehandedly invented haute cuisine. Talleyrand apparently once challenged Carême to create a year's menus using seasonal produce and never repeating. He did and was hired. Carême introduced the concept of fresh vegetables and herbs, and light sauces. His *pièce de résistance* was usually a table center-piece of sugar and marzipan several feet high and modeled as a Roman ruin or Egyptian pyramid or Dutch windmill.

In 1815 Carême was poached by one whose love of the excessive was nothing short of excessive: the British Prince Regent. Known as "Prinny." For whom Carême once did a dinner of eight soups, forty main dishes, and thirty-two desserts. And seven "other courses." The Prince Regent was, depending on your inclinations, a dissolute drunken perverted criminal fop or a charming elegant intelligent (when sober) dandy fashion-setter. Either way he was a fat sex maniac who lived ludi-crously beyond his means (at one point debts of £12 million on an an-nual allowance of £5 million), buying art, architecture, clothes, and above all, women. With whom he had an inordinate number of bastards.

Whatever was chic, Prinny had to have it. In 1818 this meant a dandy-horse, so-called because Prinny and his dandy friends all bought one. A craze for three years, the gizmo was also known as a velocipede (a bicycle before the bicycle; with no pedals you "walked" it along). Maker was Denis Johnson who'd copied the idea from a version (the "Drais-ine") invented the year before by a German forest ranger named Karl Drais. For which the local archduke made him professor of mechanics (at no university, with no such faculty).

Of course, the French claimed to have invented the bicycle years ear-lier when the Count de Sivrac produced a machine used enthusiastically by a Burgundian gent named Nicéphore Niépce. He and his brother Claude dabbled in science and invented a steam-powered boat. Claude headed for high-tech England, where people went for such mechanical stuff, but to little avail. In 1826 Claude became ill and Nicéphore turned up to look after him in Kew, outside London, where Claude was lodg-ing. And where Niépce gave a colleague of Claude's another little inven-tion: a pewter plate, covered with bitumen of Judea and exposed for eight hours to the view out of Nicéphore's window back in St. Loup de Varenne. The bright bits in the view had hardened the bitumen and Nicéphore washed off the rest with lavender oil. Thus producing on the pewter plate the first light-and-shade photographic image.

Ferdinand Bauer (Claude's colleague) showed it to the Royal Society. Not interested. So he put it in a drawer, where it was not to be rediscovered for a hundred years. So much for recognition and reward. Bauer might well have been more image-conscious. In his spare time he was drawing teacher to Queen Charlotte and his day job kept him busy, sketching and painting everything the Brit explorers were bringing back to Kew Royal Botanical Gardens. Bauer reproduced each leaf, stamen, and petal with microscopic, excruciating fidelity. Maybe the best botanical artist ever.

He'd had early practice on a four-year, two-thousand-drawing voyage around Australia he'd completed in 1805, working for the on-board naturalist, Robert Brown. Known in the trade as the "Prince of Botanists," during the trip Brown collected thirty-two hundred different samples of plant and a ton of zoology, including a wombat. In 1810 Brown's narrative of the voyage blew the Euro-botany crowd away, presenting 187 new genera and one thousand new species. It took him the rest of his life to catalogue the collection. Today Brown is best known for his 1828 footnote that down a microscope he'd seen tiny particles in a drop of water bouncing around without any apparent reason (even when there was only one particle). Brown thought that the bounce might be the effect of the "life force" popular among some scientists at the time.

This observation by Brown was instantly rubbished by Heidelberg prof. Georg Muncke. According to whom the "Brownian motion" was nothing more than light and heat creating currents in the water. However, Muncke saved most of his firepower for Lorenz Oken, leader of the *naturphilosophie* school of those who believed in the "life-force" idea. Oken's scientific version of Romanticism ("all life is one") claimed that every organism was made up of elemental bits that had all started in prehistory lying along the edge of the million-years-ago sea and looking like primordial gunk. Which Oken called "Ur-slime." For decades after he first published in 1803 this idea was taken seriously.

One of the believers was Ernst Haeckel. Who later dropped what he was doing in 1859 when he read Darwin's new book *Origin of Species*. From then on he became Darwin's evangelizer and misrepresentative all round Germany. For Haeckel evolution explained (among other, more-slime-related issues) the progress from primitive race to advanced race and implied the responsibility of the latter to take care of the former, i.e., it was okay to colonize and maintain racial purity. All the stuff that later made Haeckel Hitler's favorite noodler.

Sharing Haeckel's view to some extent was Brit philosopher and ex-railroad engineer Herbert Spencer. Spencer invented the phrase "survival of the fittest" and his version of Darwinism was known as "Social Darwinism." A few highlights: The strong make society healthy and rich; the individual is more important than the state; the "law of equal freedom" gives everybody the same chance to be successful by their own unaided efforts; a laissez-faire capitalist system offers such individuals the greatest opportunity and helps society to progress. Like Haeckel, Spencer believed that the European races were the successful culmination of social evolution. The top people.

Harvard assistant librarian John Fiske (who in 1874 wrote two volumes modestly titled: *Outlines of Cosmic Philosophy*) thought America went one better than Europe and on his extensive lecture tours promoted the evolution-based idea that as the most evolved nation on Earth it was America's Manifest Destiny to expand her borders, show lesser nations the way forward, and usher in an era of American peace and prosperity. This was not a new thought, but now it had "scientific" backing.

The fervor for American expansion came to a head in 1898 when troops were sent to the Philippines, Guam, and Puerto Rico (all of which then became American possessions). Troops also went to Cuba, where the (official) aim was to end the anti-Spain civil war going on there and where the battle for San Juan Hill gained gallant "Black Jack" Pershing a Silver Star. By 1906 he'd been fast-tracked to general and a Philippine governorship. By 1918 he was leading the U.S. Army in Europe and a year later was five-star General of the Armies. The only other five-star in history had been George Washington.

Just before returning to the United States in December 1918, Pershing awarded the Distinguished Flying Cross to a young Army Air Corps Lieutenant named Spessard Holland, who'd been flying dangerous forward-observation missions behind enemy lines. Holland was a lawyer who would go on to become Florida governor and then one of the most powerful members of the U.S. Senate (from 1946 till his death in 1971). In 1968 the law firm Holland had founded back in the 1950s turned into Holland & Knight, and by 2002 it was one of the twenty biggest firms in the world, specializing in commercial law.

In 2006 one of the partners and member of the firm's private wealth services section was RICHARD STOCKTON.

CHAPTER SEVENTEEN

Jno Witherspoon

JOHN WITHERSPOON (NJ) was fifty-three. He'd arrived in the United States from Scotland only eight years before and worked his tail off in Congress (sat on over a hundred committees and was a frequent speaker). Witherspoon had come to America to be president of Princeton College, where things were going from dire to worse. The year he arrived there were only eleven graduates. So Witherspoon hit the road to raise money (he doubled the endowments) and to recruit students. In the end he did pretty well: His pupils went on to become a U.S. president, a vice-president, nine cabinet officers, twenty-one senators, thirty-nine congressmen, three Supreme Court justices, and twelve state governors.

In 1771 Witherspoon graduated Philip Freneau, who wasn't able to be at commencement, so his schoolmate Breckenridge read Freneau's poem: "The Rising Glory of America." Don't bother. Freneau's life was one long struggling writer's attempt to make ends meet. He frequently disappeared for years at a time to earn money on trading ships in the Caribbean. At one point his ex–college roommate, James Madison (that one), persuaded him to be editor and writer for a new journal, the *National Gazette*.

Freneau wrote pieces that rambled on about how Independence was supposed to make life better for everybody and not just enrich the fat-cat merchant elite. As the only poet to flourish during the Revolution he became unimaginatively known as the "Poet of the Revolution." Much of the sharp edge to Freneau's work came from his healthy dislike of the Brits after his wartime experience in 1780 aboard the prison ship (aka "hulk") *Scorpion*. After six weeks of appalling treatment he was released, skin and bones.

Prison hulks had first appeared in England because thanks to the American War the judges could no longer transport criminals to the American colonies. This created a humongous problem, because with two hundred capital crimes and two hundred crimes-of-deportation on the books there were more jailbirds than cells. Hence the hulks. Run by contractors for profit and on which conditions were unspeakable: dysentery, fever, floggings, filth and vermin, rotten food, and guards with swords permanently drawn and palms permanently open.

In 1777 an opinionated, self-centered, devout, narrow-minded social climber named John Howard published *The State of the Prisons*, written after he'd visited 250 of them in the previous two years. Howard was a country squire who dabbled in weather forecasting, then got obsessed by incarceration and spent his life visiting prisons everywhere from Holland to Russia to Portugal. In Britain he called for crazy reforms such as clean cells, health care, purpose-built penitentiaries, and (craziest of all) salaried jailers and prison clothing. Parliament set up a committee, a parliamentary bill was introduced, and nothing was done.

Howard's bill's sponsor was his second cousin, millionaire high-tech brewer Samuel Whitbread. Whose son Sam Jr. (Eton and Cambridge, rich, ambitious) spent years in Parliament annoying aristos and being passed over for government positions because he was only a brewer. He was also a reformer: against the 1812 war with America, antislavery, pro-Napoleon. Part of Sam's problem was that he became quite hysterical over his pet peeves. The guess is that he suffered from a disease of the endocrine system known as Cushing's syndrome. This may also be why on July 6, 1815, he slit his throat.

Three years later so did his pal Samuel Romilly. A highly successful lawyer, Romilly was everything Sam wasn't. The higher he rose in the legal profession (he finally made attorney general), the more he hated what the job required him to be (as he put it: "a near spectator of selfish and degrading conduct"). As a reformer he did his best to reduce the number of death-penalty crimes (samples: picking pockets, stealing property from a boat) and to increase the frequency with which cases were argued in the presence of juries. Romilly was also keenly interested in Howard's penal reform and made much noise about corruption at the royal level.

In which regard, in 1804 Romilly was briefed to defend Mrs. Fitzherbert in the three-year-long Minnie Seymour custody case. Minnie was three and had been given to Fitzherbert by the girl's mother, who was dying from TB. Now the relatives were claiming the child back. It helped Fitzherbert that she was the illegal (because Catholic) wife of the heir to the throne, the Prince Regent. Whose passion for Fitzherbert (Roman nose, fat, curly blonde, card player, big bosom) had the prince rolling on the floor, tearing out his hair, screaming, and stabbing himself to get her attention. For twenty-six years the two of them lived together on and off (he frequently left for various mistresses), the scandal of Europe and a massive drain on public funds.

The prince was a really big spender. And a corpulent, lascivious, boozing egomaniac, who knocked down large bits of London so that he could see his new Regent's Park from his new home in Carlton House (by looking up the new Regent Street). His other great architectural overindulgence was Brighton Pavilion, erected for him in the coastal city of Brighton. Moghul Indian on the outside, Chinese and Arabian interiors. All in supremely dreadful taste but at the time the height of fashion. About which the prince cared even more than sex, drink, or gambling.

The prince's consultant in the essential matter of dress was one of the dandies with whom he surrounded himself, Sir Lumley St. George Skeffington, known as Skiffy, the fop's fop. Skeletal, with rouged cheeks, he was famous for the wave of perfume that preceded him. His clothing dictated the day's look and usually included knee-ribbons, skin-tight breeches, striped vests, and absurdly large hats.

Skiffy's obsession was the theater, and he never missed a first night or a debut, sometimes seeing four shows in the same evening. He wrote plays that were instantly forgotten and sent poems to actors who never read them. And he would hang around green rooms just to be near the players. On Valentine's Day 1831 he penned one more vacuous piece of rhyming drivel to Lucia Vestris, the toast of London, a contralto with great legs. Who titillated the entire male population by playing "breeches" parts (in men's clothing) to show off the great legs to great advantage.

The same year Vestris didn't read Skiffy's little poem, after fifteen years of success acting in burlesques and extravaganzas she bought the lease of the London Olympic Theater. As manager she remodeled the theater, staged light comedies, and brought the curtain down by eleven every night to cater to the new middle-class audience who had jobs to go to in the morning. Vestris also hired Laura Keane, a promising young actress with management ambitions. In 1835 Keane left to pursue her American dream. Like all actor-managers Keane followed the money. In her case: to New York, San Francisco, Sydney, Australia, then back to New York. In the 1860s she took her company on tour and in 1865 found herself playing a role in *Our American Cousin* at Ford's Theater in Washington, D.C. the same night actor John Wilkes Booth opened the state box door and shot Lincoln in the back of the head. Keane cradled the dying president's head in her arms.

After the assassination John Ford was jailed for a month, his theater was closed down by the federal authorities, and he was paid one hundred thousand dollars compensation. He remained faithful to Booth's family, however, arranging for Booth's body to be reburied in the family plot. Ford had a name for being astute and (unusual in the cutthroat theater world) honorable. In 1878 he was the only theater manager to pay royalties to Gilbert and Sullivan for a performance of their operetta: *HMS Pinafore*.

The show's cast included a promising young singer, Lillie West, daughter of an Iowa publisher. In 1889 she was on the verge of fame when her son died of diphtheria. Devastated, she left the stage. In Chicago her mother persuaded her to join the *Daily News* as a drama critic and for forty years (as "Amy Leslie") Lillie wrote puff pieces to encourage her readers to support the theater. In 1910 one of Lillie's colleagues sent in a report about the French craze for aeronautics.

The piece was written by correspondent Octave Chanute, who was also an American engineer and airplane buff. And who back in 1896 had developed his own experimental flight station (on the Indiana shore of Lake Michigan), where the pilots flew 359 feet in fourteen seconds on gliders whose design became basic to all modern airframes. Chanute had a difficult relationship with the Wright brothers, who later denied using his ideas in spite of the 435 letters and cables they exchanged with him between 1901 and 1910, and the fact that Chanute had been orga-nizing conferences on powered flight since 1885.

In 1913 the French mag *L'Aérophile* published a (generous, consider-ing) Chanute article on the Wrights. The same edition carried news of the new ramjet engine designed by Frenchman René Lorin. The engine was simplicity itself. Air entered a tube and was compressed by a nar-rowed section of the tube. A fuel mist was sprayed into the compressed airflow and then ignited. As the compressed air heated, it expanded and with nowhere else to go accelerated out of the back end of the tube, thrusting the tube (and anything attached to it) forward. Starting the ramjet process involved only moving the tube to cause air to enter.

In 1942 at Peenemunde on the Baltic Sea this was done with a steam-catapult launching system, which sent the ramjets, attached to wings and a bomb (an arrangement known as the "V-1") toward London. Shortly thereafter, in August 1943, more than thirteen hundred British RAF bombers returned the favor by bombing the Peenemunde launch pads, thanks in large measure to the espionage efforts of American Allen Dulles. In his Swiss HQ, Dulles (ex-banker turned Office of Strategic Services operative) ran an extraordinarily successful spy ring, whose agents included the mistress of German admiral Canaris. And a metal-lurgy expert, Edward Schulte. Who blew the whistle on the V-1 launch site.

In 1947, when Dulles was president of the Council on Foreign Af-fairs, he was involved in discussions with another ex-OSS man, John Gardner (who by this time was vice president of the Carnegie Founda-tion), at a time when the foundation was considering the establishment of a Russian Studies Center at Harvard.

Nearly twenty years later Gardner set up a Carnegie Commission on

Educational Television. The commission recommended the creation of a Corporation for Public Broadcasting. In 1967 Congress took the commission's advice and approved the formation of the Public Broadcasting System (PBS) and National Public Radio (NPR).

NPR's first board chairman was JOHN WITHERSPOON.

CHAPTER EIGHTEEN

Fras. Hopkinson

FRANCIS HOPKINSON (NJ) was thirty-nine. He was a little man. John Adams said he had "a head no bigger than a large apple." The first graduate of Pennsylvania College, Hopkinson became a chemist, mathematician, inventor, artist, playwright, satirist, songwriter, harpsichordist, and America's first composer. He was also a whiz at PR. Well connected with the English political class (he dined with Lord North two months before the Boston Massacre), Hopkinson was a late convert to the Independence cause. In Congress he doodled caricatures.

He also designed the original Stars and Stripes and organized the Grand Federal Procession in Philadelphia on July 4, 1788, eight days after the Constitution had been ratified. It was quite an affair. Kickoff was at 9:30 from Third and South streets and the procession ended up with five thousand people spread over a mile and a half. There were floats, flags, and costumes. On parade: every public official, craft, trade, and profession, plus America's military and foreign allies. Leading the way, pulled on a cart by ten white horses, came the "Grand Federal Edifice," a thirty-six-foot-high white-painted circular Greek Temple with thirteen columns, ten of which were inscribed with the initials of the ratifying states so far (not North Carolina, Rhode Island, and New York) and a dome supporting the figure of Plenty and her cornucopia.

The whole event swung along to the strains of the "Federal Grand

March" composed by Alexander Reinagle. Who'd barely arrived from London, where he had been making a name for himself and had even visited Hamburg to meet C. P. E. Bach and get permission to perform some of his old man's music. Shortly after Reinagle arrived in Philadelphia he was teaching music to Nellie Custis, Washington's stepgranddaughter. He restarted the defunct City Concerts and generally raised the musical tone of the capital with his own performances as harpsichordist and singer.

In 1792 Reinagle went into business with another new arrival, Thomas Wignall, actor (Washington's favorite) turned theater manager. Wignall returned briefly to London and then reappeared with a full backstage crew and a large wardrobe of costumes, as well as sheet music and scripts. And the names of actors keen to come out from England. All the two partners now lacked was a stage. So in 1793 they commissioned one: the first purpose-built playhouse in the United States, known as the Chestnut Street Theater. The building looked remarkably like Covent Garden Theater, London, because it was a copy built by Wignall's brother-in-law, John Inigo Richards.

Who knew the London theater well because he had been principal scene painter there since 1777. Richards was also well known for his landscapes, done in the early "picturesque" style (back then the term meant "like a painting"), and in 1768 he had been a founding member of the Royal Academy. By 1788 he was the academy secretary. That year, one of the academy's first exhibitors, John Russell, was elected to membership because he was portrait painter to the royal family. Russell did hundreds of portraits, most of them pictures of children with dogs, cats, foxes, squirrels, rabbits, and owls. Russell was also a convert to Methodism and was so devout that he wouldn't work on Sundays and tried to avoid dining out so as to avoid "loose and blasphemous conversation."

He was also a telescope freak and met (and of course painted) nightsky guru Sir William Herschel, as well as Astronomer Royal Nevil Maskelyne. Russell also painted well-heeled American loyalist Dr. John Jeffries, who ministered to the needs of other American loyalists resident in London. Jeffries had trained in Scotland, treated one of the wounded at the Boston Massacre in 1770, then left for London, then returned to fight for the Brits at Savannah, then back to London.

In 1785 came the event Russell would show in his academy painting: Jeffries on board the first cross-Channel balloon flight from Dover, with pilot Frenchman Jean-Pierre-François Blanchard. They had to jettison all the ballast and most of their clothes to stay in the air and landed three hours after liftoff, in France. Jeffries wrote it all up. Blanchard said Jeffries's version of events was a pack of lies and that his medical passenger had spent the entire flight drinking brandy. By January 9, 1793, Blanchard was in Philadelphia, charging fifty bucks (modern) per ticket to witness his flight. Present were George Washington (for whom Blanchard delivered the first airmail letter to his destination in New Jersey), as well as Jefferson, Madison, Monroe, and John Adams. In spite of this multipresidential backing, Blanchard, ever short of cash, was back in Europe the following year.

One of his earliest English supporters was anatomist and surgeon John Sheldon, who embalmed one of his patients and kept her in a glass box, designed a poisoned harpoon, visited Greenland to study whale anatomy, and was a manic depressive. In 1779 one of Sheldon's London students was Thomas Beddoes, physician, chemist, and fanatically pro–French Revolution. Beddoes developed a theory that improvements in medical chemistry would bring about an improved social order because they would prevent drunkenness, snobbery, and bad education. All this would come through the application of gases and especially laughing gas, which Beddoes tested on himself and anybody who'd risk it in Bristol, England. The riskers were Romantic poets Coleridge and Southey. In 1799 Beddoes opened what became known as the Preventive Medical Institution for the Sick and Drooping.

One of Beddoes's fellow inhalers was Joseph Cottle, a bookseller who claimed to have read one thousand books by age twenty-one. Cottle (Calvinist, antislavery, looked after orphan girls) spent much effort and money supporting the drug-addicted Coleridge and giving him unrealistically large advances. In 1798 he published Wordsworth's *Lyrical Ballads*, a financial disaster of such magnitude it drove Cottle out of business. In his poverty-stricken old age Cottle was visited by a drunken writer and forger, Dr. John Dix. The booze eventually ruined Dix's medical career and affected his writing, which consisted mainly of fantasies about nonexistent friendships and nonexistent encounters with big-name poets like Shelley and Wordsworth. After meeting Cottle, Dix lurched off to the United States, where he wrote a guide to Lake Memphremagog.

This delightful stretch of water (reportedly containing a sea monster) straddles the Vermont-Canada border and by the mid-1880s had become a major tourist destination. Two regulars were Samuel J. Barrows and wife, Isabel, who over a decade vacationed there every year. In 1887 Barrows used the experience as material for the first family holiday-under-canvas book: *The Shaybacks in Camp*. Soon happily out of print. The rest of Barrows's life was also uneventful: religious journalism and one term in Congress (voted against tariffs on imported Greek currants). His most uneventful experience of all happened while he was a student stringer for the New York *Tribune*. On June 25, 1876, he stayed in camp instead of going out with George Armstrong Custer on the day he attacked the Native Americans at Little Bighorn.

Barrows's managing editor at the *Tribune* was Whitelaw Reid. An experienced political and war correspondent, he'd joined the *Tribune* in 1868 and garnered such contributors as Mark Twain, Bret Harte, and William Dean Howells. By 1876 circulation was up over sixty thousand. In 1886 Reid introduced the linotype machine, with which a single operator on a keyboard controlled the automated pouring of lead into selected font matrices, making up an entire line of print six times faster than the previous, manual technique.

Reid's wife, Elizabeth, was the daughter of D. Ogden Mills, who'd started out as a gold dust trader and banker during the 1849 California Rush. In 1864 Mills set up the Bank of California, and by 1869 his organization was processing all the ore from the Comstock Lode. Mills moved into power generation (president of Niagara Power Company), railroads, steamships, and manufacturing. In the mid-1870s he became one of the trustees of and financial contributors to the new Lick Observatory being built on Mount Hamilton, south of San Francisco.

James Lick had spent a colorful life building pianos all over South

America and had returned to San Francisco a month before California's statehood and seventeen days before the first gold find. Seeing how the land lay he bought land. And ended up a real estate millionaire. Lick's original plan for a monument to himself was to be a giant pyramid on some land he owned in the city, but he was persuaded instead to make his mark on astronomy.

On September 9, 1892, Lick Observatory found the first new moon of Jupiter since Galileo's original discoveries. The moon was big news in the international sky-gazing community and was named "Amalthea" by one of France's greatest popularizers of astronomy, Camille Flammarion. Whose writing about inhabited planets and nonhuman extraterrestrials and above all his discovery of what looked like Martian vegetation capable of supporting a civilization galvanized public interest in other worlds.

Flammarion was also into a different kind of otherworldliness. In particular, that of Italian medium Eusapia Palladino, who convinced him that she had caused a face to appear in a tray of putty. In 1884 Eusapia was impressing bigger fish at a meeting of the British Society for Psychical Research, during which accordions played themselves, curtains billowed, tables levitated, and Eusapia grew an extra arm.

This was enough to convince Oliver Lodge, professor of physics at the new University of Liverpool, where he conducted tests in thought transference. Lodge's contribution to modern living included the invention of a major advance in electromagnetism: the "coherer." In this little gizmo loose iron filings in a tube would stick together (cohere) when hit by the arrival of a weak radio signal. The coherence would cause the filings to act as a better conductor, amplifying the signal.

Lodge was also a major player in the attempt to update the curriculum of British schools and universities with more emphasis on science and technology and less on Greek and Latin. In 1903, when the Classical Association was formed by the other side, Lodge triumphantly saw it as a last-ditch defense by the diehard school of dead-language-loving fogies.

One of whom (and Classical Association founder member) was politico Herbert Asquith, ex–classical scholar at Oxford, lawyer, and on the parliamentary way to the top. By 1903 he was already home secretary (secretary of state). In 1905 as chancellor of the exchequer (Treasury) he introduced the first state pensions. He then went on to win three terms as prime minister from 1908 until the fall of his government during World War I.

In 2003 his great-granddaughter, Helena Bonham Carter, crowned a brilliant acting career by playing Anne Boleyn in the Emmy Award–winning two-part TV drama *Henry VIII*.

The show's producer was FRANCIS HOPKINSON.

CHAPTER NINETEEN

John Hart

JOHN HART (NJ) was about sixty-four. Nobody seems to know why he slept in the doghouse (with the dog). When things went revolutionary Hart was a run-of-the-mill New Jersey Baptist mill owner with horses and acreage. He had always been vociferous about unfair Brit taxation, so in 1776 he was appointed to both the State Council and the Committee for Public Safety, which between them had fairly undemocratic powers to do whatever was necessary to keep the place in order and fight a war. Hart spent only six weeks representing New Jersey at the Continental Congress, signed the Declaration, and returned to local politics.

One of his fellow members on the Safety Committee was William Paterson. Another whose plans ("life without much hustle and bustle") were altered by the Independence fracas. A successful lawyer overloaded with cases arising from recently fled loyalists, Paterson was made associate justice of the Supreme Court in 1793 and shortly thereafter ruled on the first challenge to congressional constitutionality. One Daniel Hilton owned 125 carriages for his personal-only use (oh yeah?) and when taxed, argued that direct taxes were a state not federal matter. Paterson and the rest of the bench said nope it's an excise tax and therefore federal so pay up.

Representing government that day, legal eagle Alexander Hamilton stood before a packed court perhaps less interested in the case than in

Hamilton's already famous sexual peccadilloes. Small, red-headed Hamilton (hero, first Treasury secretary, pro-strong central government and senators-for-life, and antislavery) was in deep trouble thanks to his recent dalliance with one Maria Reynolds, lady-about-town married to an abusive swindler. Who, when he found out what she and Hamilton were up to, charged Hamilton one thousand dollars to go on doing it. Then went around town quietly telling Hamilton's political enemies that he, Reynolds, was getting insider-deal tips on bonds and such from "one who should know."

Confronted by Jefferson and others, Hamilton (expecting confidentiality) handed over letters proving he'd committed adultery but not malfeasance, resigned his secretaryship, and lost his chance at the presidency forever. Three years later Hamilton's naivete hit the fan when his erotic scribblings were published (some fingered Jefferson) by muckraking journalist James Callender, who was on the run from a sedition case in Scotland. With Callender's back-home experience as a militant radical hard man, the American political scene was sandbox stuff.

After his first success with Hamilton and with support from Jefferson, Callender produced his usual attacks on government and in 1800 got himself jailed for sedition. After he was released (and with Thomas Jefferson now president), Callender was much chagrined that not only did he fail to get his expected postmastership-for-services-rendered, but he also discovered that his ex-supporters (maybe even T.J.) were saying his wife had died of venereal disease while he frolicked in the next room. His riposte was the devastating "Sally Hemings, slave girl mistress of Jefferson" piece. By now a loose cannon, permanently drunk, and with nowhere to go but down Callender ended up in the James River.

A more adventurous fate met his old Scots fellow revolutionary Thomas Muir. Back in 1793, when Callender was hightailing it for America, Muir had been "most wanted" by the London government, which was alarmed at his far-left "Friends of the People" militant organization and his invitation to the "United Irishmen" to join a general (and violent) movement for British parliamentary reform. The authorities quickly suspended habeas corpus and arranged a fourteen-year sentence of transportation to Australia for Muir and associates.

Two years after arriving to Down-Under house arrest Muir escaped on an American ship and made his way over twelve months of adventuring and serious wounds across the Pacific to Vancouver, then California, then Mexico, then Cuba, then (in 1798) France. In Paris he was once again reunited with his old comrades in foment. One of whom, Thomas Watson, went even further than Muir, calling for blood on the streets and leading a London riot in 1794. After two years in jail he called on the revolutionary French to invade England, promising that "the people" would rise up in support. Never happened. In 1798 Watson got out of town just ahead of the sheriff and settled first in Paris, where he claimed to have taught Napoleon English, then Rome, where he spied for the Brits. Then off to Greece for who knows what. By 1825 he was back, begging in the Paris streets. Disappeared again. In 1838, back in London, he strangled himself. Checkered wasn't the word.

Watson's posthumous affairs were put in order by the man who had inspired all agitators with his street fighter's manual. "Count" Francis Maceroni was born in a Manchester suburb and spent his formative years being revolutionary in Italy and Corsica. He claimed he'd introduced the Italians to cricket. To no discernible effect. Apart from patenting a steam carriage and a rocket, Maceroni's claim to infamy was his involvement (on behalf of the Venezuelan hero Simón Bolívar) with a person even the dubious Maceroni referred to as "a coward and a mountebank."

Gregor MacGregor pulled off one of the greatest cons in history. At age thirty he was Bolívar's senior general (he married B.'s niece). One day in conversation with a local chief he swapped a bottle of booze for perpetual rights to 8 million acres of snake-infested Honduran Mosquito Coast. By 1821 he was in London as His Serene Highness Prince of "Poyais" (the acres), mingling with the high and mighty, opening a fake Poyais Legation, waving fake Poyais money, selling fake Poyais bonds and worthless Poyais land. In 1822 the first two boatloads left for their new life in MacGregor's magic kingdom, only to find there was no capital city, no mountains of gold, and that the place was bad for the health. Many died. Some made it back to sue MacGregor (now, however, long gone and running the same scam in Paris). In the end he fled back to Venezuela and is today one of the nation's heroes. Proving you *can* fool most of the people most of the time.

Key in all this fakery was MacGregor's prospectus, printed by the highly respectable William Blackwood, Edinburgh publisher of such as Sir Walter Scott and John Galt. Scott referred to Galt's work as "the worst ever seen." Galt tried business (failed), then Napoleonic sanctions-busting (failed), then literature (prolific and forgotten), then Canada. Where in 1824 he founded the city of Guelph, developed a million acres, and came home to jail for debts. But not before he'd written the preface to the memoirs of Alexander Graydon.

Graydon was a total nobody from the Philadelphia upper crust and after an uneventful War of Independence was living on a farm near Harrisburg. A dullard, yes. But his memoirs savaged a few of the great names he'd known. In spite of which he dedicated the book to a member of the establishment, Richard Rush, son of Benjamin the signer, lawyer, and over seven years U.S. minister to Britain, Comptroller of the Treasury under Madison, SecTreas under John Quincy Adams, and failed veep candidate.

In 1836 Richard Rush went back to Britain for two years to deal with the Smithsonian bequest, which was moving with the speed of treacle through the English legal system. Finally, Rush was able to ship out for home with eleven boxes containing $508,318.46 in gold. And then leave the problem of what to do with it to Indiana representative Robert Dale Owen. British-born, with a socialist background, Owen wrote on birth control, supported failed utopian communes, and then turned politically legit. After three terms in the Indiana legislature he entered the House, where he helped get the Smithsonian bequest onto the congressional agenda (it took eight bills and ten years to get things right).

Late in life Owen went slightly insane and in 1877, while recovering, wrote the first (and only, since he then died) recollection of his out-West youth for *Scribner's Monthly*. *Scribner's* had just hired a fourteen-year-old publishing fanatic (the boy already had his own printing press). Frank Nelson Doubleday went on, via mergers, acquisitions, litigation, boardroom coups, and such typical New York publishing shenanigans to become a very big literary cheese. With friends like Mark Twain, Joseph

Conrad, and Rudyard Kipling. And a strange young man who'd started life as an archeologist in 1911 digging Mesopotamian holes in Syria. And who dressed (some said "up") like the locals.

With the approach of World War I this flamboyant type was hired to provide an "archeological-excavation" smokescreen for what was really the British military survey of Sinai in preparation for events during which the Arabs were to be liberated from their Turkish overlords and in which our costumed hero was to play a major intelligence role. And thanks to his fluent Arabic (and more so, to a helpful American journalist and filmmaker) to end up world-famous as Lawrence of Arabia. Early on at Oxford T. E. Lawrence had particularly admired the spare-time poetry of his contemporary John Beazley (a whiz on ancient Greek pottery), who accumulated honorary degrees from places as far away as Salonika. And who married the stepdaughter of full-time poet Louis MacNiece, known for the power and beauty of his work.

As a boy at Marlborough College MacNiece became life-long buddies with Anthony Blunt, and in 1936 both of them went to Civil War Spain. Blunt (art historian, esthete, and homosexual) was a distant cousin of Queen Mary. Which, in the event, would turn out to be an embarrassment. At university Blunt was recruited by the Soviets and then during World War II was (incredibly) also recruited by the U.K. intelligence service, whereupon he passed at least one thousand secret files to the KGB. In 1945 Blunt was made surveyor of the king's paintings, ennobled as a sir, and recognized as the last word on French painter Nicholas Poussin. Rumors of his spying sideline were met by official hemming and hawing (something to do with his royal connections) until an American fellow traveler outed him too publicly to deny. Blunt lost job and honors, took to drink, and died.

At the height of the double-dealing, Blunt's date at gay parties was journalist Kim Philby, another Soviet spy and member of U.K. intelligence, who eventually got out of Beirut on a Russian trawler one step ahead of MI5. And who went one better even than Blunt. In 1941, as liaison officer with American intelligence, one of Philby's jobs was to teach counterespionage techniques to CIA man James Jesus Angleton. They developed a liquid-lunch friendship.

After Philby was unmasked Angleton was understandably paranoid, seeing every Soviet defector as a plant. So when in 1961 Anatoly Golitsyn defected from the KGB and said there were moles in the CIA, MI5, and French intelligence (and that everything the CIA discovered about the KGB was Russian-orchestrated, smoke-and-mirrors disinformation), Angleton believed him and gutted the agency. Three years later another defector, Yuri Noshenko, claimed that Golitsyn *himself* was smoke and mirrors. The whole of Western intelligence went into paralysis.

Finally, in 1976 a retired CIA operative was called in to sort out the mess. His conclusion: "Noshenko was real, Golitsyn was fake."

The operative's name was JOHN HART.

CHAPTER TWENTY

ABRAHAM CLARK (NJ) was fifty. And not a man you crossed with impunity. "A lively wit and very satirical," they said. Clark spent the run-up to conflict trying to make sure America wasn't getting rid of one shackle only to replace it with another. An early republican, he was against centralized government and was leery about the "greedy" businessmen who would profit from the war and then take over.

His best shot in this battle came early in the 1780s when the war started to generate a large number of small debtors (like farmers) who were land-rich but cash-poor. Clark's solution was to print one hundred thousand pounds of paper money backed by real estate and issued in loans by a New Jersey state commission. In this way people could borrow the paper money against their land, settle their debts, and pay off the loan over a number of years.

Clark's Trenton, New Jersey, money printer was Isaac Collins, who'd been turning out official documents since 1770. Isaac was a Quaker and for a while the Friends shunned him because of the way he used his first newspaper (the New Jersey *Gazette*) to raise money, supplies, and general support for Washington's army and other war-related stuff. In 1779 Collins produced the first "Family Bible." Amost all Bibles back then were designed to be carried in saddlebags, but Isaac's was big enough for the family to gather around it. Demand was so great he got three thousand preorders and the final print went to five thousand. Isaac had his kids check the proofs eleven times looking for typos. They spotted all but two: a broken letter and a missed punctuation mark.

One of Isaac's *Gazette* contributors was Quaker John Woolman, who is credited with nothing less than the birth of the modern social conscience. One of the first antislavery voices in America, Woolman spent three dangerous weeks living with Native Americans to find out what their life was like. He urged his fellow Quakers not to pay taxes for warmaking. He traveled around speaking out on these issues of conscience. When he crossed the Atlantic to England in 1772 he chose to travel steerage so as to share discomfort with the poor. Once in England, for animal-welfare reasons he walked everywhere so as not to use the "flying" (nonstop) coaches because he heard they often ran horses to death. Later that year Woolman arrived for a Quaker meeting in York, sick with smallpox.

Taken to a house outside the city, he died, tended by Sarah, daughter of local Friend William Tuke. Who'd been an antislavery activist as long as Woolman and who'd started several Quaker schools. Years later in 1790 a Quaker woman died in York Asylum for the Insane and Tuke became aware of the conditions under which the mentally ill were forced to live: treated like animals, cuffed, and without medical treatment or minimal personal hygiene. After two years of research and visits to asylums Tuke opened "The Retreat." His patients were treated as if they were sane, kept in clean, pleasant living conditions, encouraged to socialize with other patients, given decent food and occupational therapy classes. Unheard of.

Tuke's lifelong role model in mental health was a French doctor friend of Ben Franklin, Philippe Pinel. A famous painting shows Pinel removing the chains from the insane in Paris. In fact the pic was a propaganda job set up by the revolutionaries, and it was somebody else who did the unshackling. Besides mental health, Pinel's other great work was a giant book of diseases catalogued by symptom. This was the taxonomy-craze era: idea being that if you could describe a disease (and especially reduce it to as many subclassifications as possible) you could understand it. "Nosology" (as this approach to disease was called) included such gems as: "Disease: nostalgia. Symptoms: an overwhelming inclination to go home."

Over a third of Pinel's book dealt with fever treatments, one of which had been suggested by a pupil, François Joseph Victor Broussais. Remembered for his simple and effective approach to any condition. For Broussais all disease was caused by the excessive accumulation of blood. So copious bloodletting (with leeches) would effectively get rid of the accumulation. More often than not this killed the patient. But the technique was great news for the German leech industry. At the height of demand France was importing 42 million of the little German suckers. In an attempt to boost French leech-farming, Napoleon set up the Society for the Encouragement of National Industry.

Its first president, Jean-Antoine Chaptal, made paper white for the first time with his idea of using chlorine to bleach linen rags. He also invented "chaptalization": In a cloudy year with little sunshine, alcohol levels in fermenting wine could be maintained by adding sugar. It was one of his colleagues, Napoleon's inspector general of health, Antoine-Augustin Parmentier, who suggested grape juice would do the trick better.

Parmentier was also the guy who persuaded the Paris Faculty of Medicine to declare the potato edible. Ever since he'd spent time in a German POW camp back in the 1760s, forced to live off potatoes, Parmentier was a convert to the humble spud. At a time when potatoes were fed only to animals (and POWs), converting the public to the tuber required some effort. So Parmentier staged elaborate potato-every-course dinners for the likes of Franklin and famous chemist Lavoisier, sent bouquets of potato flowers to the queen, and invented an haute cuisine potato soup known to this day as *potage Parmentier*. You may have had it.

Fittingly, a close acquaintance of Parmentier was horticulture expert Philippe-Victoire de Vilmorin, who ran a seed company, married a daughter of the king's botanist, then partnered with the botanist and renamed the company Vilmorin-Andrieux. By mid-nineteenth century the firm was a national institution, collecting seeds from all over the world, producing the first-ever book dedicated to veggies (including two hundred pages on cabbages and four thousand images of every plant the company grew) and breeding the modern carrot. Every year from 1850 the company sent their clients a beautifully designed, full-color, all-vegetable poster, produced by the latest chromolithography technique. This used up to twenty thin stone plates each carrying the same design but only one of the colors in the final composition. Pressing the same sheet of paper on each plate in turn produced extremely high-quality multicolor images.

King of chromolithography was Welsh designer Owen Jones, who literally wrote the book. In this case, *Grammar of Ornament*, the definitive statement on design, which included six hundred illustrations of patterns from cultures all over the world. By the 1850s Jones was the final design authority and his stuff was everywhere: on playing cards, menus, calendars, stamps, endpapers of books, even biscuit wrappers. And at the Great Exhibition of 1851, where he designed the interiors. His bright polychrome classical-architecture "Greek Court" (he thought this historically accurate) generated such an outcry he was forced to an Apology written in 1856 with his pal George Lewes.

Who was already raising eyebrows when his wife had her second child by their live-in friend Thornton Hunt. Lewes was a second-rate poet and novelist (one contemporary assessment: "execrable") but a first-rate reviewer, essayist, and general intellectual gadfly. He wrote on everything for everybody and was friendly with Dickens. After finishing a major Goethe biography in 1855 he left home to live with and shepherd the career of novelist George Eliot (real name Mary Ann Evans). Turning to science in 1859 Lewes wrote *Physiology of the Common Life*.

Ten years later the book changed the career of a young Russian student priest south of Moscow, who dropped the habit in favor of physiology. Ivan Pavlov ended up with drooling dogs and a Nobel. The world ended up with the dubious benefit of knowing and worrying about the conditioned reflex. Pavlov did some of his early physiology lab work in Breslau with Rudolf Heidenhein, much exercised by the problem of body heat. Which he discovered was generated by muscles. Heidenhein also invented the "gastric pouch" for collecting stomach juices and was one of the first to study hypnotism in a scientific manner. One of his fellow physiologists, Viennese Joseph Breuer, made the great mesmeric leap in 1880 when he hypnotized a young woman with multiple problems: paralyzed arm, violent cough, no appetite, water phobia, and frequent delerium. After putting her under the influence Breuer talked the reasons out of her and she recovered. He told his young colleague Sigmund Freud and psychoanalysis was born.

In 1881 Freud coauthored a piece on aphasia in children with his friend and doctor Oscar Rie. Whose daughter Marianne married Ernst Kris in 1927 when art historian Kris was a curator at the Vienna Cultural Museum. A year later Kris had moved into psychoanalysis and in 1940, on the run from the Nazis, was visiting prof. at the New School for Social Research (now New School University) in New York.

A little later at Harvard the Krises' own daughter Anne met another Vienna runaway and psychoanalytic whiz, Eric Kandel, whose own rather different take on the brain would lead him into neurobiology and the epochal study of memory in the giant sea-snail *Aplysia*. The snail's chief attraction was that it had few, large, simple cells in its nervous system, which meant it was less difficult than other creatures to get to understand. For this snail-brain work, in 2000 Kandel shared a Nobel with Paul Greengard and Arvid Carlsson.

In 1968 Carlsson had discovered another basic brain mechanism: the process by which tiny amounts of chemicals pass across the synaptic gap between one brain cell and another and, on arrival, cause the target cell to fire. The discovery of these neurotransmitters and their function made it possible for drug-makers Eli Lilly to produce the antidepressant Prozac (which has an effect on neurotransmission) and create the second-biggest-selling medication in the United States.

Lilly was also cosponsor in the construction of the new Hoosier Dome at Indianapolis, where the Colts played their first game in 1984. One of the later Colts players was Todd Keene, who left football to become president (in 2005) of an evangelical group known as The Power Team. The Team's approach was to focus the interest of the congregation by performing extraordinary feats of strength (Keene's speciality was to crush concrete blocks between his arms) and then deliver their Gospel message.

In 2005 one of the Team was named ABRAHAM CLARK.

CHAPTER TWENTY-ONE

Rob Morris

ROBERT MORRIS (PA) was forty-two. By the time of Independence he was already a hardnosed middle-aged businessman doing deals in Britain, Portugal, Spain, and the Caribbean. So the war was just a minor interruption. But he gave it his full attention, joining forty-one congressional committees, in particular that of "Secret Trade." The committee agenda: get what America needed to keep on fighting. The deals for everything from bullets to flour went on behind closed doors (and even with British suppliers), so rumors flew that Morris was making more than a few bucks on the side.

In 1781 Morris was given control of the nation's finances (best described as catastrophic and getting more so) and set up the Bank of North America to borrow money from the states so as to bail out the government and the army (broke and unpaid). Morris resigned when the states wouldn't divvy up. Back in full-time trade by 1784 Morris bought shares in the first ship (the *Empress of China*) to sail from the United States to the Orient. And made 30 percent profit on a cargo of silver, wine, and Pennsylvania ginseng. Music to the ears of one Daniel Boone, dealer in bargeloads of ginseng (good for dysentery, colic, cramps, and what ails you).

Boone was nothing like the hype that surrounded him after *Adventures of . . .* appeared in 1784 and created the legend of the coonskin cap

and the bear-killing, classically educated sharpshooter and general su-
perman. In fact businessman Boone wore monogrammed buttons and,
like many, speculated in land. On one occasion, like many, he loaned
money to archswindler, ruthless charmer, and general cad Gilbert Imlay, a New Jersey ex-soldier back in the United States to get away from
romantic imbroglios in Europe.

These had included an affair in Paris with a liberated feminist writer
named Mary Wollstonecraft, already famous for her shocking best
seller, *Vindication of the Rights of Woman*. The relationship with Imlay re-
sulted in a daughter named Fanny (who was not so liberated and would
one day OD in a hotel room). After Fanny's birth, Mary looked after
Imlay's business interests in Scandinavia while he ran off with yet another actress. History settles accounts: Nobody remembers Imlay but
the world knows Mary as the died-in-childbirth mother (by a later affair) of Mary Shelley, author of *Frankenstein*.

One of Wollstonecraft's pals was minor scribbler Anne Cristall,
whose brother Joshua was painting porcelain when Mary met him and
persuaded him into full-time watercoloring. Cristall's first twenty years
were the worst, often spent living on water and potatoes. The problem
was that the Brit Royal Academy considered watercolors not to be art
but something mapmakers did, so Cristall's landscapes didn't sell well.
Then came marriage and eighteen years in bucolic nowhere, producing
more unsuccessful work. And then Cristall died. A hundred years later
he's been reassessed as "the father of English watercolors" and you
couldn't afford him.

Cristall got his start (and more than potatoes) at the house of Dr.
Thomas Monro, insanity expert (on George III's madness) who knew
nothing about insanity and was the fourth generation of Monro to run
the London Bethlehem (pronounced "Bedlam") asylum, until exposed
for cruel practices (chains, no treatment). He did better as an art maven,
inviting starving artists home (see "potatoes" above) to paint in return for
supper. No fool Monro, one of his hungry mouths was named J. M. W.
Turner.

Another one was Cornelius Varley, whose artistic ambitions (great)
outstripped his talents (small). This may have been one of the reasons

Varley patented the Graphic Telescope in 1811 to help him draw. Mirrors attached to the telescope put an image on paper and you traced it out. Not quite enough to do anything about Varley's lack of ability. His work, when remembered, is generally regarded as forgettable. The closest Varley would ever get to the big time was when his gizmo was used in 1820 by Thomas Horner at the top of the dome of St Paul's Cathedral to create a giant, full-circle panorama of London. The final canvas measured forty-two thousand square feet, and in order to show it off (for money) a speculator friend of Horner's sponsored the construction of the Regent's Park Coliseum. Where, in the first passenger elevator (the "ascending room"), you could rise up the painting. Alas, takings were low (in spite of added attractions including an aviary, organ, and Swiss chalet), and the financial backer turned out too extravagant for everybody's own good. Bankruptcy followed and the backer absconded to the United States. Followed shortly by Horner, who then went insane in Pennsylvania.

However, the Coliseum did good things for its architect, Decimus Burton, who'd trained under John Nash, helped with bits of Nash's Regent's Park terraces, and was good at producing exact copies of Greek and Roman without ever leaving his drawing board. Examples: Hyde Park Corner Arch and the Athenaeum Club. In his defense it must be said that the wonderful glass-and-iron Palm House at Kew Botanical Gardens was all his own work.

Decimus's brother James was a rum cove. After a bad start, in 1820 he managed to get to Pompeii too late to take up Sir Humphry Davy's offer of assistantship in unrolling eruption-carbonized papyri, so he headed off to Egypt to look for coal. Searching for something else to dig, he took a desultory look-around and in the Valley of the Kings (where he found a list of kings) did a bit of excavation and general tomb-robbing. Slave girls and a hookah habit then contributed to his disappearance into the Nile Delta for five years. In 1828 he resurfaced and headed back to London with slave girl and giraffe in tow (the animal slipped on ice and died; the slave girl became his spouse).

In 1839 James bumped into a distant Canadian relative and judge, Thomas Chandler Haliburton (in London looking for classy ancestors),

and the two of them discovered a family link with major scribbler Sir
Walter Scott. Haliburton, who coined such phrases as: "blood out of a
stone," "drink like a fish," and "the early bird gets the worm," was about
to burst on the Eng. Lit. scene with his own stories. Satirical tales of life
in Nova Scotia "as seen by Sam Slick, Yankee clockmaker and peddler."
The colorful Slick was a runaway best seller on both sides of the Atlantic (and netted Haliburton an honorary Oxford degree) after the
original essays first appeared as regular columns in the *Novascotian*.

The paper's editor, publisher, and printer, Joseph Howe, was already
big in local politics. After years of agitation by colonial Nova Scotians
for democratic elections, in 1867 the London Parliament passed the
British North American Act, which turned Canada into a confederation. Exactly what autonomy-loving Nova Scotians didn't want. So
Howe (by this time ex-prime minister) led calls for the act's repeal.
Then, inexplicably, he changed his tune and took a job in the new Canadian federal government. This about-face was one of the only two sig-
nificant victories in the life of Nova Scotia lieutenant governor Sir
Charles Hastings Doyle, the other being his success in foiling the Great
1866 Irish Invasion of New Brunswick.

After the U.S. Civil War the Brits, worried about a possible U.S. attack on Canada, sent over thousands of troops and trained even more
local Canadian militia. Quite by accident this was done just in time for
the botched Fenian (Irish independence movement) botched attempt to
take over New Brunswick and set up a republic in exile. On invasion day
hardly any of the Irish volunteers turned up at the appointed spot on the
American side of the border, and they squabbled when they did. When
they finally crossed into Canada, oops, in front of them was a massively
superior Brit force armed to the teeth. And behind the Fenians the
Americans were closing the border to block further Irish reinforcements
(which weren't coming, anyway).

Undeterred, the Fenians fell back on Plan B: build a submarine and
sink the British Royal Navy. Fortunately in this regard Paterson, New
Jersey, contained a sympathetic Irishman, John Holland, who'd read
Jules Verne and was nuts for the subaquatic. With Fenian backing, by
1881 Holland's thirty-one-foot three-crew *Fenian Ram* was secretly

scooting up and down the Hudson. There followed yet another internal Fenian squabble (this time about not getting their money's worth from Holland) and in dead of night the *Ram* was stolen. Alas, no Fenian could drive it and that was the end of that.

But not for Holland, who by 1900 had sold his "Holland-6" to the U.S. Navy. Minor problem: None of Holland's subs included a means to see where they were going. Enter Sir Howard Gibbs with what was to become the standard periscope for the next fifty years. From 1868 to 1926 Gibbs built any scope of any type used anywhere in the British Empire. He also developed antidazzle headlights and a sniper gunsight and ran his business into the ground. But not before he had helped to change the universe.

On May 29, 1919, one of Gibbs's gizmos (a sun-tracking coelostat, to be precise) was used at Sobral, a remote spot in northeast Brazil and one of two sites chosen by the Royal Astronomical Society to observe the total solar eclipse on that rare day. Rare because the sun was passing in front of a particularly dense lot of stars. This fact was essential to the purpose of math-astronomy-physics genius Sir Arthur Eddington (lived with mother, Quaker, bicycled, baggy tweeds), who was at the *other* eclipse site, on the island of Principe off West Africa. Before the eclipse Eddington took pix of the relevant bit of night sky. Then he photographed the eclipse. Then he superimposed one picture on the other. Sure enough, a star close to the sun had moved. Or rather, the light from the star had moved. Proving that the sun's gravity had bent the starlight, shifting the star's image. Einstein's theory of general relativity was right! Congrats all round!

Except from major thinker Bertrand Russell, who thought Eddington's scientific work was ruined by his Christianity. Russell was probably the twentieth century's greatest rationalist. His ideas left other major philosophers "thunderstruck." He was in love with geometry, got a Nobel for literature, was the author of *History of Western Philosophy* and founder of the Campaign for Nuclear Disarmament. He met Lenin and (here's the clincher) taught Wittgenstein. No slouch. Nor with women. An advocate of free love (it cost him an American university chair), he married four times.

The third left him after her torrid affair with Arthur Koestler. Variously described as arrogant, drunken, sexually predatory (there were rumors of rape), dogmatic, violent, and neurotic, the chain-smoking Koestler hit the big time with his novel *Darkness at Noon*. In 1940 Koestler joined that home of deserters the French Foreign Legion. And then deserted. He had a fling with Simone de Beauvoir. Married three times. And on one occasion urinated in a car radiator that was threatening to overheat.

Larger than life, in 1983 Koestler, suffering from leukemia and Parkinson's disease, killed himself. Later that day his wife committed suicide. Some said he'd put her up to it. Their joint bequest endowed a professorial chair in parapsychology (the only one in Britain) at Edinburgh University.

In 1983 the first to occupy the chair was American ROBERT MORRIS.

CHAPTER TWENTY-TWO

Benjamin Rush

BENJAMIN RUSH (PA) was thirty. And newlywed. And made enemies by whistle-blowing on the corruption in wartime military hospitals. After originally qualifying in Scotland, Rush wrote the first U.S. chemistry textbook, became prof. of medical theory and practice in Philadelphia, and when the city was hit with the great Yellow Fever Plague in 1793 saved hundreds (and killed a few, too) with his enthusiastic bloodletting treatment. His influence on U.S. medicine was major, not least because he taught over three thousand students.

In 1792 Rush tried and failed to set up a "Peace Office" in an attempt to demilitarize American society (he wanted the U.S. War Office door to carry the notice: "An office for butchering the human species"). These ideas were publicized in the 1793 almanac written by his pal Ben Banneker, son of a freed slave and amateur astronomer, surveyor, and mathematician, who had started sky-gazing at the late age of fifty-one with a telescope borrowed from his Maryland neighbors and mill owners the Ellicotts.

In 1790 their cousin Major Andrew Ellicott was nominated by George Washington to survey a ten-square-mile area of land between Virginia and Maryland for the new national capital. The following year Ellicott took Ben with him to start the work. Ellicott was already an experienced surveyor with various state boundaries measured. In 1813 more of the same work eventually led to his appointment as professor of math at West Point, where he managed to put studies on a more academic footing.

That same year the academy intake included B. L. E. de Bonneville. In 1825 de Bonneville escorted family friend Lafayette on the great man's triumphal good-bye tour of the Unitd States, then in 1832 took time out from the army to go fur-trapping with the financial backing of J. J. Astor. De Bonneville headed off up the Oregon Trail into the Rockies, where he wandered around for three years. In 1837 his journal of the trip was rewritten by Washington Irving as *The Adventures of Captain Bonneville*. At which point de Bonneville got back in uniform. There's some speculation that he was given military leave of absence because the real reason for heading northwest was to spy on what the Brits were up to in Oregon.

As far as Congress was concerned this was a legitimate matter for snoopery. The area was under joint U.S.-U.K. supervision and both sides traded competitively with the Native Americans and Russians. Besides which, everybody knew that the name of the game for the new Hudson's Bay Company governor, ex-London sugar broker George Simpson, was to spoil the day of any American traders on the West Coast. To make this easier, in 1838 Simpson leased the Alaska Peninsula from St. Petersburg.

In 1840 Simpson decided to check out company assets and set off on a round-the-world tour (London, Sitka, Hawaii, Sitka, St. Petersburg, London). Because of a worsening vision problem Simpson took along a seeing-eye secretary, Edward Martin Hopkins. The best thing about whom was his wife, the beautiful and talented Frances Anne Beechey. When Hopkins became head of the Montreal Department of the Hudson's Bay Company, Frances Anne accompanied him on many inspection trips across the wilderness, painting as she went. Her work is one of the very few records of the life of the *voyageurs*, intrepid canoeists who manhandled thirty-six-foot freight canoes over white water and through snowstorms and danger. Frances Anne's canvases capture with astonishing beauty the forests, rivers, and people of a time when the great northern world was empty and untouched.

Her brother had his share of the north, too. Fred Beechey spent time in the Royal Navy, freezing in the Arctic with major explorers Franklin and Parry, getting trapped in the ice, and being attacked by walruses. He also surveyed the North African coast, saw military action in America, and sailed the Pacific for four years. When the time came to retire, his great experience in tidal matters made him the navy's choice as delegate to the 1853 first-ever international meteorological conference in Brussels. Where the Beaufort Wind Scale was adopted.

Francis Beaufort was a weird type who married his own stepniece. After he died his encrypted letters were deciphered, and they revealed he had also had an incestuous relationship with his sister Hester. Royal Navy hydrographer for twenty-six years, Beaufort turned a small naval office into one of the world's great sources of oceanic data. And his Wind Scale standardized how all navigators now describe winds: on a range from from calm (0) to hurricane (12).

Beaufort also okayed the 1839–43 Ross expedition sent to search for the South Magnetic Pole. Key science tool for the onboard geeks was the high-tech dipping compass needle invented by Robert Were Fox. Having been to the bottom of his family's West-of-England mines and discovered that it got hotter the deeper you went, Fox theorized this had something to do with metal-bearing rocks, which had something to do with electricity and magnetism. Hence his needle. Which hung free to dip more or less, depending on magnetic intensity (theoretically at a Magnetic Pole it would dip vertically).

Fox's sister Caroline enjoyed her brother's scientific cronies but made her own influential friends, including Tennyson, Garibaldi, explorer David Livingstone, and philosopher John Stuart Mill. And wrote about them all in her (lifelong) journal. Which was full of little observations like that on Wordsworth: "evidently an admirer of the monologue style of conversation." Caroline was a sensible and intelligent woman until she fell head-over-heels for a married man, poet John Sterling (nothing came of it).

Sterling was an admirer of Coleridge and Wordsworth, went to Germany to "immerse" himself in the Romantic Movement, married into a Bordeaux wine company, and was involved in skullduggery for Spanish revolutionary General Trujillo, providing him and his men with false passports, arms, and money, and (no fool) being absent when Trujillo's attempted coup went sour. Sterling's other claim to fame was the Sterling Club, where diners reputedly indulged in "impious" activity. Alas nothing further is detailed.

Sterling's prolific output of poems, essays, novels, and general scribble have, fortunately, long gone from sight but at the time the stuff impressed people like Caroline Fox. And, in 1843, a visiting, one-legged American writer on religious matters, Henry James (no, not that one). By 1847 James was into Free Love and do-your-own-thing expression and behavior. All this, the subject of sell-out lectures in New York. In the 1850s James wrote for the New York *Tribune* on everything from spiritualism to alcoholism to theology. And any scandal in the news. In 1874 he created his own little fuss when a private letter he'd written about marriage, divorce, and sex found its way into a rag called *Woodhull's and Clafin's Weekly*.

In 1872 Victoria Woodhull was the first-ever woman candidate for president. Unfortunately, she was in jail on election day but in any case got no votes. Victoria had been incarcerated for using the mails to send obscene material: i.e., her mag containing a report on the long-running story (she had written earlier that year) about the holier-than-thou Reverend Henry Ward Beecher, whose sexual affair with a parishioner's wife Victoria was able to parlay into the greatest brouhaha of nineteenth century America.

Victoria had originally made her pile as a "medical clairvoyant" and hit the big time in 1868 after arriving in New York (from the Midwest) and heading straight for Cornelius Vanderbilt. Who was into table-rapping and whose prostate was given magnetic healing treatment by Victoria's lovely sister Tennessee. Vanderbilt pointed the sisters at good investments and they never looked back.

As a railroad baron Vanderbilt just got richer and richer. After he died, selling his shares in the New York Central Railroad took several years of the best efforts of his banker, J. P. Morgan. Who exercised more power in America than any elected official. Morgan singlehandedly saved the country from the Financial Panic of 1907 because he was able to manipulate financial institutions and markets. The root of the problem was America's chaotic banking system, so in 1910 something secret was done about it on Jekyll Island, Georgia. A group of six major bankers and one Treasury official met (for what was officially described as a "duck hunt": only first names were used and no records were kept) to hammer out the structure of what would become the Federal Reserve (a Central Bank in all but name). Criticized later as a cartel, the Fed became the ultimate instrument of American financial stability.

One of the groups represented on Jekyll Island was the European banking firm Kuhn, Loeb & Company. Their man Paul Warburg was the architect of the event. In 1919 the board of Kuhn, Loeb was joined by aristo Brit Sir William Wiseman, who had spent World War I as head of British intelligence in Washington, D.C. Telling his government he had top American contacts and telling the Americans he had the U.K. government's ear, he made both come true and was an effective conduit between the two powers during and after the war.

Wiseman's sidekick in D.C. was London *Times* America correspondent Arthur Willert. Whose son Paul also entered the intelligence game in 1939. Sent to the British propaganda office in Paris, he worked for Noel Coward, already a major international star and writer of *Private Lives, Cavalcade, Present Laughter,* and such hits as "Dance Little Lady," "Mad Dogs and Englishmen," and "Poor Little Rich Girl." Coward's Paris job was to spread disinformation (he studiously ignored the fact that back home in London the papers were full of scurrilous stories about him being outrageous at parties with female Polish spies). After the Germans took Paris, Coward spent the rest of the war in London making such classic movies as *In Which We Serve* and *Brief Encounter*.

Coward's interior decorator was Marion V. Dorn. By the 1920s known for her batiks, Dorn lived between New York and London, soon began to concentrate on rug design (becoming known as the "architect of floors"), and developed a long-term relationship with the Wilton Royal Carpet Company. By the 1930s Dorn was setting the fashion with such décor statements as the "all-white" sitting-room for Somerset Maugham's wife, Syrie. And with her moquette seating fabric (still in use in 1952) for the London Underground.

From 1919 to 1923 Dorn was married to her ex-tutor at Stanford, ceramicist Henry Varnum Poor, best known for his murals at the Justice and Interior buildings in Washington, D.C., and at Penn State University. In 1946 Poor was cofounder of the Skowhegan (Maine) School of Painting and Sculpture, one of America's foremost artist residency communities.

In 2005 the School's photo associate was BENJAMIN RUSH.

CHAPTER TWENTY-THREE

BEN FRANKLIN (PA) was seventy. And the oldest signer. In one sense the Declaration was Franklin's failure. From his first trip to England in 1757 up to the last-chance-saloon meeting with the Brit High Command on Staten Island in 1776, Franklin had tried for compromise and reconciliation instead of war and independence.

Apart from these weighty statecraft matters, in his London lodgings at 36 Craven Street Franklin also invented the glass *armonica* (Mozart wrote music for it), mapped the Gulf Stream (Franklin had discovered it), and taught a phonetic alphabet (Franklin invented it) to his landlady's daughter Polly. Who came to Philadelphia in Franklin's old age to look after him.

Once the War of Independence was ready-or-not unavoidable, Franklin tried (and failed) to get Canada to join in and was then appointed commissioner to France to drum up support for the cause. Everywhere he went in Paris he was lionized as the homespun American democrat, scientist, statesman, writer, and general flirt who never wore a wig (they made his head itchy). He got more than every penny of the French money Congress was asking for and was then made U.S. minister to France.

In 1779 he was inducted as the second Worshipful Master of the Paris Freemasons' Lodge of the Nine Sisters (aka Muses). The lodge was only two years old and the aim was enlightenment. All the science and arts biggies were members, including (just before he died) Voltaire. Lodge founder and first Worshipful was an ugly, egocentric astronomer with a head like an eggplant, Jerome Lalande. Who had just caused the Great French Comet Panic of 1773. Lalande had delivered a paper to the academy about how there was a one-in-a-zillion chance that planetary perturbation might make a comet change course and hit Earth. The whole of Paris headed for the hills. Lalande said, "Read my lips: one in a *zillion*." And was ignored.

Astronomically Lalande was good but no cigar. He crunched numbers and produced star catalogues. He also propositioned women (as director of the *Collège de France* he admitted them to class for the first time). And he held his professorship for forty-six bumbling years. Survived the French Revolution because he kept his head down (and, he said, because they knew he was an atheist). He also bravely hid Samuel DuPont when he was on the run.

Once the French Revolution was in full swing DuPont's previous cozy relationship with the royal government didn't help his case. DuPont had been one of Louis XVI's councillors, advising on how to keep the price of bread down and then saving both the king and Marie Antoinette from the mob in 1792. Du Pont was so highly regarded that before things got dangerous and he was forced to flee the scene and head for the States, even the revolutionaries asked his advice. His response: Don't use paper.

They ignored him. The problem was the public debt, which was close to fatal. In 1790 the revolutionaries went ahead and issued 400 million bonds (to be bought, they said, with the cash people had been keeping under the mattress). As for repayment, the bonds would later be backed by the eventual sale of church and aristo lands (a quarter of all real estate in France). Didn't work out that way because the land sales didn't happen or people didn't trust the system. So the government changed the name of the bonds to "paper banknotes." Soon more money was needed, so they printed more. Devaluing the earlier paper. Inflation set in. By 1795 the 400 million notes in circulation had become 35 billion, each worth less than one-five-hundredth the original value. Economically France went phutt.

The mess was made messier by the unhelpful activities of the count de Puisaye, minor aristo nobody with a lost-estates axe to grind. By 1794 Puisaye was in London persuading the Brits to ship him and his six thousand royalist fellow losers over to Brittany for a bring-back-the-monarchy (get-back-our-property) invasion. The whole thing was an eighteenth-century Bay of Pigs total disaster. Puisaye escaped, tried four years of Canada, then lived to a ripe old age in London. His only success (in 1794) was shipping into France a boatload of fake paper money, hastening that financial meltdown.

One of the Brits approached to do the faking claimed later he'd indignantly spurned the offer (nontheless, there were rumors, because Thomas Bewick was a well-known genius at designing money for banks and he had already come up with banknote-border designs impossible to forge). Bewick's woodcuts were so fine they looked like engravings. He first found fame in 1790 with an illustrated book on animals that became really popular and ran to fourteen thousand copies. In preparation for the work, Bewick took to visiting menageries like that of Stephen Polito, for whom he later did posters and handbills.

At the time Polito's featured show-stopper was "Monster Alpine People" (they were goiter sufferers). By 1800 the show included kangaroos, rhinoceroses, elephants, tigers, sloths, tapirs, monkeys, and lions in cages with lion-tamers. By 1811 Polito had two menageries traveling Europe at the same time. After he died his nephew John took over, running twelve caravans-full. And in 1827 in Marseilles John offered to transport George IV's giraffe back to England.

The animal, a present from the Pasha of Egypt, lasted a couple of English winters and then died. Whereupon the king had it stuffed by Britain's leading stuffer, John Gould. Already taxiderming while at school, Gould opened a stuffing office in London and then was hired as "preserver" at the London Zoo. By 1833 he was also made superintendent of birds, so he started painting them and reproducing the work in beautiful large-format lithographs. In the end: fifty volumes, thirty-five hundred plates, and a rave success thanks to his helpers, including a man whose artistic efforts have long since been forgotten.

Edward Lear never made it to big-time art with his illustrated book on parrots or the ten thousand watercolors he did during a ceaseless life of to-and-fro painting in the Mediterranean and Middle East. In spite of having given drawing lessons to Queen Victoria. Today Lear is known, instead, for the funny poems he wrote in his spare time. His 1861 *Book of Nonsense* (seventy-two limericks and drawings) went straight into the best seller list and has never been out of print. In 1867 Lear wrote the immortal "Owl and the Pussycat." As a serious artist, however, he thought this was literary tomfoolery and foolishly sold the buyout-rights-no-royalties to publishers Routledge for about five hundred bucks.

By this time Routledge was on its way to cheap and popular success with "yellowbacks," the low-price reprints they sold at railroad station bookstalls. With no copyright agreements in existence to keep them honest, they helped themselves freely to American work, starting with Fenimore Cooper and then going on to sell half a million of *Uncle Tom's Cabin*.

Routledge's success owed everything to the business smarts of W. H. Smith, who'd originally created the railroad reading market by selling newspapers and books to the new traveling public in 1848. By 1851 Smith had the monopoly for all stations on the London North Western Railways and every right-thinking Victorian approved of the way he kept smut off the shelves.

Smith's big break came in 1854 when *The Times* gave him the monopoly to sell the paper everywhere outside London. Sales went through the roof that year thanks to the Crimean War. To which the editor sent diplomatic correspondent Thomas Chenery. In Istanbul Chenery started stirring things up with reports on the appalling conditions at nearby Scutari military hospital. On October 12 the paper printed his report (no surgeons, no nurses, no supplies, no sanitation). Next day the checks started coming in. On October 14 a Letter to the Editor asked, "Why don't we have nursing help out there?" On October 21 Florence Nightingale was on the way with thirty-eight nurses.

She discovered things were worse than anybody could have imagined: no operating tables, no medication (smoking was treatment of choice), no blankets, no sheets, one chamberpot per thousand men, one surgeon per ninety-five patients, filth and rot everywhere. In 1855 after it was all over Nightingale's report eviscerated the military medical corps, noting that of the 94,000 soldiers sent to the Crimea 4,000 had died of wounds but 19,000 had died from disease.

No surprise, six years later Nightingale was being asked by Washington, D.C., to advise the Union Sanitary Commission on what it should do about the Civil War. Commission director was master administrator Frederick Law Olmsted, who organized a massive nationwide effort. Volunteers set up twenty thousand soldiers' aid societies. Five million bucks was raised in cash and $15 million in kind.

Olmsted had started out as a landscape architect. On three European trips during the 1850s he'd visited every public and private garden he could find and came back to New York to help design the new Central Park with architect Calvert Vaux. After the war the two men carried on the good work. Vaux designed and built the thirty-five park bridges, including the Bethesda Terrace with its 15,876 Moorish-design ceramic tiles made by the Minton Company of Stoke-on-Trent, England. Minton's designer and art advisor at the time was Christopher Dresser, who'd trained at the U.K. Government School of Design, studying art and botany. Dresser was probably the first industrial designer of mass-produced consumer goods such as wallpaper, textiles, toast racks, and kettles. But his main interest lay in bringing the techniques of science (and in particular, botany) to art. For which in 1860 Dresser was awarded a doctorate in botany by the German University of Jena.

Where the head of department was Matthias Schleiden, who lectured to overflow audiences after his amazing discovery that organisms were made up of cells, the basic unit of all life. One of Schleiden's early students was Carl Zeiss, whom Schleiden helped to set up an optical- and scientific-instrument company in Jena. By the early twentieth century Zeiss was a household name. In 1904 the company produced a gizmo called a blink comparator. It allowed you to switch back and forth between two photographic images fast enough (in a blink) to spot smidgen changes in the image.

Just what Clyde Tombaugh needed in 1930 at Lowell Observatory, Arizona, when he was looking for Planet X and each photograph was a field of thousands of stars. One day as he switched between plates one of the "stars" moved. It turned out to be the planet. In Oxford, England, eleven-year-old Venetia Burney suggested a name: "Pluto." Her grandfather's astronomer friend got the idea to Arizona and the Lowell people agreed. Venetia's grandfather was Oxford University Bodley's Librarian Falconer Madan.

After he died in 1935 the British Bibliographical Society endowed a library research award in his name. If the work required residence at Oxford the award holder stayed at Wolfson College. Which was also the product of an endowment in 1966 by British mail-order billionaire Sir Isaac Wolfson. In 2003 the Wolfson Foundation awarded a grant toward the cost of restoring and refurbishing a house in Craven Street, London. In 2006 it opened to the public.

The house was at number 36. The London residence of BEN FRANKLIN.

CHAPTER TWENTY-FOUR

John Morton

JOHN MORTON (PA) was about fifty-two. Up to then he had been against independence, but at the last minute changed his mind and cast the swing vote that brought Pennsylvania on the side of revolt. In one sense Morton's was the single key vote for independence, because without Pennsylvania the other states might not have decided to go ahead with the fight. So let's hear it for Morton. A year after this moment of glory in an otherwise dull, hardworking local-politics life Morton died of tuberculosis.

One of Morton's friends in the Pennsylvania Provincial Assembly had been "Mad" Anthony Wayne. Handsome and well-educated (some said rash and drunk), Wayne's "fondness for the ladies" ruined his marriage. He had a meteoric military rise to general and might have made it all the way (some said to president). Wayne's lightning march to West Point when Benedict Arnold was about to hand it over to the Brits earned him George Washington's permanent support. Later Washington would make him general of the American armies. "Mad" Anthony ended the war in debt (as did so many) and headed for Georgia to run a rice plantation. It failed. In 1791 he aimed for Congress and got unwittingly embroiled in ballot-stuffing.

The stuffer was lawyer Thomas Gibbon, who had a tendency to interpret the law rather loosely. Gibbon was a "high liver" and his pro-

Brit sentiments (and rumors of less than loyal behavior) triggered attempts to sequester his property and a duel. Gibbon was also involved in the Great Yazoo Land Scam (see elsewhere). From which he emerged smelling like a rose. And rich. Then after his wife sued him for keeping prostitutes in the house in 1817 he headed north and became involved in a fight to break the monopoly on steamboat routes between New York and New Jersey. In the end he won, after a row with the U.S. Patent Office about his own steamboat patent.

The Patent Office had been set up (and then run on a shoestring) by William Thornton. Who was also an amateur architect. Back in 1793, besides whipping up support for various South American revolutions and developing plans for a national university, Thornton had won George Washington's approval for the "noble simplicity" of his design for the proposed Capitol Building. Evidently too simple. And likely, some said, to fall down. So shortly thereafter Frenchman Etienne Sulpice Hallet (who'd come second in the contest) was called in to modify Thornton's design.

In mysterious circumstances Hallet and his partner Joseph Cerneau were then given a U.S. patent for an improved version of the Montgolfier hydraulic ram. This used the power of trapped flowing water to force more water up a tube. Known as "raising water," the technique was the main method before electric pumps. Cerneau was a shadowy figure who had spent time in Cuba before being asked to leave the island when his fellow Freemasons made "representations" to the governor. After he arrived in New York Cerneau set up an alternate Freemason organization (the "Cerneau Grand Consistory") and proceeded to make Masonic waves by inducting people and conferring ranks none of which he was empowered to confer. In 1813 a group of Masons turned up from Cuba with proof of the kind of nefarious activity Cerneau had been up to, down there, which they said would be sufficient to blacken anybody's reputation.

The official Masonic organization in America asked Cerneau to cease and desist but he didn't. His version of New York Freemasonry continued to hold meetings and do whatever Masons did. In 1824, just before he finally left for France in (no surprise) suspicious circumstances,

Cerneau managed to induct a new Masonic grand commander. None other than the Marquis de Lafayette, who was at the beginning of his triumphal farewell tour of the twenty-four states.

President Monroe's canny invitation to the lame old hero to come and say good-bye achieved its purpose. The tour revived memories of the valiant past and renewed America's sense of national pride. Everywhere he went Lafayette was overwhelmed by crowds. He opened libraries, laid foundation stones, dedicated public buildings, and had Masonic meetings. And was accompanied for a while by Frances Wright, a strange Englishwoman who wanted to be either his lover or adopted daughter but who got fed up with Lafayette's endless American groupies and dropped out of the tour.

Wright then headed to the utopian community at New Harmony, Indiana, to pick up some tips for her own similar venture planned at Nashoba, near Memphis, Tennessee. Wright's idea was that slaves could be prepared for freedom in an environment where they could mix as equals with whites. Wright dressed in tunic and trousers, wore cropped hair, and addressed "scandalous" (i.e., mixed male-female) audiences on such matters as birth control. Naturally enough she became known as the "Great Red Harlot."

Soon thereafter Nashoba went belly-up when the community overseer blew the whistle on free-love practices and miscegenation. But not before Frances had persuaded her friend Frances Trollope to come take a look. Trollope (author Anthony's mother) looked, then headed for Cincinnati. Where she wrote *Domestic Manners of the Americans* (Brits loved it, Americans didn't) and set up a money-making wax-museum project titled "Infernal Regions," featuring dummies, mechanical figures, and electrical shocks.

Most of the show's figure-modeling work was done by young sculptor Hiram Powers. Who eventually made it to D.C., where he sculpted the president and other luminaries, then headed for Florence, Italy. In 1843 he produced his blockbuster (possibly the most influential American statue ever) *Greek Slave*. The statue of a nude, shackled slave girl, her pose evoking the thought of terrible Turkish perversions, toured the United States for two years to standing-room-only prurience. Not everyone had the same reaction. At a preview in Florence, Elizabeth Barrett Browning totally missed the hint of porn.

By this time Browning was a successful and admired poet, living a blissfully happy life with her husband, Robert Browning, who had come into her life from the outside world and saved her from hypochondria, dimly lit bedrooms, and opium: Robert wrote saying he admired her writing; she wrote back saying same to you; ninety-one visits and a year later they eloped. Only one small cloud shaded their otherwise saccharine existence: Elizabeth's interest in Daniel Dunglass Home, a medium (or, as per Robert, a fake).

Things had started going bump around Home while he was growing up in the United States. The poltergeist activity proved too much for the family and Home was invited to leave home. He traveled from curtained séance to curtained séance until in 1855 he fetched up in London where big names including Ms. Browning held hands as tables tilted, levitated, and rapped while instruments played, phantom figures appeared, and Mr. Home extended himself. In the era of credulity Home couldn't fail. There followed marriage to the tsar's goddaughter, a twenty-four-thousand-pound gift from a woman believer, and a U.S. tour. And meetings with the pope, the French emperor, and the king of Bavaria. And the establishment of a posh spiritualist center in London.

In 1871 Home was given the ultimate cachet: Victorian England's leading nerd fell for the mumbo-jumbo. William Crookes was president of scientific everything and held forth on the same number of subjects. He was Victoria's Victorian sage (and chemist, and physicist), who turned his experiments into money (water treatment, sewage treatment, cow-pest treatment), cultivated other science biggies like himself, and nearly discovered X-rays. Like many others at the time, Crookes was into sending electrical discharges through rarefied gases. During which procedure he produced a "stream" or "ray" that fluoresced whatever it hit, was warm to the touch, and cast shadows. In the 1890s Crookes was able to do all this with his "Crookes Tube" (cathode ray tube), a high-vacuum glass tube with two electrodes in it. The mystery rays went from the cathode to the anode (i.e., from one end to the other).

In 1896 telephone billionaire Alexander Graham Bell had a Crookes tube at his mansion in Nova Scotia and was forecasting the use of X-rays to produce three-dimensional pictures of the inside of a body (a prediction of the modern CT scan). In 1903 Bell also suggested using tiny pieces of radium in tiny vacuum tubes placed inside a cancer to destroy it. By this time the great man was enjoying well-earned retirement, experimenting with electricity, radioactivity, and flight, while his patents made him richer by the minute.

In the United Kingdom, Bell's patents were owned by the National Telephone Company. In 1914, Mick Mannock, one of their clerks looking for advancement, took off for Istanbul to work on an NTC subcontract, rigging up a telephone network for the city. A few months later World War I happened and Mannock and all other expat Brits were interned until an exchange agreement in 1915 set them free.

Mannock returned to Britain and by 1917 was a Royal Flying Corps fighter ace in a squadron equipped with the latest Nieuport 17. The Nieuport was a highly maneuverable French airframe built by designer Gustave Delage and used by all the air forces in the war. Carrying a synchronized machine gun that fired through the propeller, the plane had an unusual feature: The upper wings were twice the size of the lower wings. For this reason the Nieuport was designated a "sesquiplane" (one-and-a-half wing). Only one minor tendency detracted from its many good points: In a steep dive the lower wing could sometimes come off.

After the war, as private flying became fashionable, the same wing design was taken up again by a New York company, which produced over two hundred sesquiplane Brunner-Winkle "Birds" for such flying elites as Lindbergh's wife. Another enthusiast was Russian-born aeroengineer Alec Ulmann, who flew his Bird around Europe in the 1930s while working for international companies such as Goodyear.

In 1950 Ulmann, who was also a high-performance car buff, set up a new twelve-hour endurance race at Sebring, south of Orlando, Florida. In the early years the race attracted all the great names: Stirling Moss, Graham Hill, and Mario Andretti. Driving Porsches, Ferraris, Maseratis, and Jaguars.

The race is still run today. In 1994 the winner was JOHN MORTON.

CHAPTER TWENTY-FIVE

GEORGE CLYMER (PA) was thirty-seven. Tax returns show he was one of the richest men in Philadelphia. Throughout the war he sat on innumerable committees. Clymer was obsessed with points of order and such bureaucratic noodling, so after things settled down he got the job of persuading late-paying states to ante up their share of the war debt. Served him right.

In 1791 Clymer was just the man to be tapped as collector of revenues in Pennsylvania. Where everything hit the fan. After fighting an international war over unfair taxation, farmers all along the western frontier were less than amused when Congress authorized a tax on whiskey and sent in a corps of excise inspectors to find farmers' stills and take farmers' money.

In western Pennsylvania the local response was to burn down the inspector's house and threaten to shoot him. Government warnings didn't work, so in 1794 George Washington issued the relevant proclamation, collected nearly thirteen thousand troops from Virginia, Maryland, New Jersey, and Pennsylvania, and headed west into whiskey country. Washington's almost royal progress had a salutary effect on the rebels, who melted away ahead of the army. Those few caught were amnestied. The new Republic's first major crisis was over. Phew.

Some said that farmer, ex–land speculator, and ex–French teacher Albert Gallatin was a Whiskey Rebellion ringleader. Others claimed that he had helped calm things down. Either way his involvement on behalf of the locals won him six years in Congress, where in 1801 Gallatin's Swiss financial acumen persuaded Jefferson to make him secretary of the Treasury. Gallatin used cost-cutting techniques to pay off the war debt and then turned his attention to getting the economy on its feet. His 1803 proposal for a federally funded National Road raised cheers. Farmers donated land for the sixty-six-foot-wide strip that started in 1811 and eventually went from Cumberland, Maryland, to Vandalia, Illinois. Gallatin knew it would be jammed night and day with traffic, mostly Conestoga wagons that would ruin a gravel road. So he opted for a road surface designed by a Scot who had once turned up in America just in time to be a loyalist and go home again.

John McAdam's road was easy to make: a foot-deep base of seven-inch stones carrying an upper layer of three-inch stones carrying a top layer of crushed stone. Plus drainage ditches. By 1820 McAdam's company was building and maintaining roads all over Britain. That year he was approached by the administrator of the Royal Military Hospital at Greenwich to McAdamize lots of Northumberland (northeast England) where the hospital owned big estates with coal mines that needed access roads. The contract came from Edward Locker, running Greenwich Hospital after a navy career much of which had been spent as secretary to the commander-in-chief, Mediterranean fleet. Which is why in May 1814 Locker had found himself on the Italian island of Elba showing paperwork for the upcoming peace treaty to uninterested ex-emperor Napoleon.

By now Napoleon had been "Emperor of Elba" since his abdication a month earlier and was already getting used to being a tourist target for the Brits who turned up by the dozen to gawp. And in some cases sketch. Back in the glory days, Napoleon had been impressed by young London artist Henry Barker, who had visited him with a great plan for a great panorama depicting Napoleon's greatness. So the great man ordered seven great circular buildings to be built in the Champs Elysées to show more panoramas of great French victories. Alas, neither victories nor panoramas nor buildings happened. So in 1814 on Elba Henry

Barker was having another go, doing preliminary sketches of Napoleon and his island. Back home Barker's giant pix were making him a fortune. Standing-room crowds queued for hours to look for hours at all-round giant paintings of all-round giant events. Including Barker's most successful show of all, the battle of Waterloo. Another box-office smash was his view of the departure (for Spitzbergen and points north) of a four-ship fleet commanded by Captain David Buchan.

This was yet another of the neverending attempts to find the Northwest Passage (from Atlantic to Pacific over northern Canada). Of course they didn't find it. After doing meteorology, magnetic everything, and sea temperatures (and any other measurements they could think of), Buchan's fleet ended up like everybody else: hitting ice, ice, and more ice. Then going home. One of their number wasn't giving up that easily, though. In 1819 John Franklin headed off again to spend three more years in northwest Canada, mapping, starving, freezing, and "eating his own boots" (and, it was rumored, any of the team who died). Then back to a hero's welcome. In 1825 crazy Franklin was off yet again. Three more years of raw meat and frozen toes. Then back to a hero's welcome. After which, a brief and disastrous interval (1837-43) proving great explorers didn't make good governors of Tasmania. Back in the United Kingdom, the obsessive Franklin headed out yet again for you-know-where. This time he didn't come back. His wife, Jane, financed five expeditions to find him. All they found were skeletons.

Jane then headed off round the world to meet people: Hawaii (Queen Emma), Japan (emperor), Brazil (emperor), Salt Lake City (Brigham Young), and Rome (pope). Her purpose was to wave the flag of "enlightened" colonialism. Which was partly why she had earlier ruined her husband's tour as governor in Tasmania, when her too-liberal intentions took her on a fact-finding mission into the women convicts' prison. She'd got the idea from her friend Elizabeth Fry. Whose own epiphany had been in Newgate Prison, London. Where back in 1813 Fry'd been persuaded to take a look at conditions for female prisoners. And had staggered out, shocked to the core at the filth and degradation in which lady inmates were forced to live. Fry became a nationally known power for reform: education for inmates, fresh straw bedding, clothing, and above all the separation of male and female prisoners. In no time Fry was an international figure, meeting such worthies as the pope, the tsar, and the kings of Prussia and Italy.

The man who had originally sent her into the cells was a French exiled aristo who claimed to be the last living person able to identify the Lost Dauphin (crown prince) of France. Etienne de Grellet had run away from the French revolutionaries because of his royal connections, then arrived in the United States, turned Quaker, and finally ended up in London (hence the connection with Quaker Elizabeth Fry's family). The Lost Dauphin mystery gripped everybody. Once the Dauphin's mom and pop (Louis XVI and Marie Antoinette) had been guillotined, the lad should have become Louis XVII but for the minor inconvenience of the French Revolution. During which he disappeared. There were rumors he was being kept in a secret prison, masked and unrecognizable to would-be supporters. Others said he was dead. Eleaser Williams, missionary in Wisconsin, claimed to be him.

Williams was checked out (and flunked) in 1841 by visiting Prince Joinville, youngest son of King Louis Philippe of France. Joinville then returned to Europe and (in his other role as French admiral) scared the Brits with an article saying that if France had a couple of paddle-steamer warships the United Kingdom would be a pushover. Panic reigned in London. In 1859 a Defense Commission was set up under Sir William Jervois, who soon became Mr. Fortifications. His plan: build forts in the sea off the main English ports. Some were built. None with guns. Meanwhile Jervois was off all over the world checking out other people's defenses. Which was why in 1863, after a period studying such stuff in Canada, he was to be seen risking life and limb in a rowing boat pretending to be an artist sketching the harbor walls in Portland, Maine. And in fact sketching them.

This was a dangerous occupation, because the Civil War was still going on and the place had just witnessed the capture of daring Confederate raider Charles Read after he had crept up and stolen a U.S. Revenue cutter. In the previous months Read had nobbled twenty-two Union commercial ships and generally created mayhem in the shipping lanes. So after Read's capture off Portland he was interned. A year later he was prisoner-exchanged and was soon back at his old tricks until captured for the last time in 1865. When he was interrogated (possibly because he knew Confederate president Jefferson Davis) by no less than Allan Pinkerton.

Who went on to immortality with the first U.S. detective agency, employed mostly as strike breakers and infiltrators of terrorist groups such as the Molly Maguires, active in the Pennsylvania coalfields. By the time Allan Pinkerton died in 1884 the "Pinkerton man" was a national figure chasing bandits and train robbers like the James brothers. And spying on cash-register clerks who might have their hand in the till. Such sneaky behavior was an after-sales service provided by National Cash Register Company founder and president John Patterson. Who also invented everything that makes modern U.S. business tick: annual sales conferences, employee-training programs, company ethics, a two-hundred-page manual on "How to Sell" (complete with memorizable script), sales quotas, and above all the concept of "creating demand."

In 1906 Patterson hired young engineer Charles Kettering, the propeller-head's role model, whose inventions included premature baby incubator, automatic transmission, safety glass, electric railroad gates, shock absorbers, and a version of Patterson's cash register that could be opened by an electric motor at the press of a button. This last gave Kettering the idea for his greatest gizmo: the electric automobile starter motor. Did away with hand-cranking in 1911 when the first one appeared in a Cadillac.

Kettering had his starter-motor manufactured by fan-makers Robbins & Myers of Springfield, Ohio. In World War II their precision-engineering techniques were employed making the Norden bombsight. The Norden was a small gyro-controlled computer and was so cosmic secret it was loaded on the plane before a mission by armed guard and unloaded the same way afterward. When linked with the autopilot, the Norden used input on the plane's direction, airspeed, altitude, and angle of drift to fly the aircraft through the bombing run to the target point and then release the bombs. The data required for all this to happen was punched into the Norden computer by the aircraft's bombardier.

During the War forty-five thousand men and women were initially to do this work, starting on the B-17 Flying Fortress. In 1942 one of the bombardier training staff applied for combat operations and went on to twenty missions, six battle stars, a Distinguished Flying Cross, an Air Medal, and the rank of brigadier general. This war hero was film star Jimmy Stewart. Born in the small Pennsylvania town of Indiana.

Where in 1805 land for the county seat was donated by GEORGE CLYMER.

CHAPTER TWENTY-SIX

JAMES SMITH (PA) was about sixty-three. And thinking ahead. When he wrote his name on the Declaration, Smith was already on the committee set up to plan the structure of postwar government. Although colleagues called Smith eccentric he was essentially a quiet, no-fireworks, behind-the-scenes guy. Smith had started in law, then given that up for iron-making, then given that up for law again.

In 1784 he acted as counselor for Pennsylvania in one of those half-forgotten affairs that occurred so often immediately after Independence while things were still settling down. Or in this case, not. Smith's legal brief regarded a disagreement that hadn't been resolved in more than a hundred years. Back in 1684 King Charles II had relied on guesstimate maps to grant Pennsylvania a charter for settling a piece of land. Unfortunately the grant-to-settle rights for the same land had previously also been given (by the same king, using a different map) to Connecticut. Seems crazy but back in those days, who knew?

The location in question was the Wyoming Valley in western Pennsylvania (or Connecticut, if you saw things that way). In 1783 Connecticut settlers were driven out of the valley by Pennsylvanians at a cost of 150 lives and thousands of refugees. But all was not over. In 1786 Ethan Allen arrived with some of his Green Mountain Boys, offering the Connecticut Wyoming settlers help in setting up a new state (to be called

Westmoreland). Allen had done the same state-forming thing once before when he'd declared independence from New York state of an area of green mountain country on the Canadian border.

Before the place (Vermont) was finally admitted as a state of the Union, Allen had even flirted for two years with the idea of secession to Canada (see elsewhere). At one point during all this he was involved in naming a town (St. Johnsbury) after a French friend, Hector St. John de Crèvecoeur, who wrote a book of fictional letters from a "Farmer James" describing life in rural America and asking for the first time: "What is an American?" (Crèvecoeur's answer: a new man, with new principles, free of European prejudice.)

Neutral during the war, Crèvecoeur made several U.S.-France trips. Back in Paris he was hailed as his own best example of "American new man" and became the darling of salon chatterers. After a first publication (successful) in London, in 1793 his *Letters from an American Farmer* appeared in Philadelphia published by Matthew Carey, aka "Scriblerius O'Pindar." The pseudonym was for Carey's protection, since he tended to make powerful enemies for whose jugular he'd journalistically gone. On the run from British-ruled Ireland (for penning revolutionary stuff about giving Catholics the vote), Carey met and impressed the Marquis de Lafayette, who loaned him four hundred dollars to start his first American newspaper, the Pennsylvania *Herald* (it failed). Carey also produced the first American atlas, started the first American Sunday school society, and had a very boring brother.

John Carey taught classics, French, and shorthand in London. He wrote essays (now long forgotten), edited a series of fifty classical texts (now long unread), and produced the best insomnia cure of all time: *Latin Prosody Made Easy*. In 1803 he had an idea: save souls from shipwreck by shooting (at them, from the shore) a wooden ball on a line. Said endangered souls would then haul in the line attached to rope with which they would then be then pulled to shore. Carey did nothing more about it. In 1808 George Manby came up with the same idea, inspired by the loss of the *Snipe*, which foundered (and all aboard were drowned) within sight and sound of the beach. Manby (at one point he had been shot in the head and tended to behave oddly) went on to invent ways of catching people jumping from burning buildings or saving those who had fallen through ice, as well as the first pressurized portable fire extinguisher and a harpoon. This last he tried out on a trip to Greenland in 1821.

Around 1810 Manby took another of his bright ideas (how to assassinate Napoleon) to an old political pal, the Honorable Charles Yorke. Who turned down more government jobs than most: ambassador to Russia, governor of Madras, governor of Jamaica, surveyor of forests, and member of the board administering India. He accepted secretary of war, wrote a book on Egyptian monuments in the British Museum, and generally made no mark on parliamentary history. He did, however, support the launch of the Royal Military College, Sandhurst.

Whose architect was James Wyatt. You loved or hated him. He had an infuriating tendency to enthuse about a project till it started and then lose interest. Nonetheless, at twenty-six he was architect of choice if you had a falling-down country mansion to renovate. Wyatt traveled an amazing four thousand miles a year in his coach complete with office and drawing board. After sprucing up the abodes of royalty (Windsor Castle) and various dukes, Wyatt turned to the restoration of Gothic cathedrals. Wyatt's "restoration" meant ripping out anything later than medieval (such as carved screens, chapels, and porches) as well as moving tombs and other memorabilia into neat, orderly rows between the aisles. This good work earned Wyatt his nickname: "the destroyer."

Not everybody hated Wyatt's stuff. One fan was a philandering German dissolute, Prince Puckler-Muskau, a dashing ex–cavalry officer who dyed his hair and was also an accomplished landscape gardener. In 1827, having spent all his wife's money and then divorced her, he was in England taking in the sights, meeting royalty and Sir Walter Scott, and sleeping with every woman he could persuade. His predilection seems to have been for vicars' daughters, sisters, and actresses.

After his England visit he published a selection of the letters he'd written home. The book caught the attention of Sarah Austin. Just the kind of woman Puckler-Muskau fancied. Sarah was beautiful, sensuous, and married to a cold-fish professor of jurisprudence who had bad health and hangups. Sarah spent a year in Bonn learning German and in

1832 translated Puckler-Muskau's work as: *Travels of a German Prince in England*. She also began a correspondence with him that verged on the pornographic. There was much talk of dreams. By 1835 after Puckler-Muskau had offered to come and "visit" and she'd said no, the prince headed for Africa.

Sarah turned to another translation job which she referred to as "dry." *Report on the State of Public Instruction in Prussia* had been compiled in 1832 by France's leading thinker and molder of public opinion, Victor Cousin. It outlined the kind of educational system Cousin wanted France to have: compulsory primary school attendence for both boys and girls (and punishment of parents who failed to send them), standardized curriculum, textbooks produced by the state, state control over teacher training, and of course, state funding.

When Sarah's translation of Cousin arrived in America, the book was just what Horace Mann was looking for. Mann was secretary to the Massachusetts Board of Education and he had already opened a couple of teacher-training schools. Mann also visited Germany during his honeymoon in 1844 and came home fired up for reform. Above all Mann wanted to take religion out of schools. Over the next few years Mann increased teachers' salaries by 50 percent, opened fifty new public high schools that used standard textbooks published in Boston, and finagled more than $2 million out of the state to pay for it all. The rest of America soon followed Mann's inspiring example.

In the early 1850s Mann's sister-in-law and her short-of-cash husband came to stay on their way to Liverpool, England, where the husband (Nathaniel Hawthorne, by this time famous as the author of *The Scarlet Letter* and *The House of Seven Gables*) was to be U.S. consul. After Liverpool in 1857 the couple headed for Italy where they met the expat community toughing it out in Florence. These lotus-eaters included poets Robert and Elizabeth Browning and Walter Savage Landor.

Leader of the esthete Florentine layabouts was Seymour Kirkup, a Brit painter with (it was said) too much money and not enough talent. And who by this time had been in Florence for more than thirty-three years complete with three mistresses and offspring. Kirkup had been a disciple of the London-based Dante scholar Giuseppe Rossetti and

knew about the Lost Giotto Portrait of Dante Hidden Somewhere in
Florence. On July 21, 1840, he found the fresco, covered over with
whitewash, on a wall in the Bargello. So he sent a tracing to Rossetti.
Who showed it to his son Dante Gabriele.

Who painted *Giotto Painting Dante's Portrait.* D. G. Rossetti was part
of the group of artists known as the Pre-Raphaelite Brotherhood whose
aim was to return to the medieval simplicites of art before Raphael.
Great if you liked spun sugar. Or woodsy wallpaper such as that produced by fellow PRB member William Morris, designer to a middle
class now yearning to forget the industrial world outside their windows.
In 1870 Morris spent a year in Iceland (where the communitarian
lifestyle fired his socialist imagination) and then translated a medieval
Icelandic saga. He went on to do the same for the Anglo-Saxon epic
Beowulf.

This medievalist aspect of Morris's work (and indeed the entire Pre-
Raphaelite range of product) was, between 1936 and 1945, to inspire
Anglo-Saxon scholar J. R. R. Tolkien to write the great *Lord of the Rings*
trilogy. At the time Tolkien was professor at Pembroke College, Oxford,
where one of his colleagues was modern historian Ronald McCallum.
Whose forte was political analysis (he coined the word "psephology":
the study of polls).

Of all the students who attended McCallum's tutorials, perhaps the
most famous was William J. Fulbright, who spent from 1924 to 1928 in
Oxford as a Rhodes Scholar studying modern history. After which, a year
in Europe with journalist Mikhail Fodor meeting major political figures.
In 1942, back in the United States, Fulbright began a thirty-two-year
congressional career. Fulbright was prosegregation, anti-isolationist,
pro–peaceful coexistence with the U.S.S.R., and anti–Vietnam War. He
also believed in internationalism as a means of keeping the peace, so he
supported America's involvement in the U.N. To the same end in 1946
he set up an international exchange program in graduate studies, which
became known as the Fulbright Scholarship.

In 1968 Thomas Heck was a Fulbright Scholar in Vienna studying
the history of the classical guitar and in particular adding to his collection of first-edition manuscripts of music by Giuliani (guitar composer,

1781-1829). In 1973 Heck set up the Guitar Foundation of America to act as a storehouse for his (and then others') guitar-music collections. Since then the organization has acted to provide guitarists with materials, a library, a society, a publisher, and educational resources.

In 1985 the Guitar Foundation president was JAMES SMITH.

CHAPTER TWENTY-SEVEN

Geo. Taylor

GEORGE TAYLOR (PA) was about sixty. And did his bit for victory by making cannonballs. Not much is known about his beginnings in Ireland. When he signed he was a well-to-do ironmaker, a justice of the peace and member of the Pennsylvania Provincial Assembly. And the replacement for a delegate who refused to sign the Declaration. John Dickinson argued that war would be a mistake since the states hadn't even agreed on a constitution among themselves. Nor (at that time) did America have any allies, nor was the country in any military shape to fight, nor did the states even have proper governments of their own. In Congress Dickinson's logical and persuasive thoughts hit a stone wall. So he went home.

In 1782, after a two-month period as president of Delaware, Dickinson became president of Pennsylvania and donated five hundred acres at Carlisle, on the frontier, for the foundation of a new college. Dickinson College (as it's now known) was the first chartered college in the United States and opened for business in 1805. In 1811 ex-Brit noodler Thomas Cooper (reckoned by Thomas Jefferson to be the most informed man in the country) arrived as Dickinson's first professor of chemistry. Most of his knowledge of molecules came from his long-term U.K. friendship with ex-Brit noodler Joseph Priestley (discoverer of oxygen and lots more), who ran away to the United States with Cooper when things got too hot for them back home (both men were dangerously pro–U.S. independence and pro–French Revolution, so Priestley's house was ransacked and burned by a carefully government-arranged "mob").

After Priestley died in 1804 Cooper's comprehensive survey of the great man's work formed the basis for a chemistry textbook. Cooper also wrote a book on cookery. He also did debris-scatter studies and fragment analysis on the new terror weapon used in the War of 1812: the Congreve rocket (as in "rockets' red glare").

William Congreve's father ran the lab at the Woolwich Military Academy in London so the son grew up a geek. Some of his inventions: canal lockgate, parachute, rocket-propelled whaling harpoon, perpetual-motion machine, gas meter, and unfakeable banknotes. Congreve's rockets were regarded in some quarters (*Morning Chronicle*) as "tomfoolery," but they had done a lot of damage to Copenhagen in 1809 and most important of all impressed the Prince Regent, a fat buffoon who asked Congreve to add some excitement to the August 1814 London event when crowned allied heads would get together to celebrate the recent victory over Napoleon. Congreve obliged with fireworks and rockets galore.

Before which, while the sky was still safe, others amazed the crowds. John Sadler rose in a balloon and dropped programs. Sadler's father had already done over forty ascents (one to thirteen thousand feet) and his balloon trademark was being used to sell soda water. Son John was by this time an established member of the scientific establishment, having been chemical assistant to the Royal Institution since 1800. The RI had originally been formed to provide instruction to artisans on the latest gizmos and techniques. Unfortunately the artisans didn't turn up. But from 1801, once the charismatic Humphry Davy had begun lecturing, the street outside was so jammed with the carriages of ticket-holder royalty and nobility that the traffic had to be one-way-only for the evening.

Davy's brilliant style made science fashionable. He also identified tannin in tea, discovered that sunlight caused pond weed to give off oxygen, experimented with laughing gas and suggested (decades before it was used) that the gas be administered during surgery, cofounded London Zoo, received medals and a knighthood, and was one of the inventors of the miners' safety lamp. When he was president of the Royal

Society in 1823 Davy was approached for support to open a new club for artists, scientists, and writers.

The idea that the Athenaeum Club would bring thinkers together to counter the public trend toward sensationalism and trash (aka Romantic Movement) originated with John Wilson Croker. Who had recently been accused of killing John Keats with his attack on the poet's "Endymion," causing (it was said by the Keats crowd) a rush of blood to the lungs that killed him. In fact Keats died of tuberculosis. Croker was a politico and writer who believed that the Romantics were flushing British culture down the toilet and that the previous century had seen the end of good literature. Croker also raised hackles by exposing scams organized by royal mistresses and public-fund embezzlement by bureaucrats, and (most of all) by the way he helped to push through Parliament the first income tax bill.

In 1815, once the Napoleonic Wars were over Croker headed to Paris to have fun with his old friend William Vesey-Fitzgerald. Five years later Vesey-Fitzgerald was in Stockholm (not having fun) as British minister empowered to renegotiate the Guadeloupe Fund. In 1813 Britain had taken the island from the French, then given it to Sweden to compensate King Charles XIV for loss of his estates, confiscated when (as Napoleonic general Jean Baptiste Jules Bernadotte) he had left France to become Swedish king. The Fund also covered Sweden's Napoleonic Wars costs. After the war Guadeloupe went back to the French and Britain gave Sweden twenty-four million francs indemnity for loss of Guadeloupean income.

By 1820, however, there was talk of the Swedes giving some back. Unfortunately, Charles XIV had already spent the money on (among other things) the Gota Canal. Linking the Baltic and North seas, the canal was Sweden's biggest infrastructure project, built by fifty thousand shoveling soldiers and with the consultant help of Britain's top waterways person, Thomas Telford. By this time (1808) Telford was a legend for his suspension bridges, harbors and docks, restored churches, public buildings, the amazing Welsh Pontycyllte aqueduct (1,007 feet long and 126 feet up), and the Caledonian Canal through the Scottish Highlands.

Inevitably, Telford was also asked advice on the Welland Canal around Niagara Falls. Chief Welland engineer was David Thomas. Whose real passion was fruit. His son John was even more fruitily inclined and ran one of the best nurseries in the country where he produced the Tillotson peach, started and edited the *Country Gentleman*, invented the smoothing harrow, and wrote such gripping pieces as "The Fruit Culturalist" and "Farm Implements and Machinery." Not surprisingly John set up the American Pomological (apple-study) Society with a fellow fruit, Andrew Downing.

Who wrote about what to do with the rest of the garden around a house (landscape gardening, ornamental additions, statuary, romantic views). Downing is also credited with popularizing the front porch. In 1850 he spent six months looking at gardens in England, then returned to a presidential commission landscaping the public grounds of Washington, D.C. (the strip from Capitol Hill to the Washington Monument site). Alas, before he could create this first public park in the United States he died in a steamboat disaster. His Pomological Society colleagues paid for a Carrara marble memorial urn.

Urn sculptor was Robert Eberhardt Schmidt von der Launitz, the doyen of mortuary monuments. You name it, he carved it: stone angels, recumbent girls with flowers in hair, firemen rescuing children from flames, lambs. He also got a good share of the Civil War monuments going up all over the country. Launitz's pupil Thomas Crawford went to Italy and settled there. In 1849 on a visit back home he read in a Boston newspaper of the plan to erect a monument to George Washington in Richmond, Virginia. Crawford put in a bid and got the job: Washington on horseback, with the standing figures of Patrick Henry and Thomas Jefferson, plus two shields, thirteen wreaths, and stars. For nearly fifty-three thousand dollars. For an additional nine thousand dollars apiece he added John Marshall, Thomas Nelson, Thomas Mason, and General Andrew Lewis. The whole gigantic bronze thing was forged at the only mid-nineteenth-century place capable of handling such a piece, the Royal Bavarian Foundry in Munich.

Son of the foundry boss was Oskar von Miller, who was crazy about electricity. In 1882 Munich City commissioned him to set up the first electricity exhibition, at which he wowed the crowd with a supply coming from thirty-five miles away. Two years later he opened the first small power plant in Munich. In 1883 Oskar teamed up with Emil Rathenau to run what eventually became known as AEG, a counterpart of General Electric in the United States. Rathenau had a head start in the marketplace because he owned the German patent for Edison's light bulb.

By 1889 Rathenau had two thousand employees and his catalogue included curling tongs, cigar lighters, irons, tea kettles, and hotplates. And he was the first to employ a designer for factory buildings as well as appliances. In 1903, switched on to the future commercial potential of radio, AEG teamed up (as "Telefunken") with Siemens, a company dealing in the larger uses of electricity. Siemens had already laid a telegraph line from London to Calcutta and had introduced the first German electric railroad, tramcar, elevator, and streetlights.

In 1902 the Siemens office in St. Petersburg hired a young Polish engineer to equip the Russian navy with radios. Joseph Tykociner turned out to be the man movie history forgot. By 1918 he was teaching at the University of Illinois, where he developed a sound-on-film system. Speech from a microphone modulated current to a light, making its brightness vary. The varying light then varyingly exposed a moving strip of celluloid negative. When a projector was used, the printed (varyingly light and dark) film strip let varying amounts of light through to hit a photoelectric cell. Which in reaction generated varying current to a loudspeaker. Which then reproduced the original sound. In 1923, Tykociner was beaten to the patent by Lee De Forest's similar system.

By the late 1930s talking pictures were getting into their stride, and in 1937 a young sports radio announcer on a visit to Hollywood took a screen test for Warner Brothers and landed a seven-year contract. His first starring role was in *Love Is on the Air*. A 1932 graduate from Eureka College, Illinois, he had lettered in football. One of his fellow players went on to a distinguished career as a coach.

When the coach retired in 1972 the actor (now governor of California and future president of the United States Ronald Reagan) sent a message of congratulations to his old gridiron colleague GEORGE TAYLOR.

CHAPTER TWENTY-EIGHT

James Wilson

JAMES WILSON (PA) was thirty-three. He'd been in America for only ten years. Back home in Scotland his St. Andrews University background had netted him an offer to teach at the College of Philadelphia. Once there, his politically left background showed in the way he was soon speaking up on the Independence issue: power came from the people, and since the American people weren't represented in London (PS, the same went for most Scots), they owed no allegiance to England. This powerful democratic streak in Wilson's character made him almost the only signer to support the notion of direct election of the U.S. president.

Wilson was also involved in several questionable land and manufacturing deals, spent much of his time in debt, and died owing seventy thousand dollars (back then, a lot). Curiously, in 1780 he was a founder member of the short-lived Bank of Pennsylvania (a model for the U.S. National Bank). One of Wilson's fellow directors was Philadelphia upper-crust Thomas Willing.

Willing did very nicely out of the war. Already rich from business, he supplied the revolutionary armies with blankets, bullets, guns, and medicines. And between 1770 and 1790 made a million. He was president of the Bank of North America and then of the First Bank of the United States. And as is often the case with plutocrats, his socialite daughter

Anne married money. Her well-heeled new spouse, William Bingham, had traveled Europe in 1773 and was then sent by Congress to do intelligence work in the Caribbean and to negotiate a possible wartime alliance with the wait-and-see French. Mixing business with these politics inevitably made him even richer and he became a major stockholder in the Bank of North America. Turnpikes and land made even him more boodle. By 1800 he was the richest man in the United States.

So who did his two daughters marry? Two Barings, members of the richest banking family in the United Kingdom. Alexander Baring (who married Anne Bingham) was a hot young financier in 1795 when he turned up in America to buy 1,225,000 acres of Maine from Bingham. Acting for a consortium of Baring's Bank and the Hope Bank of Amsterdam, Alexander later negotiated a $5 million loan to the U.S. government and then in 1803 pulled off the greatest deal of his career, arranging an $11,250,000 loan for America to buy the Louisiana Territory from France.

One member of the Hope Bank kept well out of the business world: Thomas Hope was too busy spending his megabucks on the arts. Patron, neoclassical buff, scholar, writer, and above all (to be expected, given his bankroll) collector, Hope was known for his conceit, tactlessness, effeminacy, and sickly looks. He bought everything and especially classical vases of which in 1806 he owned fifteen hundred. His antique and art collection grew so big he issued tickets to selected friends to come to his house and view.

Naturally, Hope also commissioned work from the greatest sculptor of the day, Antonio Canova, renowned for the velvety texture of his stone. By the time Canova was twenty he was well on the road to international fame and fortune. He worked for several popes, as well as Napoleon and family, the king of Naples, the king of Spain, the Archduchess Maria Christina of Austro-Hungary, and minor nobodies such as royal dukes. His erotic nude statue of Napoleon's sister Pauline shocked Europe. His heroic Washington went into the South Carolina State House. His masterpiece, the *Three Graces*, inspired an Italian to poetry.

Ugo Foscolo (he wrote "The Three Graces") had the doubtful honor of being professor of Italian eloquence at the University of Pavia until he gave his first lecture. In which he said that the duty of literature was to investigate the nature of national identity. At a time when Italy was occupied by France and then Austria these words were an invitation to have all chairs of Italian eloquence shut down. They were. Nationalist patriot Foscolo was then more or less permanently on the run for producing poems like one summoning the mighty dead from their graves to refight their great national battles. Not subtle enough for the censor. In 1816 Foscolo headed for the haven of all political troublemakers, London. Where his work on Dante, Boccaccio, and Petrarch gained him kudos with the intelligentsia but not enough money to live on. Before dying in extreme poverty Foscolo managed a series of affairs with well-born ladies, including Lady Caroline Lamb (see elsewhere).

Top-drawer, outrageous, and unbalanced, Caroline became famous for calling her lover Byron "mad, bad and dangerous to know." Talk about pots and kettles. Caroline's string of infidelities (the noisiest was with Byron) nearly ruined her husband's political career and caused the Lambs to feature in at least six novels. Caroline was godmother to the daughter of Isaac Nathan, composer and con artist, who set Caroline's poems to music (and had also done so for Byron). Nathan fared badly: operas and books failed and his debts mounted. At one point he tried to blackmail a member of the U.K. royal family. Things went badly wrong with the scam and in 1841 Nathan had to skip town for Australia. Where he was a leading light in the darkness of Sydney's concert scene. He even experimented with aboriginal music.

In 1846 Nathan wrote "Leichhardt's Grave" to commemorate the disappearance and presumed death of the German naturalist and explorer who'd failed to get a job in the local botanical gardens and had gone off with a suspect bunch of fellow explorers (plus a convict and 180 sheep, 270 goats, 40 bullocks, 15 horses, and 11 mules) to find a way across the north of Australia from Brisbane to Arnhem Land. And so far hadn't come back. Later the same year Nathan was obliged to write "Home Again" when Ludwig Leichhardt turned up alive and well to a hero's welcome.

When Leichhardt really died some years later he rated an obit from one of Germany's leading geographers, Friedrich Ratzel. Who had started out as a travel writer and spent 1874 in the United States discovering his true vocation: humans and their environment. His studies of the fate of Native Americans and the living conditions of German and Chinese immigrants led Ratzel to the then-extraordinary thought that cultures might be influenced by location. Based on this idea, his *Human Geography* was an entirely new approach to the subject, investigating the way in which individuals and communities were affected by constraints placed on them by their surroundings. This led him to the 1901 essay (for which he has become famous) on the need for any healthy community of plants or animals to have room to expand and grow. He termed this expansion-space *lebensraum* (the necessary room to live). A generation later the Nazis would use the concept as justification for war.

In 1896 one of Ratzel's earlier works (*The History of Mankind*) was translated by boring British bureaucrat A. J. Butler, who spent years in government education and in the public record office. His spare time was spent in translations of such as Ratzel and in mountaineering. An early member of the Alpine Club and editor of its mag from 1882, he was also one of the "Sunday Tramps," a group of walkers organized by lit. crit. guru Leslie Stephen.

"Long Leslie Stephen in his velvet jacket," as Robert Louis Stevenson described him, was the archetypal U.K. second-rank intellectual. As a Cambridge undergraduate he famously walked the fifty miles to a London Alpine Club dinner. By 1861 he had climbed every Alp and reached the top of Mont Blanc. Then it was essays and reviews all the way to editorship of a major lit. mag, commissioning Hardy's *Far from the Madding Crowd*, friendship with Longfellow, Oliver Wendell Holmes, Emerson et al., marriage to Thackeray's daughter, and as Stephen himself put it: "going on writing, as an habitual drunkard goes on drinking."

His daughter by a second marriage became known as Virginia Woolf. In spite of (or because of?) incestuous and lesbian affairs, plus shaky mental health (suicide attempts), she outdid even her father with nine novels, four thousand letters, four hundred essays, and thirty volumes of diary. In 1941 she drowned herself, weighted down with stone, in the River Ouse. Today Woolf is best remembered as one of the Bloomsbury group of literary and philosophical noodlers that flourished around 1906 and included people like novelist E. M. Forster and economist John Maynard Keynes.

At the time, the homosexual Keynes (Bloomsbury was avant garde about such things) was still hanging on at Cambridge hoping for a fellowship (it came only later). By 1913 he was writing authoritatively about Indian finance. By 1915 he was in the Treasury handling interallied war loans. It was a no-brainer that at the end of World War I he would have much to say on the matter of German reparations. Keynes's view was that the Allies would cripple Germany with war-damage repayments on a scale the country could never afford and that in creating an economically ruined country with no hope of recovery the Allies would be activating a political time bomb. In this prescient view he was joined by his associate and Boer, Jan Smuts.

Who by this time had wide and varied experience of what it was like to be defeated. As in the Boer War, started in 1899, in which Smuts's commando guerrilla troops wrought havoc on the Brits until, outnumbered, the Boers agreed to a cease-fire in 1901. Moving into politics, by 1909 Smuts had brokered the Union of South Africa. During World War I Smuts was tasked with defeating the German East Africa commander Paul von Lettow-Vorbeck, as great a master of guerrilla warfare as Smuts had earlier been. In the end it was only the 1918 armistice that brought von Lettow-Vorbeck's surrender.

Back in 1913 on the ship out to Africa von Lettow-Vorbeck had met and been charmed by Baroness Karen Blixen, a Danish aristo on her way to join her new cousin-husband (and philanderer, who would give her syphilis) at their farm in Kenya, where over the next eighteen years Blixen would try (and fail) to run a profitable coffee plantation. While also producing what many believe to be the most beautiful book ever written about the continent: *Out of Africa*. After separating from her husband, Blixen fell in love with an Englishman, Denys Finch Hatton, who flew her around in his yellow Gypsy Moth airplane. In 1931 he crashed and died and Blixen went back to Denmark.

Where, in 1989, came the premiere of an opera commemorating her life: *Grinning at the Devil* by composer JAMES WILSON.

CHAPTER TWENTY-NINE

GEORGE ROSS (PA) was forty-six. He'd started out as a royalist but changed tack when independence became an option. As a revolutionary he was a moderate, urging everybody to go careful but keep at it. As a member of the Congressional Committee on Safety, Ross wrote the military rules of engagement. He argued (on civil-rights grounds) against the loyalty oaths being suggested for would-be citizens. His great moment came when as a judge of the Pennsylvania Admiralty Court he ruled on the case of Gideon Olmsted.

In 1778 privateer Olmsted and his crew were captured by the British sloop *Active*. Heading for New York and prison, they jumped the *Active*'s crew and took over. They were then stopped and boarded by the Pennsylvania brig *Convention*, whose captain claimed the *Active* as a prize. Back in court Olmsted argued that the prize was his by right of first jump. George Ross's jury awarded Olmsted one-quarter of the *Active*'s value. Olmsted asked for the money, but Congress turned him down. Ross then took on the Feds, arguing they couldn't overturn a jury decision. The case dragged on for thirty years and was the first major states'-rights litigation in the new Republic.

Olmsted had an unlikely ally in Benedict Arnold (at that time military governor of Philadelphia), who paid Olmsted's legal costs in return for a quarter of the prize money, if awarded. Later, when Arnold was under threat of court-martial for other matters and also accused of corruption, he thought up a scheme to hand over the plans for West Point to the Brits and then defect with lots of Brit money. So his career took a turn for the fugitive. After failing to get a business off the ground in New Brunswick, Arnold ended up in London, where in 1792 he was slighted by the earl of Lauderdale and challenged his earlship to a duel. The earl refused to fire and Arnold missed.

Lauderdale was that rarest of birds, a democratic aristo. Scots lawyer and active left-wing MP, in 1792 Lauderdale founded the Society for the Friends of the People (arguing for "a more equal representation of the people in Parliament") and was inspired by such democratic crazies as Tom Paine (of *Rights of Man* fame). Lauderdale was of course strongly pro–French Revolution (called himself "Citizen"), defended civil liberties, and opposed the 1794 British suspension of habeas corpus.

Colleague in this risky behavior (and fellow member of the Friends) was Richard Brinsley Sheridan. Gambler, drunk, womanizer (preference: upper-crust wives and their governesses), and promoter of such wild ideas as freedom of the press, Sheridan was Parliament's most extravagant and theatrical MP. No surprise, since he was already a famous actor and playwright (*School for Scandal* and *The Rivals*, featuring such unforgettable characters as Lord Backbite, Lady Sneerwell, and Sir Anthony Absolute). In 1799 Sheridan's politics found voice in his new, boffo-success play *Pizarro* (Peruvian independence struggle against Spain).

The play's success was guaranteed by its female star, the iconic Sarah Siddons, greatest tragedienne of her day and possibly of all time. In 1788 at a packed Drury Lane Theater, London, her Lady Macbeth caused grown men to cry and women to faint. Siddons had been brought to London by Sheridan in 1782, painted the following year by the great Sir Joshua Reynolds, and could do no wrong. Behind the scenes life was very different. Married to a sleep-around who gave her VD, in 1796 she became embroiled in a four-way affair with her daughters Sarah and Maria and young painter Thomas Lawrence.

Lawrence and Siddons had first met in Bath when Lawrence was ten and doing his first child-prodigy portraits. Lawrence was self-taught (he also had only two years of formal education) and by 1787 his "fresh, crisp" art was supporting his family. His move to London heralded a meteoric rise. By 1792 he was royal painter and by 1810 was probably having an affair with the Princess of Wales. That year he painted Charles Vane, third Marquis of Londonderry, a vacuous twit known as the "golden peacock." Vane was yet another aristo example of blimpish lack of talent promoted beyond capabilities. After years spent in military service (being dangerously incompetent) he was made general and ended up as a diplomat at the post–Napoleonic Wars Congress of Vienna. Where he frequented the Vienna brothels, pinched every bottom, and had nonstop affairs with the wives of his colleagues. These included Lady Priscilla Burghersh, who had her own fling with the Russian tsar and whose husband Charles was a carbon copy of Vane.

Lord Burghersh's one redeeming feature was his violin-playing. He also composed (prolific and fortunately forgotten). Even his diplomatic activity at the Congress was regarded as entirely useless. As a result he was made minister to the Grand Ducal Court of Florence, Italy. To which in 1821 he moved with Priscilla and where he met Walter Savage Landor, poet and professional expat who had helped establish Florence as the place-to-be for artistic Brits looking for somewhere cheaper to live. Landor was a man of slim volumes, unending debts, and a laid-back lifestyle. Apart from a brief three-month flurry fighting for Spanish independence, he spent his life writing poems nobody reads anymore, having affairs, and generally acting as host to the visiting celebs who turned up in Florence in search of adventure. These included Romantic poets William Hazlitt and Leigh Hunt and saloniste man-eater Countess Blessington (see elsewhere).

In 1832 a tubercular young ex-pastor from New England arrived in Florence on a tour of Europe, during which he hoped to meet his heroes Coleridge and Wordsworth. Ralph Waldo Emerson was about to burst on the American scene with his Transcendental Romantic stuff but for the moment he was still a relative nobody in search of inspiration. In 1832 he found it (in Scotland) in the person of Thomas Carlyle, whose American agent Emerson would become.

After several years failing as a minister and a schoolmaster the prolix

Carlyle (try: *Past and Present* and good luck) was on his way to becoming the Victorian's Victorian and the intimate of such major harrumphs as Tennyson, Dickens, Thackeray, and Ruskin. Tortured, brooding, the visionary libertarian wracked by the social agonies of an industrializing society, Carlyle had Victorian health problems stemming from inner turmoil and insanitary living conditions. So in 1851 he went for a water cure at the Malvern establishment of Dr. James Manby Gully.

Gully was well qualified (Edinburgh and Paris) in the latest medical knowledge but his cure for absolutely everything was sleeping in cold wet sheets, up-and-down cold-water douches, rides on donkeys, and many glasses of cold water. Every personality including royalty visited his hydrotherapy center between 1831 and 1873. That last year a beautiful young woman called Florence turned up on the run from a drunken husband and Gully fell. Florence left the husband. She and Gully headed for Germany and Italy. Where Gully got her pregnant and performed an abortion. And she left him.

Early in 1876 Florence married a rising young lawyer, Charles Bravo, and in November of the same year Bravo died of poisoning. In proceedings that had the nation gripped, the court decided it was "murder by persons unknown" in spite of the ruthless cross-questioning of Florence by George Lewis, attorney for Bravo's parents and guaranteed front-page. Lewis, who wore a monocle and a fur coat even in hot weather, was soon counselor to the rich and famous, specializing in borderline stuff: homosexuality, transvestites, indecent assault, infanticide, blackmail, perverted husbands, and (after an introduction to Bertie, Prince of Wales) aristo and royal mistresses. Including the prince's own, Lillie Langtry.

For three years the extraordinarily beautiful Mrs. Langtry (complaisant husband) scandalized society with her royal affair, hung out with Whistler and Oscar Wilde, and was ostracized by all right-thinking people. Inevitably Prince Bertie got bored and Lillie moved on to another royal. In 1881 she took up acting and estabished her own drama company. In 1882 the American impresario Henry Abbey masterminded a well-paid, five-year tour of the United States.

In 1883 Abbey took on management of the new New York Metropol-

itan Opera House with his partner Maurice Grau, who specialized in
European performers. In 1903 Grau persuaded a new Neapolitan star to
come and sing. Enrico Caruso had had a fairytale start. While working
as a mechanic, he sang in churches and bars, was talent-spotted in 1896,
and became an instant legend. In the following seven years he played St.
Petersburg, Buenos Aires, Moscow, Warsaw, Monte Carlo, London,
Lisbon, Montevideo, and Paris. The New York Met now became his
home, and over eighteen seasons he sang 607 times.

Five years after Caruso arrived at the Met a new conductor turned
up. Gustav Mahler had just finished ten years at the prestigious Vienna
Opera and was already known (loved or hated) for his composing ("brilliant and innovative" or "self-indulgent trash"). After a season in New
York he returned to Vienna to discover that his wife, Alma, was having
an affair with a young architect, Walter Gropius.

In 1915, after Mahler died, Alma married Gropius, only to divorce in
1923. By which time Gropius had already begun the functionalist work
for which he and (after 1919) his Bauhaus school in Weimar, Germany,
would become world-famous. The Bauhaus was soon a center of avant
garde art, architecture, and design. In 1933 the stark modernism didn't
appeal to the more Teutonically minded Adolf Hitler, who closed the
place down. Gropius ended up at Harvard and was a major influence on
American architecture.

As was his contemporary (whose own work had influenced Gropius)
Frank Lloyd Wright, maybe America's greatest-ever architect. In 1943
Wright was commissioned to build a museum unlike any in the world to
house the art collection of Solomon Guggenheim. The New York City
site (on Fifth Avenue between Eighty-eighth and Eighty-ninth streets)
presented unique problems of space. There wasn't enough. So Wright
designed an upside-down pyramidal structure, the central feature of
which was a spiral ramp.

One of Wright's assistants on the project was Arthur Holden, who
had spent a lot of time on public housing and municipal projects, and
(since he also knew the New York building comissioner) was able to help
Wright deal with the often-lunatic challenges presented by the city
building codes. Even so, it still took until 1952 to satisfy all the require-

ments, and the museum didn't open until 1959 after Wright and Guggenheim were already dead.

Back in 1931 Arthur Holden's architectural firm had laid off a young man named Alfred Butts. Out of work during the Depression, Butts decided he'd make money by inventing a game. Inspired by an Edgar Allan Poe story about cracking a code with letter frequency analysis, Butts came up with a word-game in which letters had values based on their frequency of use. By 1939 he had named it "Criss-Cross Words." Nothing much happened until 1952 when it suddenly took off, selling over two thousand sets. The following year, eight hundred thousand sets. Then a world craze.

By now the name had changed to "Scrabble," and there were annual world Scrabble competitions. In 2004, at the U.S. National Scrabble tournament, placed number twenty-one in division seven was competitor GEORGE ROSS.

CHAPTER THIRTY

CAESAR RODNEY (DE) was forty-seven. And loaded. And by the time of Independence, deep into the murky waters of local Delaware politics. On July 1 he was in South Delaware on antiloyalist business when he heard from a colleague in Philadelphia that the third Delaware delegate (of three) was going to vote against the Declaration and that Rodney had to get there fast to tip the balance. Riding all night through thunderstorms, he arrived on July 2 just in time for the vote. Never mind Paul Revere.

Rodney's younger brother Thomas was equally busy throughout the war as a militiaman and member of Congress. In 1803 Jefferson made him U.S. judge for the Mississippi Territory, and he moved to middle-of-nowhere Natchez. Where he met the extraordinary Harman Blennerhassett, a tall, stooping, shortsighted Irish aristo who, having incestuously married his young niece and scandalized the local Irish upper crust, was obliged to leave for America. Where he bought an island in the Ohio River near Parkersburg and spent most of his money building a great mansion with library, landscaped gardens, and a music room where he played the violin. In this other Eden the Blenerhassetts put on Shakespeare plays and entertained anybody who turned up.

In May 1805 one such turner (in more senses than one) was recent ex–vice president of the U.S. Aaron Burr. Who came to dinner and blew away Blennerhassett with tales of a Mexican empire, to be grabbed from Spain and which would include the (newly American) Louisiana Territory. Burr would be emperor and Blennerhassett would be involved in some well-paid capacity. Fellow plotter in this hugger-mugger was James Wilkinson, general of the American armies and governor of Upper Louisiana. And double agent for the Spaniards. Blennerhassett started recruiting soldiers and building boats.

In 1806 Wilkinson got cold feet and told President Jefferson (almost) everything. Jefferson ordered troops to find Burr and Blennerhasset. They did. In 1807 at the trial for treason in Richmond, Virginia, the case was dismissed for lack of evidence. At the same time without Jefferson's knowledge Wilkinson had already sent a spy into Spanish territory. Lieutenant Zebulon Pike had no idea what Wilkinson was up to but his reconnaisance mission was supposedly to check out what the Spaniards were doing on the southwest border of Louisiana and tell Wilkinson.

Pike headed west and ended up on the Rio Grande, where he was jumped by the Spaniards (who it turned out had been advance-warned by Wilkinson) and escorted back to American territory. By this time Wilkinson was on trial, so Pike had nobody to brief on his trip. Pike's interpreter on the expedition had been Antoine Vasquez, whose brother worked for Manuel Lisa, one of the heroic figures of the early fur-trapping days. Lisa was a general merchant in St. Louis (flea-pit, sewage in the streets) selling everything from guns to chamber pots to such as explorers Lewis and Clark.

In 1811 a competitor arrived on the scene. W. P. Hunt had been hired by New York financier John Jacob Astor to travel to the mouth of the Columbia River in Orgeon where Astor wanted to set up a fur-trading colony. Lisa was worried that Hunt would gate-crash his market and chased after him. Starting three weeks and 240 miles behind Hunt, Lisa plunged into one of the greatest keelboat chases in American history. He caught up with Hunt on June 11, the two men sorted things out, Hunt headed on for Oregon, and Lisa started back for St. Louis with Hunt's two English botanists.

One of whom, John Bradbury, sent all his specimens back home when he got to St. Louis. Some of the plants ended up with Aylmer

Burke Lambert, a chaotic botanizer who exasperated his colleagues because typically he'd heap together collections of dried plants and then leave them uncatalogued. Lambert's real passion was prehistoric English burial mounds, which he excavated with his lifelong pal William Cunnington, the first proper archeologist. Cunnington opened over 450 funeral chambers and found bones and gold in almost every one. His careful scraping and cataloguing also revealed fossils, which he sent to William "Strata" Smith with notes on depth, distribution, etc.

By this time surveyor Smith was all over Britain digging holes and telling people (from the fossils he came across) whether they would find iron, coal, or clay. In an industrializing, raw-materials-hungry time, Smith's was a valuable skill. He also identified the best routes for canal builders. And produced the first stratigraphic geological map of Great Britain, initially pooh-poohed by academics but belatedly recognized, as was Smith. In 1838 he was invited to join a government stone-hunting commission.

The stone was needed for the greatest building project of the British nineteenth century: the new British Houses of Parliament (the old ones had burned down in 1834). Out of fourteen hundred design submissions from ninety-seven architects, the winner was Charles Barry, already busy on public buildings such as the Reform Club and also able to turn anybody's ancentral home into Renaissance, Egyptian, Classical, or Arabesque.

The government had decided that the new Parliament building should be Gothic. The resultant fake-medieval extravaganza by Barry kicked off the entire Gothic Revival. But if the ornate scrollwork of Parliament's exterior caused eyestrain, the real excesses were to be found inside. Interior decorator Frederick Crace's firm was the one-stop shop for all social climbers (to whom he sold heraldic wallpaper), and in the Houses of Parliament Crace gave new meaning to "over the top," swamping the place in curlicue woodwork, gilding by the bucketful, lush canopies, silk walls, flowery carpets, heraldic escutcheons on walls, green-gold brocades, and swags and tassles with everything. The place became (and still is) excess-with-umbrella-stands.

Crace also did the royal interiors at Windsor and Buckingham Palace, including a "Gothic" bedroom for Prince Albert. The mind boggles. In 1852 Crace also founded the Photographic Society. Fellow member was a snake-oil type who had recently opened a photographic studio in London. Jabez Meal had spent several years in Philadelphia learning the trade and calling himself "Professor Highschool." Back in 1847 London he changed his name to John Edward Mayall, set up the American Daguerreotype Institution, and encouraged everybody (including Queen Victoria) to think he was American.

In 1847 Mayall photographed a seventy-three-year-old man he took to be a judge. It was J. M. W. Turner, the most famous painter of the day, who quizzed Mayall about the rainbow effect in Mayall's photo of Niagara. Turner was either idolized for his dazzling modernist color poems or reviled for the same reason. In over fifty years of work he traveled constantly, sketching and painting prolifically for exhibitions and book illustrations (for poems, Bibles, travel books, and the neverending "Views of . . .") Today the collection of (only some of) Turner's work at the Tate Gallery in London totals three hundred oils and nineteen thousand watercolors and sketches. And the erotica long thought to have been burned by his admirer and friend John Ruskin.

Who had first met Turner in 1840 because his father had been one of Turner's early patrons. The twenty-one-year-old John had just left Oxford for reasons of ill health and soon afterward headed for the Continent to recover. In 1842 he read some of the attacks on Turner and decided to defend the painter in his major multivolume *Modern Painters*. In which Ruskin began to develop a theory of art and imagination that moved away from the Romantic view. He also started writing acerbic art reviews that frightened everybody.

In 1851 Venice he began his greatest work: *The Stones of Venice*, a full-blown reassessment of the Renaissance and a revival of the long-ignored Byzantine and Gothic. The book woke up the entire literary and artistic community and made Ruskin famous. Result: In the later 1850s he met and became cheerleader for the new Pre-Raphaelite painters (Rossetti, Holman Hunt, Burne-Jones, and Millais) and encouraged rich friends to commission their work. One of these well-heeled buyers was a new American friend, Boston Brahmin Charles Eliot Norton.

After a quick visit to India for the family business (and a look around at the culture) in 1850 Norton began twenty years of one-night stands around Europe, using his family contacts to meet English scientists, French painters, Scots aristos, even Swiss peasants. He learned Italian. Then came essays on Coleridge, Native American burial practices, and politics for the *North American Review* and eventually his own mag, *The Nation*. His essays continued eclectic: everything from the Vatican Council to the English class system and the *Rubaiyat* of Omar Khayyam. By 1874 Norton was Harvard (and the first U.S.) professor of art history.

Shortly thereafter Ralph Waldo Emerson, one of Norton's fellow members at the snooty Saturday Club, gave a Shakespeare lecture in nearby Amherst and changed the life of Henry Folger. Folger was so inspired by Emerson's talk he dedicated his life to setting up the world's biggest collection of Shakespeariana, and when the Folger Shakespeare Library finally opened in 1932 it held seventy-nine of the 240 extant first-folio copies of Shakespeare. And scads of associated period stuff.

Needless to say, Folger wasn't a fan of Elizabeth Gallup, who in 1899 wrote her first book about how Shakespeare wasn't Shakespeare but Francis Bacon. By 1916 when she was deeply into decoding the cryptograms she had "discovered" in the Shakespearean texts and was revealing more extraordinary "facts" about the Bard and Bacon, Elizabeth was assisted briefly by Elezebeth Smith, who subsequently interested fellow researcher William Friedman in her deciphering work. And then married him.

The Friedmans went on to become America's top cryptographers, and in 1939 William's group of codebreakers cracked the secret of the Japanese PURPLE encoding machine. In 1941 an American cypher team visited their Brit counterparts at the Bletchley Park cypher research center, where they exchanged one of their copies of the Japanese machine for the design of the German Enigma, which had just been decoded by the team in Bletchley's Hut 8.

One of the Hut 8 geeks was Hugh Alexander, British chess champion and stamp collector. After the war Alexander returned to his job as head of research for the John Lewis department store in London. One of his colleagues there, a department chief named Rudolf Bing, was an Austrian immigrant who had managed the Glyndebourne Opera until World War II closed it. In 1945 Bing suggested a new world-class festival to make up for the (temporary, postwar) loss of Salzburg. In 1947 Bing directed the first Edinburgh festival.

By 1997 the Edinburgh event welcomed hundreds of performances by amateurs, that year including the American Theater High School Festival. For which an American school group perfomed the play *The Night Thoreau Spent in Jail*, directed by their art drama teacher Eddy Seager.

In 1998 Seager won the competition to design a new U.S. quarter. It became known as the Delaware Quarter. Seager's design featured a man riding a horse.

The rider was CAESAR RODNEY.

CHAPTER THIRTY-ONE

GEORGE READ (DE) was forty-two. He had first refused to vote for Independence but when the majority went for it, Read signed. Already an experienced local politico and Delaware attorney general at thirty, Read became acting president of Delaware in 1777 after the Brits snatched the president. Overall he spent twenty years in the Delaware Assembly, and as a moderate in a colony where there was little extremism he helped to ease Delaware through to statehood without too much fuss.

Read's great pal was Samuel Wharton, who by the time of the signing had spent nineteen years in London working with Ben Franklin and Thomas Walpole (a relative of the U.K. prime minister) trying to persuade the British government to agree to sell to Wharton and his fellow investors 2 million acres south and east of the Ohio River. The plan was to set up a new colony called Vandalia (named after George III's German queen, who claimed descent from the Vandals) and make scads of money by reselling the land to new settlers. Wharton's dream was to be Vandalia's royal governor.

For a moment in 1772 it looked as if the deal would go through. Then the American rebellion started and that was the end of Britain selling bits of America. The Vandalia project's prime opponent was gone, too. Lord Hillsborough, wimp and Brit secretary of state for

America, had resigned earlier in 1772 after failing to block the pro-Vandalia decision. Hillsborough loved opera and the sound of his own voice. He worked hardest at self-promotion, trimming whatever sails were required so as to stay in favor with whomever was in power. In spite of which, Hillsbrough's fifty years in Parliament left not an echo. And as was often the case in politics at the time, he came out of the experience with a nice little nest egg: ennobled as baron, marquess, viscount, and earl. Who says incompetence doesn't pay.

Nobody was happier to see Hillsborough stagger away under the weight of his titles than the egregious Granville Levison-Gower, one of the disappointed would-be Vandalia investors and (here we go again) a marquess, son of an earl, married to the daughter of a duke. How could he fail? By age thirty, Gower was a lord of the Admiralty. Then came an almost comic-opera series of old-boy jobs: lord privy seal, royal master of the horse, royal master of the wardrobe, lord chamberlain, lord president of the Council, and knight of the garter.

Gower owned large bits of the county of Staffordshire in the English Midlands so he used his influence help the potters for which the area was famous, promoting a network of turnpikes and canals to help bring in clay and fuel and take out finished pieces. Naturally one of Gower's main men was Britain's crockery maven, Josiah Wedgwood. Who once said his ambition was to be "Vase-Maker-General to the Universe." He got pretty close. Back in 1763 he had hit the big time with a cream-colored product that took the fancy of Queen Charlotte (aka "Vandalia"). Wedgwood got her royal okay to call the stuff Queensware and found himself selling an instant conspicuous-expenditure must-have for every upwardly mobile wannabe. And in 1774 Catherine the Great of Russia ordered a thousand-piece dinner set.

Wedgwood was also a power in the industrial landscape. He mixed with other geeks like James Watt, Erasmus Darwin, Matthew Boulton, and the rest of the Lunar Society, who met to discuss nerdy stuff at full moon (for safer riding home afterward). One of these noodlers (with whom Wedgwood became fast friends) was a Unitarian minister with a bad stammer named Joseph Priestley. Who went on to discover oxygen, invent soda water, teach school with a new science-and-modern-language-based curriculum, and become a major brain. Things went badly wrong when Priestley made too public his views on such dangerous matters as freedom of speech, equality, American rights, and what was good about the French Revolution (i.e., loss of royal heads). It didn't take much for the authorities to arrange for a mob, and in 1791 everything Priestley possessed (Birmingham lab and house) was destroyed in two days of patriotic rioting.

There was only one place for Priestley to go. By 1794 he was in Northumberland, Pennsylvania. And still speaking out. So in 1797 when things Franco-American turned sour Priestley's pro-French stance had him in trouble again. Only his friendship with President Adams saved him from deportation under the new (1798) Alien and Sedition Acts, which blocked free speech, deported noncooperative noncitizens, and imposed a hundred-thousand-dollar fine (in modern money) and five years in jail just for having "bad intent to oppose the government's measures."

The man trying hardest to get Priestley on a ship back to where he came from was Timothy Pickering, secretary of state and general weasel. Pickering altered his convictions when it suited his political book (from American loyalist to revolutionary and then in the French case from revolutionary to monarchist). He was rude, intolerant, and never involved in any important committees. He failed as Washington's adjutant general, as a merchant, and as a land speculator and by 1790 was in terminal debt. A job negotiating with the Native Americans then earned him a (brief) secretaryship. During which he prosecuted the first sedition case in U.S. history, against Matthew Lyon. Who had for some time been a thorn in government flesh.

Six-foot-six, 350-pound muscleman Lyon had spent time as a Green Mountain Boy helping to prise Vermont from the clutches of what he referred to as "New York aristocrats." By 1796 Lyon was in Congress, making waves about scandals and generally whistle-blowing in his newspaper. One issue of which wrote that President Adams "had an unbridled thirst for ridiculous pomp." This earned Lyon a twenty-thousand-dollar fine and four months in jail. During which he was re-elected to Congress. In 1800 he cast the deciding vote in Jefferson's election, then headed for Kentucky, then Georgia and lack of money.

In 1820 President Monroe helped him out by giving him a job as U.S. factor to the Cherokee in Arkansas. Their leader at the time was one-eighth-Native-American-the-rest-Scots John Ross. Who'd made money in trade and then took up tribal matters, acting as president of the Cherokee Legislature from 1819. By 1828 he was first principal chief and resolutely opposed to white-man forked-tongue pressure on the tribe to move west. Ross failed. Ten years later four thousand Cherokee would die heading for Oklahoma on what became known as the Trail of Tears.

One of Ross's fellow tribesmen (supporting the move west) was Stand Watie, a half-Cherokee who in 1837 moved to the new tribal lands with his brother (who'd anglicized his name to Elias Boudinet), settled down, and made a success of his life. Until 1871 when the Cherokee Tobacco Company (which he and his brother had set up) got stung by the U.S. Supreme Court for back taxes. The case was the first of its kind and established that Native Americans were "independent, dependent" nations living within the United States and therefore subject to federal laws whether or not these clashed with earlier treaty agreements.

The judgment was given by one of the Court's more forgettable chief justices, Noah Swayne, who'd been appointed in 1862 by Lincoln and is described by modern scholars as "mediocre at best." The minority dissenting opinion in the Cherokee case (that treaties ought to be observed and in this case no taxes levied) came from Justice Joseph P. Bradley. A brilliant mathematician and lawyer who had campaigned for President Ulysses S. Grant and in return was awarded the Supreme Court seat. Then in 1877 the Tilden-Hayes presidential contest triggered a crisis. Democrat Tilden had 184 electoral-college votes and needed only one more to win. The Democrats were confidently expecting victory. Hayes had 165 votes. The remaining 20 votes would swing it one way or the other. Accusations of fraud and violence caused these 20 votes (from Florida, Louisiana, South Carolina, and Oregon) to be contested. Congress formed a fifteen-man commission to adjudicate and Bradley (a Democrat all his life) gave the deciding vote in favor of Republican Hayes. Immediately he began receiving threats on his life.

His friend Navy Secretary George Robeson arranged for detectives to guard him. In 1869 Robeson was the man who opened the world's only military research station dedicated to torpedo development on Goat Island, Rhode Island. That year the U.S. Navy was offered (for seventy-five thousand dollars) the rights to produce a ready-made torpedo designed by Brit Robert Whitehead, who was at the time working in an Italian engineering company making ships' engines for the Austrian navy. Whitehead's torpedo was propelled by compressed air and its secret was called the "Secret." Inside, the weapon had a barometric pressure sensor that kept the depth right and a pendulum that kept the up-or-down right. By 1891, after numerous attempts to make their own torpedo, the United States opted for the Whitehead model, and it remained in the Allied arsenal till well after World War I.

During this time its only serious competitor was the German Schwartzkopf torpedo, which carried a high-explosive charge manufactured by the new Haber process. Fritz Haber was a chemist who realized that there was soon going to be a crisis: the urgent need to find an artificial replacement for bird-droppings, aka guano fertilizer, on which Euro-food supplies depended. By 1910 supplies of the stuff were short and getting shorter. So Haber came up with a trick for passing very hot hydrogen and nitrogen gas over iron filings to produce ammonium (the essential ingredient in plant food). It also produced nitric acid (the essential ingredient in explosions). Hence chemical plant food and torpedo warheads.

One of Haber's pupils was English chemist Owen Wansbrough-Jones, who went on to become scientific advisor to the British army and keen on chemical warfare (ironic, since it was his teacher Haber who had first used chlorine gas during World War I). Wansbrough-Jones's brother Llewellyn was chief administrator of the Allied Control Commisson after World War II. In 1946 the commission coopted German ex-U.K.-internee economist E. F. Schumacher to advise on postwar German economics and industrial recovery.

Schumacher had been a Rhodes Scholar in 1930, left Nazi Germany, and then burst on the international scene in 1973 with a series of essays titled: "Small Is Beautiful." Schumacher's philosophy can be summed up as anti-industrialist, anticapitalist, agnostic, prolocal, pro-small-scale, pro–appropriate technology. His emphasis on human-scale economics, decentralization, and environmentally friendly "intermediate" development struck a chord across the planet.

In 1980 Schumacher's ideas inspired the creation of the Canadian "Small Party." In 1983 it was renamed the "Green Party."

In 2005 the leader of the Alberta Green Party was GEORGE READ.

CHAPTER THIRTY-TWO

SAMUEL CHASE (MD) was thirty-five. And either a "universally de-spised . . . foul-mouthed rabble-rouser" or a man of "energetic elo-quence." On the day of the Declaration vote this lawyer arrived in Philadelphia after a hundred-mile dash from Maryland where he had just persuaded the Assembly to reverse its opposition to Independence.

After working on thirty revolutionary committees, Chase left Con-gress accused of insider-dealing in the flour market. This didn't prevent him from being appointed to the U.S. Supreme Court in 1795. Where after launching a political attack from the bench on Jefferson (Chase thought the Republicans would let the country be ruled by "moboc-racy") he was impeached. And then aquitted.

Back in 1783 Chase had acted for Henry Harford in the latter's at-tempt to regain the lands he had lost during the Revolution. The acreage in question was no less than the whole of Maryland, because Harford was the heir (and one of the many illegitimate children) of Lord Baltimore, rake, debauchee, and until lately owner of the colony. The new Maryland Assembly wasn't about to give back the entire state, so Harford compromised and accepted the lost rental income backdated to his inheritance in 1771. He got the then-colossal sum of one hundred thousand pounds.

Harford's guardian in 1771 (he was under age at inheritance) was lawyer Robert Morris, who had sucessfully defended Henry's dad in a scandalous rape case. In 1772 Morris (aged twenty-eight) created his own scandal by eloping with twelve-year-old Fanny, another of Baltimore's bastards. She then left him. Morris (no surprise, disbarred for immoral behavior) took to the life of a highwayman. In 1785 he married a farmer's daughter and went straight. Till the wife died four years later, whereupon Morris headed off for India. Where the local judges wouldn't let him practice so he went round the jails urging prisoners to revolt and escape.

This was reported in the local rag, *Hickey's Bengal Gazette*, written and published by lawyer William Hickey. No angel himself, Hickey was in India because his "propensity to women," gambling, general unemployability, and numerous scandals obliged his father to get him out of town. In India Hickey set up as a lawyer, started the first English-language paper, had innumerable liaisons with English and Indian ladies, and for thirty years lived a relatively successful professional life. At one point he became clerk to Sir Henry Russell, Calcutta Supreme Court chief justice.

Russell had arrived in Calcutta in 1896 at the age of forty-seven and proceeded to impress all and sundry. Chief exception, the Brit he sentenced to death for burning an Indian's hut and killing him. On the extraordinary grounds that Indians had the same rights as Brits. Apart from this Russell did nothing untoward, and when it came time for him to retire he got the usual golden handshake and address of thanks.

Russell's children's governess was Frances Burney, who took the job because her father's virtuosity at the harpsichord didn't pay the bills. Burney was a literary type with her own personal library of books in Greek, French, Latin, German, and Italian. In 1818 she produced three awful melodramas (for private performance only, since no respectable lady wrote for the theater). She also suffered from chronic jaundice, which evenutally killed her in 1828.

Her aunt, Fanny Burney, was made of sterner stuff, making quite a reputation with an anonymous novel titled *Evelina*. The book caused a sensation when it came out in 1798 and created a new genre: the lives of women in contemporary settings, described with wit and social realism.

The resultant fame led to Fanny's being groped by her father's pal, the lecherous literary buffer Samuel Johnson. Fanny's second book, *Cecilia*, was even more successful (the last chapter inspired Jane Austen to change her title from whatever it was to *Pride and Prejudice*). In 1793 Fanny married Lafayette's dashing aide-de-camp Alexandre d'Arblay and the two of them spent the next few years in and out of France, depending on whether Napoleon was in or out of power. In 1811 Fanny's character was tested to the extreme by a mastectomy performed without anesthetic (see elsewhere).

The operation took only twenty minutes because it was performed by the fastest surgeon in France, Dominique Jean Larrey. Larrey was also one of the first to suggest the therapeutic use of maggots in wounds. And he was the only senior French medical figure to support the crazy idea of an unknown young English country surgeon, Henry Hickman, who unbelievably wanted to render patients unconscious before operating on them. Hickman had used carbon dioxide to knock out dogs, cats, mice, and rabbits and then done various surgical things to them. Later (he said) the animals awoke, recovered, and healed. Unwilling to try the trick on humans, he described his experiments to the French Medical Academy who (except for Larrey) pooh-poohed the idea. As did the senior British medical journal, *Lancet* (describing Hickman's idea as "surgical humbug").

Hickman did no better when he wrote to Thomas Knight. This may have been because although the scientific Knight was a fellow of the Royal Society he was more interested in peas (one variety of which bears his name). Knight was a country squire who investigated the formation of ice at the bottom of rivers, sheep meat, and cattle-breeding. In alarm at the decline of British fruit, he then turned horticulturalist. Knight lived in a castle and in 1805 had been elected to the Royal Society for his article on tree-grafting. President of the Horticultural Society from 1811, Knight designed a water-powered, centrifugal gizmo to measure the effect of gravity (or lack of) on plants and seeds. Knight would also have beaten geneticist Gregor Mendel to the punch if he had understood why his pea cross-breeding experiments produced the results they did.

Knight's downfall came over Horticultural Society expenditure on offices, library, gardens, overseas specimen collection, and fetes at which bands played and wine was consumed. This last splurge triggered a nasty, anonymous article by cantankerous lawyer Charles Bellenden Ker. Who spent years heading a commission on criminal law (and earned from the *Law Review* a reference to his "eminent inability.") Questions were also raised regarding Ker's commission expenses. Ker was one of the first amateur orchid growers and a founding member of the Arundel Society (dedicated to producing prints of Old Masters). Fellow founder was Ambrose Poynter, architect and general failure.

After training in the offices of John Nash (who designed Regent's Park and Street, London), Poynter spent his life building ghastly pseudo-Gothic or imitation-Tudor houses, restoring churches (he got the medieval bits totally wrong), and building fake-Renaissance bank buildings. And being a heraldry freak. As government inspector for provincial schools of design, he failed to keep them up to date. His son made up for all this.

Edward Poynter spent time in Paris and then took up Egyptian and Classical genre paintings in works such as *Israel in Egypt* and *The Catapult*. In the 1860s he was a leading member of the "mosaic revival" and did mosaic bits of the Albert Hall and the Houses of Parliament. In 1871 Poynter became the first Slade Professor of Art at London University where he made life classes respectable. His greatest (and biggest) work came in 1890. *The Visit of the Queen of Sheba to King Solomon* included fifty figures and took six years to finish. Talented in mosaics, portraiture, etching, glass, engraving, ceramics, fresco, and theater design, Poynter's career went up and up, ending with directorship of the National Gallery and an aristo title.

The life of his fellow artist in Paris James Whistler went much the other way. There are those who see Whistler as a great fake: self-proclaimed southern gentleman (he wasn't), dashing South American revolutionary (he wasn't), army officer (he flunked West Point), and painter of apparently meaningful compositions with names aimed at impressing the media (*Arrangement in Grey and Black, No. 1*). Whistler's *Symphony in White No. 1* caused a flurry of interpretative comment in London. In the painting what did the girl in white mean, if anything? Ruskin said "Nothing" and sledgehammered the work. Whistler sued and won a cent in damages. The legal costs bankrupted him and ended his career.

One of Whistler's more unexpected friends was Fleeming Jenkin, a crusty prof. of engineering at London University who indulged in such gripping stuff as trades-union organization, the standardization of electrical measurement, urban sanitation, and an overhead electric package-delivery system that never got off the ground. Jenkin also adventurously proposed that British universities give engineering degrees. And he taught Robert Louis Stevenson. Although he was prone to seasickness Jenkin's full-time job was undersea communications, and from 1857 to 1861 he was employed by R. S. Newell, a cable-making firm.

In 1868 Newell was contracted by a new Danish consortium to lay cables between Scandinavia and Denmark and between Denmark and England. The consortium later became the Great Northern Telegraph Company, with cable-laying activities as far away as Russia and Japan. Head of the company was Danish entrepreneur and financier C. T. Tietgen, who in 1873 set up Tuborg as a rival to Carlsberg.

The Carlsberg brewery owners, the Jacobsen family, were generous patrons of the Royal Danish Academy of Art. To which in 1914 came a young Icelandic painter, Johannes Sveinsson (he later changed his name to Kjarval), who would end up painting more than six thousand works. Kjarval was eccentric: He dressed as an outlaw, placed "orders of the day" in newspapers, either gave his paintings away or charged a fortune for them, and in 1929 went to the *Thingvellir* (site of the ancient Icelandic Parliament) to paint dozens of pictures of the lava and moss there. He was soon the most famous artist in Iceland, and at a 1955 exhibition of his works more than 10 percent of the entire population turned up.

Kjarval was immortalized in song by Iceland's greatest pop singer, Björk, whose 1977 first album (including her Kjarval piece) sold five thousand copies while she was still only twelve. In 1993 her music video *Human Nature* was directed by Frenchman Michel Gondry, whose 2004 film *Eternal Sunshine of the Spotless Mind* (starring Kate Winslet) collected rave reviews.

The generator operator on the *Mind* film crew was SAMUEL CHASE.

CHAPTER THIRTY-THREE

Wm. Paca

WILLIAM PACA (MD) was thirty-five. And smart, good-natured, well-spoken, and elegant enough to be called a dandy. A rich, London-trained lawyer, Paca married money and built the first Maryland Georgian mansion with ornamental garden. Paca was a pro-Independence member of the Maryland Assembly. And while his colleague in Congress Samuel Chase did the handwaving and rhetoric, Paca was strategic and reasoning.

Paca had two wives, three terms as governor, and became the first judge of the Federal District Court of Maryland. In 1783 he persuaded the Assembly to approve setting up Washington College in Chesterton, the first U.S. College to be chartered after independence. Paca's partner in this educational effort was the quarrelsome and slovenly William Smith. Who had been provost at the College of Philadelphia from 1751 until the establishment was closed down in 1789 after an outbreak of political and religious backstabbing. Smith's unfriendly attitude to his ex-supporter Ben Franklin didn't help. Nor did the rumors that Smith was less than revolutionary and more than drunk.

In Philadelphia one of Smith's grads was the wealthy Jacob Duche, who visited London and then returned to the College of Philadelphia as professor of oratory. Logically enough he turned out to be good at preaching and was asked to be chaplain to the Continental Congress and give the opening prayer in 1774 and again in 1776. Things went oops for Duche when he wrote to Washington suggesting the Declaration of Independence be torn up. The letter was leaked to the papers and by 1778 Duche was an exile in London, chaplain to the Asylum for Female Orphans in Lambeth and getting deeply into the mystical Swedenborgian sect. Protestant and extremely serious. In 1780 Duche asked Francois Barthelemon, a rising star on the London musical scene, to write the music to a hymn: "Awake My Soul."

Barthelemon wrote operas, concertos, ballets, and symphonies, and on one occasion wrote the music for a song while looking over the shoulder of the poet (David Garrick) as he was writing the words. Barthelemon conducted every major orchestra in London (including those at Sadlers Wells, Drury Lane, and Covent Garden), played the violin at Windsor Castle, and on trips abroad entertained the aristocracy and royalty of Germany, France, and Italy.

In 1791 fellow composer Joseph Haydn came on a visit from Austria and gave music lessons to Barthelemon's daughter. Haydn was already a European music superstar with hundreds of compositions under his belt. Included in Haydn's amazingly prolific output were his settings to 398 Scottish songs commissioned by persuasive Edinburgh publisher George Thomson. Whose friend Dr. Henry Reeve visited Haydn in Vienna in 1805 during a year-long continental tour visiting the medical sights (i.e., important doctors, professors, asylums, hospitals) before returning to London to write up his experiences. This included a paper on cretinism and a report of experiments he had conducted in Germany on the torpidity of hamsters and hedghogs (he said the cold sent them to sleep).

Reeve's brother-in-law Richard Taylor also had Germanic connections in the shape of Friedrich Koenig, inventor of the mechanized printing press, which he developed with financial help from Taylor. Koenig's steam-powered machine used a system of rollers to deliver ink to a leather roller, which then inked the typeface (moved into position by another roller). Paper on yet another roller was then pressed onto the inked typeface. In 1814 the Koenig press could print both sides of eleven hundred sheets in an hour and the London *Times* bought two.

At the time the paper's owner, John Walter II, was trying hard to boost sales from the low level to which his father had let them sink. By the time Walter finished the *Times* was the greatest newspaper in Europe. Walter hassled governments of the day, lobbied for parliamentary reform, and gave the paper a reputation for in-your-face political independence. Walter also hired continental correspondents who mailed translations and comments on foreign-language newspaper reports. Also a London editor, six reporters, and a theater critic, Barron Field.

Field's job was to break with tradition (paid-for puff pieces usually written by the playwright himself) and write unbiased reviews, accept no free tickets, and not socialize with the playwrights and theater managers. In his spare time Field was studying law and in 1814 left the paper to become a judge in New South Wales, Australia. He hated the country ("the after-birth of Creation"), wrote two poems ("Botany Bay Flowers," and "The Kangaroo"), and collected his pay. When his contract ended it was not renewed, and in 1824 Field headed happily back to London. To a welcoming epistle in verse from his old friend and fellow scribbler Leigh Hunt.

Hunt's work has generally been eclipsed (with good reason) by that of his close pals Byron, Keats, Shelley, and Lamb. He spent most of his life between sickness and debt, saddled with an alcoholic wife and being bailed out by the others. Still, his mag, *The Examiner*, lasted for thirteen years, contained some of his best essays and reviews, and brought the Romantic poets to public attention. On the occasion when Hunt called the Prince Regent a "libertine" the libel got him put in jail for two years. His single major poem ("The Story of Rimini") shocked the public with its incest-adultery theme.

One of Hunt's helpful friends (who provided him with a piano in jail) was Vincent Novello. At the age of sixteen the myopic Novello had been hired as organist for the Portuguese embassy chapel in London. Then he became obsessed with publishing music, because at the time sheet music was handwritten and scarce. Novello scoured the British Museum, churches, chapels, and his friends' libraries looking for manuscripts and then printing the music together with notes on performance and instrumentation as well as how-to remarks for conductors. Modern printed sheet music begins with Novello.

Unsurprisingly, his daughter Clara was one of the best vocalists of her generation (Queen Victoria was a fan), married an Italian count, and inspired Rossini to give her lead roles and become a lifelong admirer. By the time Clara met Gioacchino Rossini he was already the greatest Italian composer alive and an international star with prestige, money, acclaim, and influence. And a dish had been named after him (by the great French chef Carême): *tournedos Rossini*. Rossini wrote at breakneck speed. *The Barber of Seville* took only three weeks to write, and many of his operas were finished in a month. He churned it out, saying once: "Give me a menu and I'll set it to music."

Most of the time Rossini was helped by good librettists like Eugène Scribe, who in 1828 wrote the words of *The Count Ory*. It was only Scribe's third opera after nearly 150 musical-comedy scripts. Scribe's work was production-line stuff, with assistants to provide jokes, storylines, ideas, dialogue, and a card-index of plots. He wrote more than 450 plays to the same formula: Things go complicatedly wrong and then hilariously resolve. He took a percentage of the receipts and by the age of forty was a millionaire.

Scribe's audience was the new French middle class, which is why the young poet and critic Théophile Gautier attacked him for being bourgeois. Which Gautier was trying not to be, with two mistresses, three illegitimate children, a possible affair with Princess Mathilde Napoleon, star of everybody's salon, leader of the more off-the-wall Romantics, and painter turned writer of plays, poems, essays, reviews, and poetry. He also wrote the storyline of one of the most popular ballets of all time: *Giselle*. His major novel, *Mademoiselle de Maupin*, rocked the bourgeoisie with its sexual themes. Above all Gautier's writings popularized the concept of "art for art's sake." And the use of hash.

Once a month in the 1840s he and other experimenters would visit a particular hotel to eat the green paste and hallucinate. All of this under the observant eye of eminent psychiatrist Dr. Jacques-Joseph Moreau, the first to suggest that insanity wasn't caused by physical damage in the brain but by chemical changes in the way it worked. Moreau discovered this by watching the effects of varying doses of marijuana on his patients (and pals) and observing that the drug caused long-term personality change. In 1845 he wrote it all up as *Hashish and Mental Alienation*.

In the United States, Moreau's work was reviewed by Dr. Amariah Brigham, Connecticut psychiatrist and director of the Hartford Retreat for the Insane. It was Brigham who introduced the process of institutionalization and behavioral therapy that would become standard treatment in modern psychiatry. Founder of the *American Journal of Insanity*, Brigham wrote about the influence of evangelism on mental health because he was worried that the contemporary Millerite revivalist movement posed the threat ("greater than malaria") of what he called "religious insanity."

By this time preacher William Miller's message ("Get Ready for the Imminent End of the World!!") was packing hundreds of thousands into tents for prayer meetings at which believers went ecstatic, saw visions, heard voices, and more. When Miller's predicted date for the Second Coming (1844) came and went the movement nearly disintegrated. Many of the faithful were at a loss. These included the charismatic Sojourner Truth (aka Isabella Baumfree), a freed slave. Who turned to abolitionism and made her name speaking out against slavery, together with the movement's major figure, Frederick Douglass.

Sojourner (she said the Holy Spirit had suggested the name change) was also the object of Harriet Beecher Stowe's admiration and an essay. Sojourner met Lincoln and failed to get the Washington, D.C., streetcars desegregated, or western land given to freed slaves. Sojourner also fought hard to stop the transportation of emancipated African Americans to Monrovia, Liberia, a practice begun back in 1820 by the American Colonization Society.

In 1858 the Navy's SS *Niagara* took another boatload to their new life in Africa, a year after the ship's maiden voyage, during which she had laid the first (failed) transatlantic cable. It took three more attempts before success in 1866 when linking the main twenty-three-hundred-mile cable with the Irish shore station involved a special twenty-seven-mile stretch of twenty-tons-a-mile, ninety-tons-breaking-strain armored connector line. Manufactured and put in place by the W. T. Henley company.

Which in 1913 hired a fourteen-year-old draftsman named Alfred

Hitchcock. By 1920 Hitchcock was designing silent movie titles. In 1925 he directed his first film: *The Pleasure Garden*. Over the following decades he became an international cinema figure with such successes as *The Lady Vanishes* (1939), *Rear Window* (1953), and most famous of all, *Psycho* (1960). In 1959 Hitchcock directed a comedy thriller, *North by Northwest*, starring Cary Grant. A bit-part ("A Farmer") in the movie was played by Andy Albin.

In 1972 Albin acted in the film *1776*, playing the role of WILLIAM PACA.

CHAPTER THIRTY-FOUR

Thos: Stone

THOMAS STONE (MD) was thirty-three. A relative unknown in terms of what he got up to in Congress. A country squire with a fancy family mansion near Port Tobacco, Maryland, Stone's ancestor had been royal governor. Some of his fellow revolutionaries thought Stone might have been a touch less than fervent about breaking with Britain, but he joined in with the rest.

In 1785 Stone was on the commission that okayed the Potomac Canal, George Washington's dream of an economic link between the capital and the interior. Building the canal wasn't going to be easy because right in the path there were three waterfalls. The worst was at Great Falls (hence the name) where the water dropped eighty feet in a mile and where any locks would have to be staired and cut out of the rock. But the real problem was that there were no American engineers to do any of this. And foreigners wouldn't take the job. So the politicos (essentially, George Washington) designed everything.

Organizing the whole effort was ex–cavalry major Henry "Lighthorse Harry" Lee, a southern gent who was great stuff at leading a charge but no good at counting the cost. He bought a large stretch of western land, which then turned out to be half the acreage he'd paid for without reading the fine print. He then bought even more land in order to build the town of Matildaville (named after his wife) as headquarters for the Potomac Canal construction workers, with a mill, an inn, boarding houses, a housing barracks, and several small homes. Then he discovered his contract said he couldn't charge rent on any of the buildings. Permanently in debt, at one point Lee even gave George Washington a bad check. Not many people did that.

Lee's canal superintendent was ex-blacksmith George Rumsey. Who decided a year later to switch careers and become an inventor. Rumsey shipped out for London with his great idea: a steam-powered jet-boat. Following a meeting with the famous steam-engine-builders Boulton and Watt, the pair offered Rumsey a partnership. Rumsey dithered, badly advised by an agent with his own agenda. B&W withdrew the offer. After a couple more years of work (and heavily in debt) in 1792 Rumsey was ready to try out his *Columbian Maid* on the Thames. The day before the event he died and the project went west.

Benjamin West had given Rumsey some useful introductions because West knew people in high places. Twenty years as history painter to the king, one of the founders of the Royal Academy, and by now celebrated as the first American public figure in European art—all this had inflated his already considerable ego. West had first made his mark with bigger and bigger paintings of historical and religious subjects, as well as doing renovation work at Windsor Castle and conducting nonstop self-publicity. Byron called him "Europe's worst dauber." The untrained West had made it to the top by sheer force of complacent arrogance.

At one point around 1802 West turned for technical advice to a young surgical anatomist. The issue in question was how a recently dead corpse would hang on a cross. John Constantine Carpue obligingly crucified the body of a newly executed criminal and made a plaster cast. In 1816 Carpue also perfected a fifteen-minute no-anesthetic operation to reconstruct a nose. The technique had originated in medieval India: trim the stump, then make a wax nose and set it in place covered by a skin flap hanging down from the forehead and cemented onto the wax with African root pulp. Leave for three days. Result: a nose, said Carpue, which would sneeze and smell. And could be blown without coming off in your hand. In 1818 German doctor Carl Ferdinand von Graefe improved on Carpue's technique. Graefe published several papers on the subject, invented a Greek name for the procedure ("rhino-plasty") and became known as the first modern plastic surgeon.

Graefe was one of the six professors in the new medical faculty of the new Berlin University. Where the dean was the best-known doctor in the country, Christoph Hufeland. Who had made his name in 1796 with a book describing his holistic approach to medicine and titled *Macrobiotic* (a word later hijacked by nutrition freaks). An instant success, within four years the book was translated into every European language. Hufeland was a pioneer in public health, came up with the idea of a twenty-four-hour body clock, and promoted his "nature cure": colonic irrigation, ventilation, bathing, veggie diet, herbal remedies, and copious quantities of mineral water. Paving the way for modern naturopathy.

One of Hufeland's patients was none other than the great Johann Wolfgang von Goethe: poet, playwright (*Faust*), philosopher, educator, political analyst, physiologist, botanist, anatomist, major influence on European thought, reverenced by such heavies as Schiller, Herder, and the other German Romantics. And subject to doctoring of a different kind. In 1807 when Goethe was fifty-eight he met the twenty-two-year-old Bettina Brentano, who fell for him and (she later said) jumped into his lap. Bettina was the sister of Romantic poet Klemens Brentano, and in 1811 she married his fellow versifier Achim von Arnim (the Brothers Grimm came to the wedding dressed as storks). Bettina had also met and charmed Beethoven (who played for her every day), but she reserved her passion (platonic, it says here) for Goethe.

In 1834, when Goethe was dead and unable to defend himself, Bettina wrote a now-it-can-be-told exposé of her "affair" titled *Correspondence with a Child*. In the book she doctored Goethe's rather formal letters to her, described their first meeting as having happened when she was thirteen, included Goethe's poems to her (in fact written to other women), and generally told fibs. Twelve years later in Concord, Maryland, a fourteen-year-old American girl found a translation of Bettina's book and went into the same unrequited mode, writing (unsent) letters to and leaving flowers on the doorstep of the object of her crush, writer Ralph Waldo Emerson. Whose money was helping the financially strapped Alcott family.

Emerson also encouraged Louisa May's literary ambitions. In the end, her 1868 *Little Women* was one of the greatest international best sellers in history. On the way to fame and fortune Louisa May also wrote pseudonymous bodice-rippers (e.g., *Pauline's Passion and Punishment*) that she later referred to as "dangerous for little minds." Louisa May also became a feminist, seamstress, governess, domestic servant, teacher, and (from 1860) wrote for the new *Atlantic Monthly*, founded by a group of writers including her hero Emerson and another family friend, Henry Wadsworth Longfellow.

Who had just achieved international fame for his 1855 *Song of Hiawatha*, a poetic version of Native American tales collected by the ethnographer Henry Schoolcraft. In 1836 Longfellow had returned from the second of two European trips (both trips were in order to study languages in preparation for college jobs: the first at Bowdoin, the second at Harvard). During the second trip Longfellow spent time in Sweden where he was introduced to Finnish and bought a teach-yourself book. And then got excited by the newly published *Kalevala*, a poetic collection of Finnish folk tales. Years later *Hiawatha* used exactly the same poetic meter as *Kalevala* and some of the same themes.

The original Finnish collector of the *Kalevala* folk material (some dating back a thousand years) was doctor Elias Lönnrot, who spent ten years on the Finnish-Russian border treating patients and writing down their ancient songs and poems and tales. Lönnrot ended up helping to get Finnish nationalism off the ground, becoming professor of Finnish at Helsinki University. And impressing Germans like Jakob Grimm.

By this time (1845) Grimm and his brother Wilhelm were famous for their collection of folk stories known as *Grimms' Fairy Tales*, which included "Sleeping Beauty," "Cinderella," and "Snow White." Expurgated before publication to remove references to such unpalatable stuff as anti-Semitism, necrophilia, and incest. The Grimms' obsession with the German past led Jakob to involvement with German language and philology (he was the first to take a scientific approach to the Germanic languages) and at the Berlin Academy while Jakob was reading *Kalevala* he and his bro were already starting on their great German dictionary. Both men were dead by letter F, and the work was finished only in 1960.

Jakob was especially known for his study of the process of German con-
sonant mutation over time. Riveting stuff.

The Grimms' colleague Johann Peter Gustav Lejeune Dirichlet (in
the Berlin math department and who married Mendelssohn's sister) was
famous for equally arcane noodling, i.e., his "box principle" (if one
distributes more than n objects in n boxes then at least one box must
contain more than one object). For such epoch-making revelations
Dirichlet became Germany's foremost mathematician.

Dirichlet taught Heinrich Schroeter, who wrote incomprehensible
tomes about the second-, third-, and fourth-order plane curves and
went off to teach at the University of Breslau. One of his pupils was a
hunchback who later on took the name of Charles Proteus Steinmetz
and whose socialist views led him to depart Germany for Switzerland,
where he picked up his Ph.D. in electrical engineering. Then he was off
to American citizenship and (in 1893) a job at the recently founded
General Electric Corporation.

Over the next twenty-eight years Steinmetz filed 195 patents and
wrote the definitive book on alternating current (key to the development of the American electrical industry). An early supporter of pollution control, solar energy, and electric automobiles, Steinmetz even
managed a year in 1919 as a member of the briefly socialist city government of Schenectady. He eventually made his name as the greatest electrical engineer in the country and helped General Electric to success.

Original financial backing for GE had come from the Ames family,
famous since 1805 for Ames shovels. And for having used them to lay
the transcontinental railroad track in the 1880s. And do all the other
digging required to build nineteenth-century America (the head of the
Ames family was known as the "King of Spades").

The Ames corporation was first headquartered in the iron-making
town of Easton, Massachusetts, about twenty miles from Boston. By
2004 the company was long gone from the town, but the Ames corpo-
rate archive was still there and the Easton museum still contained several hundred Ames shovels.

Ably protected by Easton fire chief THOMAS STONE.

CHAPTER THIRTY-FIVE

CHARLES CARROLL OF CARROLLTON (MD) was thirty-nine. The only Catholic signer, the "slender, handsome" Carroll was also the only millionaire in Congress. A planter, businessman, and investor, he attended school in France and then went to London to study law but skipped classes in favor of dancing, fencing, drawing, and learning Italian.

After he got back home he helped to run the family business (a three-hundred-slave, 12,500-acre plantation and an ironworks). By 1774 Carroll was into politics, fighting to keep the revolution from turning out too egalitarian and lobbying against the confiscation of loyalist property, but otherwise generally impressing people so much that when he died in 1832 (he was the last signer to die) the federal government closed down for the day.

Carroll's only major stumble was when he was on the commission that failed to persuade Canada to join the fight against Britain. The other commission members were Ben Franklin and Carroll's cousin, Catholic priest John Carroll. Who'd been educated at the Jesuit College in St. Omer, France (there were no Catholic schools in Maryland, or Catholic voters, lawyers, or public officials).

Once he had become a priest John Carroll returned home to missionary work in Maryland. Gradually he earned a reputation for defending Catholic rights, for pushing the use of English in the liturgy (instead of

Latin), and above all for preaching the view that American Catholics should support American values of equality, individual freedoms, and the separation of church and state. In 1788 the pope made him first American Catholic bishop.

Episcopal ordination had to be at the hands of another bishop. There were none in America so Carroll went to England and in 1790 did the necessary at the chapel of Lulworth Castle, Dorset. Castle owner Thomas Weld had overlapped with Carroll at school in St. Omer and was the first English Catholic of importance to be officially visited by Protestant George III.

Weld gave room and board to Catholics on the run from the French Revolution. He even set up a Trappist monastery in his castle grounds. And then donated one of his many estates (together with its very big house) to twelve fugitive Jesuits from St. Omer. By 1792 the house (at Stonyhurst, Lancashire) had become Stonyhurst College Catholic School (today it's the biggest Catholic school in England). In 1796 one of the school's new boys was Charles Waterton, who signaled his future zoological interests by becoming a fanatical rat catcher.

Waterton's family had estates in South America, so between 1812 and 1824 he went into the jungles on four separate expeditions. On one he came out with curare (and his later experiments with its knockout capabilities led to general anesthetic use). On another expedition Waterton searched (in vain) for the fabled city of El Dorado. On all his trips he collected everything he could find, from aardvarks to sloths and (above all) hundreds of birds, which, in a lifelong pursuit, he stuffed. Waterton built a wall round his English estate and turned it into the first nature reserve (no guns, only observation hides). Waterton was also well known for being able to scratch the back of his head with his big toe.

Strangely (given his animal-loving propensities), Waterton went fox-hunting with his friend Harry Vane. Born the son of an earl, married to the daughter of a duke, and then himself becoming a marquis and a duke, Vane's second marriage might have seemed a trifle down-market (she was the daughter of a gardener). But in the lady's defense it must be noted that she had previously been the mistress of one of the richest men in London, Thomas Coutts.

From 1800 the Coutts Bank was a major player in the financial market and had among its many clients George III and his spendthrift sons. Thomas Coutts himself ran the organization (he called it "my shop") with a rod of iron. Unlike other bankers, he built no country house and lived modestly. He was a big fan of American independence. He carried a volume of Shakespeare with him wherever he went. He was also a theater enthusiast and friends with actor-manager David Garrick. Above all, Coutts was known for his discreet handling of customers' affairs. And his own.

His first marriage (to his brother's daughter's governess) stayed secret for seven months. His second marriage came at the end of a secret ten-year affair with famous actress Harriot Mellon, darling of the Georgian stage. Harriot was thirty-seven when she married the seventy-nine-year-old Coutts, so she featured in the dailies as a gold-digger. In fact she knitted shawls and made soup for him and they appeared blissfully happy. After he died in 1827 Harriot (ever the social climber and now aged forty-nine) married the simple-minded twenty-year-old Duke of St. Albans and got the title she'd always wanted.

When Harriot died she skipped the generation of her ducal husband's family (who had looked down their noses) and left the income from her entire estate (modern money: $50 million and change) to her granddaughter Angela Burdett, who was obliged by the will to add "Coutts" to her name. Angela Burdett-Coutts became the greatest Victorian philanthropist of all. Given the size of her inheritance, Angela was an instant celeb and in 1838 got invited to Victoria's coronation. Naturally she was also deluged with offers of marriage. Her social circle included scientists, artists, writers, churchmen, actors, and royalty to whom her bank loaned money. Liszt played for her. Hans Christian Andersen was a house guest. She bankrolled the (white) rajahs of Sarawak.

The extent of Angela's philanthropy was impressive. She built churches, gave support for poor-children schools, built homes for ex-hookers, founded colleges, Bible classes, soup kitchens, nursing programs, homes for donkeys, and drinking troughs for dogs and horses. And was involved in major colonial social programs. She built model homes for workers, funded science scholarships at Oxford, and when she was thirty-three proposed marriage to the seventy-nine-year-old Duke of Wellington. He gently declined. In 1871 Queen Victoria (who loved Angela) made her a baroness.

Angela's philanthropy advisor was Charles Dickens. Whose only blot on his famous-author copybook was the 1840 visit to the United States. Where he visited asylums, schools, prisons, hospitals, and other such social institutions as well as the Lowell, Maryland, textile factories. Already an international star and mobbed wherever he went, Dickens was appalled by the amount of tobacco spit and by the general American ignorance of the world (fostered, he said, by the American press). "This," he complained, "was not the Republic I came to see." When his scathing *American Notes* came out in the United States the book succeeded like a case of acne, and it would be years before he was invited back. In spite of this Dickens made one American friend, Cornelius Felton, professor of Greek at Harvard. A major educator (he ended up president of Harvard), Felton's claim to fame was that he tried (and failed) to make classical Greek a major subject on the American college curriculum.

Felton's brother made more of an impression. Samuel Norse Felton was a Harvard-educated civil engineer and in 1861 was running the Philadelphia, Wilmington, and Baltimore Railroad when an Illinois lawyer named Abraham Lincoln was due to travel to Washington, D.C., for his inauguration. A plot was discovered to assassinate Lincoln (while he was changing trains in Baltimore) and then to cut the Washington telegraph lines and take over the capital in a military coup. Felton arranged a private train for Lincoln, sent a "special package" on Lincoln's original ticket (to fool the plotters), and on the day of the journey had security men "whitewashing" every bridge on Lincoln's route in case of trouble. Lincoln made it safely to the ceremony.

In 1863 President Lincoln met young Prussian army officer Count Ferdinand von Zeppelin, who was visiting America to observe the Union Balloon Corps. In 1874, after his return to Germany, Zeppelin was further enthused to take up an aeronautical career when he heard a speech in which postal chief Heinrich von Stephan talked about sending the mail by air. Zeppelin began the experiments that would end not with airmail but with airships bombing London in World War I. Meanwhile von Stephan was nationalizing the Prussian mail services. Which meant that things got less lucrative for the Thurn und Taxis family, who'd had the postal monopoly for the entire Holy Roman Empire since 1490 and were doing very nicely thank you. Now they had to make do with a government indemnity of only several zillion dollars.

They also carried on marrying into every royal and noble family in Europe. The seventh Prince Thurn und Taxis was called Maximilian and his wife was Helen Duchess of Bavaria. Her sister Sophie had been jilted (lucky girl) by her cousin, mad King Ludwig II of Bavaria, the lunatic who built Neuschwanstein Castle (the model for Snow White's castle at Disneyland; it included fake Byzantine-Gothic architecture, flush toilets, and electricity). Ludwig had the hots for Richard Wagner (or any passing young man) and Teutonic everything. Finally declared officially insane by the government, Ludwig walked into a nearby lake and drowned.

His grandfather Ludwig I had had an equally unusual existence, high point of which was his affair with the Irish ("Spanish") dancer Eliza Gilbert (aka "Lola Montez," famous for the remark, "Whatever Lola wants, Lola gets"). In spite of this, Ludwig was a devout Catholic and set up a foundation to support German Catholic missions in Asia and America. In 1838 a German Benedictine, Boniface Wimmer, set off with fourteen others for the United States, where in 1846 he founded St. Vincent College seminary at Latrobe, Pennsylvania.

In 1855 Rome made St. Vincent's an abbey and in 1892 an archabbey. In 1929 Archabbot Father Aurelius Stehle went for a spin at the local Hill Airport. And decided to add aeronautics to the college curriculum.

The Hill Airport manager (and later director of the aeronautics program) was CHARLES CARROLL.

CHAPTER THIRTY-SIX

Th Jefferson

THOMAS JEFFERSON (VA) was thirty-three. A young lawyer with only seven years' experience in politics, he already had a reputation for clear thinking and better writing. So he got the job of drafting The Document. One committee, one Congress, and eighty-six text changes later they scribbled their signatures and it was all over bar the shooting.

Jefferson's career (governor of Virginia, vice president, and twice president) wasn't roses all the way. Apart from successes like fighting off the old guard who didn't want anything to change, making sure the country stayed democratic, liberalizing America's international trade, and introducing decimal coinage with dollars and cents, most of the reforms Jefferson tried back home in Virginia failed (except the one setting up the university).

In 1785, after a major row, the Virginia Assembly rejected (by one vote) Jefferson's proposal to scrap the death penalty. Jefferson got the idea from a minor government official in Milan, Italy. Cesare Beccaria was a shy little man who in 1764 anonymously published a small book: *On Crimes and Punishments*. An instant rave with such as Catherine the Great of Russia, Empress Maria Theresa, Voltaire, John Adams, and all intellectuals.

Beccaria effectively invented modern criminology and penology. His key criticism of capital punishment: "It's absurd that laws which punish murder should commit one."

Beccaria also standardized Milan's measures, basing his idea on astronomy and suggesting that there ought to be an internationally accepted "universal" measurement system. At this time France had seven hundred different kinds of measures, depending on city and materials being measured, so for the French revolutionaries (with their mania for standardization), Beccaria was music to the ears.

The astronomical bit of Beccaria's idea called for setting up a standard international length equal to one-ten-millionth of a line from either pole to equator. Not easy to measure, given the oceanic interruptions. The only way to do the job without falling in the water was to use just a tenth of the pole-equator distance (for example from Dunkirk to Barcelona, which was all land and mostly France). Two measurers were chosen, Jean-Baptiste Joseph Delambre and Pierre-François-André Méchain. Delambre would go Dunkirk to Rodez, Méchain Rodez to Barcelona. In 1799 they finished and the meter was established.

Delambre was famous for the incredible accuracy of his noodling. In the Dunkirk-Rodez case (which involved calculations to an eye-smarting nineteen decimal points), each of Delambre's measurements along the route was accurate to 1/36,000. By 1801 Delambre was secretary to the French Science Academy and a very big scientific *fromage* and winner of every honor in zee book. So in 1809 the French minister of war jumped when Delambre said let that Englishman go.

The chap in question was James Macie, a minerals freak on one of his frequent trips to Europe (in spite of Napoleon-versus-England war) to look at guess what. Got caught playing with crystals in Hamburg (French at the time) and jailed. Then freed by Delambre. The illegitimate Macie became famous for three things. One: He discovered calamine. Two: After he changed his name to that of his natural father (Duke of Northumberland), whose family name was Smithson, he then left $508,318.46 to be used to establish the Smithsonian Institution. And three: In 1791 he published a paper on a queer stone (tabasheer) found in bamboo joints.

In 1819 tabasheer caught the interest of the great David Brewster, Scottish science king of all reflection-refraction-diffraction matters (he also invented the kaleidoscope). If something related to light Brewster was on it like a ferret. In the case of tabasheer he discovered it was a form of opal that phosphoresced when hot, reflected a curious bluish-white light, and was more holes than solid, so it absorbed liquid. In India it was used to suck out reptile venom and was known as "snake-stone."

Brewster had wanted to be a preacher but once at a dinner fainted when asked to say grace, so opted for science. In the end he jolted St. Andrews University out of its medieval torpor, founded the British Association for the Advancement of Science, and for years was editor of the *Edinburgh Encyclopaedia*. One of his less-famous contributors was Dr. John Bostock, sneezer.

Bostock was an Edinburgh U. grad living in Liverpool and keen on botany and literature. For two months in the summer of 1819 (and then every year thereafter) Bostock developed itchy eyes, runny nose, wheezy breathing, and sneezes. Over the next nine years he found and studied twenty-eight others who were doing the same. In 1828 he published his results, identifying what he called *catarrhus aestivus* (hay fever). Since neither he nor any other GP had noticed this (today, common) ailment, it was probably caused by pollution in the newly industrializing environment of the time.

A fact confirmed a little later by the irascible Dr. John Elliotson. Elliotson was a hot-shot clinician who also published on prussic acid treatment, opium medication, and the medical properties of creosote. He expressed his unconventionality (first doc to wear a beard, and donning trousers rather than breeches) by getting deeply into head-bump-reading and then mesmerism. By 1837 he was professor at University College Hospital, London, and used the hospital theater for some astonishing mesmeric shows attended by the rich and famous. Elliotson would mesmerize and then cure sufferers from all kinds of diseases. In 1838 the authorities decided this might be charlatanism and threw him out.

Elliotson dreamed about one kind of mesmeric treatment he was never going to be allowed to do. It was practiced in India where Dr. James Esdaile was carrying out surgical procedures with the anesthetic aid of the mesmeric technique (waving hands over the body and breathing onto the face and head). Finally, in 1850 at the Calcutta Hospital, his down-to-earth bosses (all Brits) watched him do it and said it seemed to work. Then chloroform arrived on the medical scene and that was the end of "look-into-my-eyes-and-feel-sleepy" operations.

Both Esdaile and Elliotson had been influenced by the "mystery force" discovered by German count Karl von Reichenbach in 1844. Reichenbach was a scientific entrepreneur who invented a more efficient charcoal oven and analyzed the gunk by-product. In which he found (and named) creosote and paraffin. He also built metallurgical factories, grew sugar beet, and investigated meteorites. Reichenbach's mystery force was called "Od" and was supposed to be an invisible kind of gravity that allowed some sensitive people (mostly women) to see (in the dark) the "Odic light" being given off by objects. Naturally enough, Reichenbach was slaughtered by his science peers, especially the one he visited in Leipzig and failed to convince.

Mind you, Gustav Fechner had his own little foibles. In 1838 Fechner started thinking about the relationship between psychology and physiology, especially the origin and meaning of the afterimages people saw when they'd been staring at bright light. He chose the sun and stared. And went blind for three years. On recovery he "saw" the "souls" of plants. This led (of course) to investigation of the link between mind and body. And to experiments with light, weights, and sounds. Fechner was looking to quantify awareness: How much extra light, weight, or sound did you need before you noticed things had changed? He discovered there was a constant. With light the just-noticeable increase had to be more than one-hundredth of the original, with weight one-fortieth, and with sound one-tenth. He called this stuff "psychophysics."

Fechner's work on subjective impressions got universalized by Austrian physicist Ernst Mach, who by 1873 had a paper bag on his head while being spun round on a revolving chair. Mach's observation: Once you were up to speed the awareness of spinning went away. You felt no movement at all. Within your own frame of reference and with no external clues to help, it felt as if you weren't moving. So this had to be true about the entire universe and any observations we might make about it. Everything was affected by our frame of reference and the frame of reference was affected by where it was and what it was doing in relation to the rest of the universe. Everything, in other words, was relative. Enter Einstein.

In 1909 Mach was recommended for (and got) a Nobel because his proposer (German chemist Wilhelm Ostwald, already a Nobel) thought Mach could do with the money. Ostwald was the guy who standardized color. In 1920 his *Atlas of Color* was used by two Americans to produce today's definitive *Color Harmony Manual.* Ostwald also invented his own artificial language ("Ido") and developed a theory about "Energetics" (everything could be explained in terms of energy). He also got deeply into social theory with the idea that the individual was a cell in the collective human organism.

Ostwald's day job was chemical catalysis (for which, the Nobel). So he got very excited by the work on chemical reactions being done by fellow geek William Ramsay. Ramsay was another one of those Victorian multitalents, fluent in several languages, member of the British royal sewage commission, and popular science writer. And he was hot stuff with frozen air. Which he allowed to boil off, then distilled out the known ingredients like oxygen, nitrogen, carbon dioxide, and so on, then examined what was left. By 1898 this technique had revealed the existence of gases that were so "do-nothing" (inert, so no evidence of their presence) they were really hard to find. Besides which, there were only teeny-weeny amounts of them in air: argon was one part in a hundred, neon was one part in eighteen million, krypton was one part in a million, and xenon was one-tenth of one part in a million. So Ramsay got a Nobel.

Xenon turned out to be just what Harold Edgerton was looking for. Electrical engineer Edgerton had begun in the Nebraska Power and Light Company and faced the problem of diagnosing malfunctions in power generators while they were still spinning. Moving target was putting it mildly. In 1926 Edgerton had begun research (which continued when he joined the faculty at MIT) that ended with the stroboscope: illuminating spinning turbine blades with a light flashing at the same speed as they were spinning, thus "freezing" the image of a single blade for examination. By 1938, using a xenon discharge lamp, Edgerton could flash a million times a second and produce famous photos like the bullet hitting the apple.

Then Edgerton got into oceanography, sailing with Jacques Cousteau, developing underwater cameras and a towable side-scan sonar that mapped a profile of the ocean floor. By 1994 this gizmo was being used (together with a multibeam version) on board the USNS *Littlehales* naval oceanographic survey vessel to make very high-resolution maps of the seabed off the coast of Albania. Four years later, the U.S. Navy was able to use these maps to position ships accurately enough to fire Tomahawks into Yugoslavia during the Balkan conflict. In 2003 the *Littlehales* was given to the National Oceanic and Atmospheric Administration.

It took on a new name: that of the president who sponsored the first U.S. coastal survey back in 1807: THOMAS JEFFERSON.

CHAPTER THIRTY-SEVEN

Benj Harrison

BENJAMIN HARRISON (VA) was forty-nine. "An indolent, luxurious, heavy gentleman, of no use in Congress," said John Adams. No surprise, rich landowner Harrison was against independence at first but turned his coat when he saw how things were going. During the war Harrison was involved in the network set up by the colonies to exchange defense information. After it was all over Harrison opposed the idea of a federal government because he thought northern business interests would grab power.

At the first Continental Congress in Philadelphia Harrison (and George Washington) lodged together with Harrison's brother-in-law the aristocratic Peyton Randolph, a London-trained lawyer and owner of a fancy town house and two plantations. When people started talking revolution Randolph argued instead for a trade embargo on Britain, but then decided to go with the flow. And did so well that he ended up on the Brits' "Most Wanted" list.

Peyton's brother went entirely the other way. John Randolph (had the ear of Washington, played violin duets with Jefferson) was a loyalist and in 1774 left for England, selling his violin to Jefferson for five dollars. He also wrote the first American book on vegetable gardening (good stuff on artichokes). In exile he prepared plans for reconciliation with America and wrote a letter to Jefferson asking him to tear up the Declaration.

On his arrival in England Randolph stayed with John Murray (aka Lord Dunmore), ex-governor of Virginia. Dunmore had shipped out his family in 1775 and stayed behind to fight the Americans. He tried (and failed) to get the slaves to revolt on Britain's side. In 1776 he left for Britain. In 1781 he was back again, ready to take over at Charlestown when Cornwallis won. Cornwallis lost, so Murray was shunted off to the Bahamas as governor and organizer of buccaneering sorties into Spanish Florida. Things were going pretty well for him when he was suddenly fired. Reason: In 1792 his daughter Augusta (known as "Goosey") secretly married Prince Augustus Frederick, one of George III's sons. This was illegal since they hadn't received the king's okay. And weren't about to. So the marriage was declared invalid and Goosey was paid off.

Augustus Frederick (asthmatic, weedy, liberal, and grand master Freemason) was a nerd, a popular after-dinner speaker, and had a fifty-thousand-book library. And (being who he was) became president of the Royal Society in 1830. His brother Prince Frederick Augustus did even better. A bishop when he was six months old, Fred entered the army in his teens and was royally fast-tracked: colonel at seventeen, general at nineteen, field marshal at thirty-two. In 1799 he was put in charge of the invasion of Holland, made Duke of York and spent much time marching his army up hills (and back down). To give him his due he also started proper officer training (he founded the Royal Military Academy), provided clothing for soldiers, and started rooting out army corruption. Ironically, everything went down the latrine when he lost his own job over a matter of corruption. By his mistress, Mary Anne Clarke, who was busy selling army commissions for lots of money.

It was easy. She just added somebody's name to the list and the prince signed without reading. This helped Mary Anne meet the cost of an extravagant lifestyle, which included "entertaining" gentlemen. As the prince's mistress, however, she was sailing close to the wind. When a failed ex-army man, Gwyllym Wardle, exposed the commissions-for-cash scam, the prince dumped Mary Anne. After which she and Wardle got together in a plan to cook the prince's goose. Mary Anne threatened to publish their love letters and was given about half a million (modern) in hush money and a pension. In 1809 the prince resigned from the army. Wardle got medals and cash, but not enough to pay the bills, which included furnishings for Mary Anne's new house. In spite of temporary financial help from friends, Wardle headed off to a cheaper existence in Italy.

The friends-to-the-rescue had included Timothy Brown, well-heeled banker and brewer. Brown's bank also loaned money to agitators, and after 1812, when he became a founder member of the revolutionary Union for Parliamentary Reform, Brown went onto the government's usual-suspects list because he also received foreign newspapers. "Equality" Brown also helped pay for the publication of Tom Paine's libertarian work *Age of Reason* and a translation of the French philosopher D'Holbach's book questioning the divinity of Christ (this ran afoul of the blasphemy laws). In 1815 Brown wrote in defense of religious toleration for the *Political Register*, a London mag run by William Cobbett. Who, two years later, was running the journal from a farm in Long Island.

Years earlier Cobbett had spent almost a decade in Philadelphia writing anti-American articles bylined "Peter Porcupine." A threatened libel charge forced his departure for England where he started investigating government corruption and urging workers to insurrection. Neither activity was good for the health, so soon Cobbett had to hightail it for Long Island. After two years there he would return to write his famous *Rural Rides*, about working conditions in the countryside, become a politician, and wait for the British revolution that never came.

Meanwhile on Long Island Cobbett gave lodgings to a young schoolboy, J. J. Mapes. Who grew up to be a chemist. By 1834 Mapes was in New York working as an expert witness in patent cases, secretary of the National Society of Inventors, professor of chemistry at the National Academy of Design (a colleague was Sam Morse), and president of the Mechanics' Institute. In 1847 he started a farm in Newark, New Jersey, and turned to agricultural chemistry. In 1852 he was the first American manufacturer of superphosphate fertilizer.

Mapes also became friends (and fellow photography researcher) with another chemist, John W. Draper. English-born Draper was professor of chemistry at NYU and in 1839 had taken the first photograph of the moon. He conferred the first Ph.D.s in America, wrote numerous textbooks, did basic early work on radiant energy, and then moved into science-and-society stuff. At the 1860 Oxford meeting of the British Association for the Advancement of Science he droned on about Darwin's new theory and caused the famous row between T. H. Huxley and "Soapy" Samuel Wilberforce about us all being "descended from apes."

Draper was best known for his view that science had always been held back by religion, after he found the idea in a book by French "positivist" thinker Auguste Comte. Comte, a workaholic whose breakdown led to his jumping into the Seine (fished out), saw history in three stages: theological (myth and religion), metaphysical (philosophical speculation), and finally "positive" (scientific). Comte lectured to such science stars as Alexander von Humboldt and Jean Baptiste Joseph Fourier on math, astronomy, physics, chemistry, physiology, and the social sciences. He also invented sociology, dividing it into two parts: "statics" (the study of what holds society together) and "dynamics" (the causes of change). And he believed that the most powerful influence on humans was their environment.

Comte's disciple Hippolyte Taine took things further, arguing that race, environment, and circumstances shaped everything in human behavior. And that understanding people, now or in the past, involved seeing them in terms of those three "natural" elements. Taine's "naturalism" turned up in works by scribblers such as Zola, Dickens, and Thackeray. As the thinker's thinker, Taine also attended the *dernier cri* salon of Princess Mathilde Bonaparte (as did everybody in the arts) and met the good-looking young composer Gabriel Fauré, an organist-composer and pupil of Saint-Saens.

Nothing much happened for poor Fauré till he was fifty. In spite of turning out songs and piano pieces and half-finished symphonies, plus a marriage, several affairs, and some travel (met Liszt, who couldn't play Fauré's stuff because too difficult), Fauré was stuck in second gear till 1891. Then things took off. Ten years later he was chief organist at the posh Madeleine Church in Paris, director of the Paris Conservatoire, had finished his big *Requiem*, taught Ravel, and was music critic for *Le Figaro*. Things like that happened when sewing-machine heiress Winnaretta Singer took an interest.

Winnaretta was a millionairess at eighteen, married a prince, divorced him, and then married another (at which point she became Princesse de Polignac). Her gay second husband suited her lesbian lifestyle (which included an affair with the daughter of the king of England's mistress). Winnaretta was also a major figure in the music world. She gave money to Boulanger, Rubenstein, Horowitz, the Ballets Russes, and the Paris Opera. She commissioned work from Stravinsky, Satie, Diaghilev, and De Falla. And she knew everybody else. In 1929 she asked a young Swiss architect to design accommodation for single homeless women in Paris. So Le Corbusier built the Salvation Army Refuge.

Le Corbusier was by now well on the way to becoming one of the twentieth century's most influential architects, with his concepts of entire cities composed of skyscrapers set in parklands and linked by aerial pedestrian bridges. Socialism in grass and glass. In 1930 Le Corbusier invited a young German to become an apprentice. After a year, Horst Horst moved on to find his true vocation taking fashion photographs for *Vogue*. For the next sixty years Horst dominated the rag trade with his surreal style. In 1939 just before leaving for the United States his last photograph showed a model whose Mainbocher corset was coming undone.

Horst and Mainbocher had met at *Vogue*, where the American couturier was designing clothes for the rich and famous. In 1934 he had introduced the first strapless evening gown and in 1937 designed the Duchess of Windsor's wedding dress. Back again in the States in 1939 he made clothes for such as Gloria Vanderbilt. In 1942 the wife of the assistant secretary to the navy asked Mainbocher to design the uniforms for the new naval women's force: the WAVES. By 1943 twenty-seven thousand women were wearing Mainbocher's creation.

Many WAVES had their three months' basic training on the campus of the Georgia State College for Women, in Milledgeville, Georgia. Where they got mail from home thanks to the town's postmaster, BENJAMIN HARRISON.

CHAPTER THIRTY-EIGHT

Th.^{s} Nelson jr.

THOMAS NELSON (VA) was thirty-seven. The year before, he and some pals had their own (York River) Tea Party. A plump, red-haired businessman, plantation-owner, and reckless spender with a lavish lifestyle, Nelson was land-rich and cash-poor. Like many of his class he preferred a trade embargo to outright war but gradually came to see that there was only one way out of the mess.

During the war Nelson put up his estates as collateral for loans taken out by the state. He was never reimbursed and died in poverty. As a young man Nelson had been sent to England and educated at Cambridge under Beilby Porteus, who in 1787 became bishop of London and then chaplain to the king. Beilby was born in Virginia and his family knew the Nelsons well. He was a leading figure in the Society for Enforcing the King's Proclamation against Immorality and Idleness and in the fight against slavery. He also persuaded George III not to play cards on Sunday. And worked hard to stop people Sunday-promenading (but failed).

When he heard that humble workers were selling their Bibles to buy copies of Tom Paine's *Age of Reason*, Beilby indicted Thomas Williams, a bookshop owner, for selling one of Paine's books. He hired Thomas Erskine as prosecutor. Erskine visited the poverty-stricken Williams (two kids had smallpox) and then urged mitigation. The judge went easy on him: only three years.

Erskine was a brilliant lawyer and specialized in military cases, adultery, and radicals. He defended many clients free (including a man who had taken a shot at George III) and at age fifty-six was made lord chancellor (head of the legal profession). Erskine was an animal lover (he kept dogs, a goose, and a macaw) and introduced a "Prevention of Cruelty to Animals" bill in Parliament. He also owned two pet leeches named after the eminent surgeons Everhard Home and Henry Cline.

Henry Cline inclined to the political left, often appeared in the witness box as a medical expert, and would have gone from history unnoticed but for his major medical moment in 1777 when he identified (and developed a surgical procedure to treat) a disease of the hand in which fibrosis of the tissue of the palm pulls on the fingers causing them to contract like hooks. For some strange reason, by 1833 Henry's role in this had been forgotten when the entire matter was revisited by a French surgeon who then got all the glory (the condition is now known, after this French person, as "Dupuytren's contracture").

In 1794 Baron Guillaume Dupuytren was in the first class to graduate from the new Paris Medical School, where he was taught the cutting-edge stuff with which French medicine was leading the world: clinical observation, progress charts, ward visits, and the rest. Dupuytren became known for great pathology, dissecting every death that occurred in his wards. Dupuytren's other moment of glory came on the evening of February 13, 1820, when he was called to the Théâtre Louvois in Paris where the Duke de Berry (nephew of the French king Charles X) had been stabbed in the chest by a deranged republican supporter of the Bonapartes. Dupuytren tried the usual treatment for a stabbed man: bleeding him. Unsurprisingly the duke expired.

De Berry (and his pregnant duchess) had been enjoying the latest chart-topper: *Le Rossignol*, a comic opera that played to packed houses no fewer than 227 times (some said because there was little else worth seeing). Composer Louis-Sebastien Lebrun was a tenor turned composer who churned out many other comic operas (now thankfully dusted off only for Ph.D. research work). *Le Rossignol* has survived because of the virtuoso duet between the soprano and the flute, whistled (as they say) in every Paris street.

A few years later a guitar arrangement of this amazingly popular piece was done by guitarist and publisher Jean-Antoine Meissonnier. This was the era of guitar mania in France, and Meissonnier even wrote an arrangement of the overture to *The Barber of Seville* for violin and guitar. Avoid it if you can. In 1814 just after he started his Paris publishing business Meissonnier met a Catalan guitar virtuoso who was to become a major client. Fernando Sor had left Spain for Paris that year, then moved on to London the following year. In both places he was an overnight rave. Nobody'd ever heard the instrument played so brilliantly. Sor developed the basic modern classical guitar technique and by the 1820s he was an international star playing St. Petersburg, Moscow, Berlin, and Warsaw before settling in Paris for the rest of his life.

One of Sor's pupils was a young Irish actress, Fanny Kelly, who at age seven had debuted at Drury Lane and after a brief tour in the provinces returned to the theater for the next thirty-six years. In 1816 she was shot at, onstage, by a lunatic who missed. In 1819 the drama reviewer who habitually gave her good notices finally proposed marriage. She turned him down primarily out of concern about the insanity that seemed to run in his family. Back in 1795 he'd spent time in an asylum and a year later his sister Mary had stabbed and killed her mother in the kitchen. After a period in an asylum, she had been released into her brother's care.

In spite of Fanny's marital no-thanks, she and the shy, stammering boozer Charles Lamb remained good friends. Already well known for his children's book *Lamb's Tales from Shakespeare*, Lamb was by now using his spare time (from an undemanding job as an accountancy clerk) to write the *Essays of Elia* for which he would be famous as the best English writer in the genre. Semiautobiographical, gentle in tone, full of whimsy and observation, the essays ran in the *London Magazine* for thirteen years. And gained him the friendship of Keats, Coleridge, and the Wordsworths.

One of Lamb's own favorite reads was the 1824 *Our Village* by Mary Russell Mitford. Whose main reason for writing was a gambling, high-living father who spent it faster than Mary could earn it. She tried her hand at the kind of blood-and-guts historical tragedies popular at time: Her *Foscolo* featured two deaths from joy, two poisonings, two assassinations, and a hero killed. In spite of which the play bombed. As did all her others except *Rienzi*, all about the fourteenth-century governor of Rome assassinated for his cruelty. In 1828 a smash hit at Drury Lane. Mary's one and only success.

Rienzi also did well at New York's Park Theater, where it featured the rising American tragedy star Charlotte Cushman. In 1844 Cushman arrived in London and was acclaimed as the Next Big Thing. After five years of success she returned triumphant to the United States where she earned so much money that by 1852 she decided to retire to Rome with her English lover Matilda Hays. Soon after, Cushman switched her affections to live-in American sculptor Emma Stubbs, with whom she would cohabit from then on.

During one of their frequent return journeys to London and America, in 1861 Cushman and Emma went to Fontainebleau, near Paris, to the château of (another lesbian) painter Rosa Bonheur, famous for animal painting. Her specialty was horses, and the château had been bought with the proceeds from three equine paintings: *Ploughing in the Nivernais, Horse Fair,* and *Haymaking in the Auvergne.* In the 1880s Bonheur became fascinated by Buffalo Bill Cody and after meeting him she visited the Wild West Show in Paris in 1889 and produced several works including *The Buffalo Hunt,* the image used from then on to give Cody's publicity a distinctive look. And to differentiate the show from its imitator.

Sam Cody, "King of Cowboys" (a Texan whose real name was Franklin Cowdery), toured Britain with his own act, dressing and looking (long hair, beard) just like Buffalo Bill. In 1900 Cody's theatrical show *Klondike Nugget* made him enough money to concentrate on his passion for kites. By 1901 he had a man-carrying version. Small "lifting" kites set at intervals on a cable raised the main kite. Once it was flying, a man-carrying trolley, hung from a wheel running on the cable, could be hauled up to just below the kite. By 1906 Cody was hoisting artillery observers as high as twenty-four hundred feet and had become chief kite instructor to the British army.

In 1907 Cody's work excited the imagination of army engineer Ernest Swinton, who included an essay ("The Kite") in a series on future warfare he was writing for *Blackwood's* magazine. In 1914 Swinton was sent as a war correspondent to the trenches, where he saw the murderous effect of machine-gun fire. This gave him the idea of an armored vehicle capable of breaking down barbed wire and overrunning machine-gun emplacements. By 1916 Swinton's idea (the tank) was in action at the battle of the Somme. The new fighting vehicles had one minor problem: They were blind. No window and no periscope.

Unfortunately most optical glass was made in Germany. With that supply cut off there was a desperate need to find other ways of making the glass, now also needed for telescopes, binoculars, and rangefinders. In America one of the scientists coopted to solve the problem was University of Illinois chemist Edward Washburn, who specialized in ceramic engineering. His other speciality was electrical conduction in concentrated solutions. This esoteric discipline was to prove earth-shatteringly important.

In due course Washburn became chief chemist at the National Bureau of Standards in Washington, D.C. Meanwhile, in 1931, Harold Urey had discovered deuterium, a hydrogen isotope (a different element with the same number of protons in its nucleus as hydrogen). Using electrolysis Washburn succeeded in concentrating deuterium oxide in water. This process drove off the hydrogen and left a concentrated solution of deuterium known as "heavy" water. Which turned out to be part of the process controlling atomic nuclear reactions.

Deuterium was also used to fission (split) atoms during the effort to develop the atomic bomb. In 1940 Urey was put in charge of separating out fissionable uranium-235 from nonfissionable uranium-238. He succeeded and U-235 was exploded successfully over Hiroshima in 1945. Urey's Manhattan Project team included a young graduate student, Paul Doty. Who in 1973 founded the Belfer Center for Science and International Affairs at Harvard.

In 2005 one of the center's international council members was THOMAS NELSON.

CHAPTER THIRTY-NINE

Francis Lightfoot Lee

FRANK LEE (VA), aka Francis Lightfoot Lee, was forty-one. The only mild-mannered member of an aggressive and outspoken family of four brothers, after sixteen years in the Virginia House Frank became a busy revolutionary responsible for army supply.

His brother Arthur was an entirely different kettle of fish. The best-educated of the brothers (Eton, Edinburgh University, and the London law school), Arthur socialized with the movers and shakers during his years in Britain. In 1777 together with Franklin and Silas Deane he acted as commissioner negotiating to buy French weapons. A year later it was Lee who blew the whistle on what he thought was corruption (it looked as if Deane was taking profit from the funds). It's possible that Lee just misunderstood diplomatic wheels-within-wheels, but in any case he was outmaneuvered by Franklin and recalled.

But unknown to the others Lee had spent the previous eighteen months involved in cloak-and-dagger stuff (laundering war-finance money to America) with the chief French undercover agent and fake aristocrat Caron de Beaumarchais. Who had begun his career making wristwatches for Louis XV's mistress. Then taught the king's daughters the harp. Then wrote two plays: *The Marriage of Figaro* and *The Barber of Seville*. Then turned deniable royal spy.

The king sent Beaumarchais to England, from where he reported that the Brits secretly wanted to get rid of the American colonies. In an associated bit of double-dealing, Beaumarchais arranged for the high-tech ironmaking Wilkinson brothers (who also made cylinders for James Watt's engines) to deliver forty miles of piping to the new Paris water-supply company in which Beaumarchais himself had shares. The "double" bit of the dealing was that the Wilkinsons' latest cylinder- (and cannon-) boring machine would also be delivered, labeled as "piping."

The French plan was that this cutting-edge machine would then be used to make new cannon to replace the ones sent to the Americans under the (first) secret deal brokered by Lee and Beaumarchais (who had set up a fake company to charter forty ships to take guns, tents, ammunition, gunpowder, and money to the Caribbean for onward shipment you-know-where in exchange for sugar, cotton, tobacco, and rice from you-know-who). In the end the return shipments never happened and the deniable Beaumarchais lost a fortune.

Meanwhile, by 1783 the Paris water supply system was up and running and being tested by Charles Augustin Coulomb, physicist, military engineer, and superintendent of water supply and fountains (at this time, high-tech stuff). Over the years Coulomb put together more than three hundred reports for the French Academy of Sciences on everything from British hospitals to French canals, harbors, machinery, and engineering projects in general. Later in life Coulomb would be a major influence in setting up the French secondary education system. His fame, however, rests on his work in electricity and magnetism and especially his development of a gizmo for measuring electric charge. Which may be why an electric charge is now measured in "coulombs."

Early in his career Coulomb also got to spend time on the Atlantic coast (at Rochefort) working with the Marquis de Montalembert, inventor of a new kind of fortress (old-buffer military fortress designers forced him to delay design publication for fifteen years). Montalembert changed the shape of a fort from the previous complicated arrangement of bastions and angled walls to a simple polygonal or even circular structure. Key innovation: The fort was built to be aggressive, not defensive. Guns were placed in enclosed positions (roofed against the downward killing power of the new shrapnel) all round the fort, so as to be able to shoot in any direction. Great for clobbering a passing fleet, when time to shoot was short.

In 1807 New York Harbor this kind of ship-sinking trick was just right for Lieutenant Colonel Jonathan Williams, looking for a way to discourage any Brits who might be heading that way. His Montalembert-inspired "Castle Williams" was circular, with two tiers of protected cannon. And in terms of Brit discouragement Williams was right. In 1812 the threat of Castle Williams's firepower persuaded the Brits to bypass New York and set fire to some other city farther south. Alas for Williams, he never got the credit he deserved. And worse, when he was superintendent of West Point (where he modernized the curriculum) and then at Castle Williams, regular army officers objected to having an engineer in command.

Williams's case wasn't helped by Secretary of War William Eustis, one of the least-qualified holders of the office in American history. Eustis was a doctor with limited military and political experience (as an army surgeon and in Massachusetts local government), appointed by Madison to reform the army. The new secretary proposed a publicly funded volunteer force of fifty thousand plus nine thousand extra infantry and several new military departments. He pushed ahead with equivocation and incompetence.

When war came in 1812 Congress was still arguing about Eustis's plans. And thanks to his bumbling nothing was ready for the attack on Canada. General Hull surrendered Detroit without a shot because Eustis hadn't told him war was imminent. Buffalo and Washington, D.C., were attacked and burned. The country went into uproar and Eustis suddenly became minister to Holland. The irony was that on June 18, 1812, when Madison declared war, the immediate reason for the conflict (the British Orders in Council preventing America from trading with France) had just been provisionally repealed. But the news would take six weeks to get to the United States, by which time it was too late.

The repeal of the Orders had been the result of lobbying in Parliament by Henry Brougham, a brilliant young lawyer representing U.K. manufacturers who were losing a bundle because the trade embargo was being counterenforced by the Americans. Brougham was a politico to his fingertips (opportunistic, depressive, boozer, eccentric, scheming, charismatic, hypochondriac) and argued for reform of Parliament, anti-slavery laws, the legal profession, education, bankruptcy, charities, and much else. He was also a founder of London University and authored hundreds of articles in the *Law Review*. And ended up lord chancellor (top lawyer), loved or hated.

Re love, Brougham had numerous affairs, the most widely publicized of which involved a foreign holiday with Caroline Lamb. Lawyer George Lamb, the cuckold in question and known by his mother as "unsatisfactory George," was a red-faced, red-haired uncouth drunk (hence Caroline's trip) who fancied himself as a dramatist and wrote un-successful Gothic stuff full of brigands with daggers. In 1815 he was on the new management committee of Drury Lane Theater when Byron showed him a play he'd been sent by Sir Walter Scott (who was a finan-cial supporter of the author). Lamb loved it and in 1816 *Bertram* hit the stage for a sensational forty performances.

Bertram was to be the only great moment for Irish cleric and play-wright Charles Maturin. His other works (with Irish plots full of coded references to English usurpers and invaders) pretty much flopped. As did his clerical career. Maturin was an extravagant dresser and crazy for the quadrille, which he would dance in the daytime with the curtains closed.

This unusual behavior was shared by his nephew's wife, Lady Jane Wilde, who always closed the curtains when she entertained, dressed like a tragedy queen in flowing silk, and wore so many portrait brooches she looked like "a walking family mausoleum." During the potato famine in 1846, Jane began to write the nationalist poems and prose that would make her famous. Six feet tall and strikingly handsome, she was an active feminist, translator (French and German), writer of travel books, pal of George Bernard Shaw and Yeats and above all, mother of Oscar. For twenty years after her husband died bankrupt she eked out an existence in London still holding weekly salons in the dark.

One of Jane's many admirers was William Hamilton, child prodigy math nerd. By age thirteen he spoke French and Italian and could read Persian, Arabic, Greek, Latin, Hindi, Sanskrit, Malay, and Hebrew (for relaxation, he said). To the nonmathematician his work is total gob-bledygook. He invented quaternions (a major stage in the development of algebra, it says here) and helped establish the wave theory of light. He also developed some arcane mathematical thing known as a "Hamil-tonian." He was also the Irish royal astronomer at age twenty-one and never did much.

But in 1839 he got the first look through the Earl of Ross's new giant telescope. Ross was rich enough to have fun making giant telescope mirrors. In 1844 he produced an even more giant scope known as the "Leviathan." Carrying a six-foot mirror that took three years to perfect, the telescope stood fifty-six feet high and was for sixty years the biggest telescope in the world. Almost immediately it discovered the Whirlpool Galaxy Messier 51, gave the distinct impression that nebulae were actu-ally dense star clusters, and seriously improved the study of the night sky. So Ross won prizes and the presidency of the Royal Society.

Sixty years later his youngest son, Charles Parsons (aristocrats' titles and their family names are often different; it's a Brit thing), was made society vice president. Parsons started out as an engineering apprentice, and by 1884 was so fed up with the clunky old steam engine that he de-veloped a turbine alternative. High-pressure steam hit turbine blades mounted at an angle on an axle and made them spin eighteen thousand times a minute (more than ten times the speed a steam engine could achieve). By 1894 Parsons's spinning-axle turbine-powered propellor-driven yacht *Turbinia* could reach thirty-four knots. Faster than the fastest ship in the navy. By 1899 Parsons had a turbine in a destroyer. He used gearing to slow turbine speed so it could be used by cargo vessels.

Early on, Parsons also used his turbine to spin copper wire loops through a magnetic field and generate electricity. In 1884 the license for this clever trick was snatched up by American George Westinghouse, at the time busy fighting the "War of the Currents." Westinghouse made alternating-current electricity: The electron movement (electricity) went back and forward in the copper wire as the spinning wire loops "al-ternatingly" cut the magnetic field first one way then the other. West-inghouse rival Thomas Edison's direct current used a commutator to turn this two-way electron flow into "direct" one-way electricity. Alternating current could be stepped up to high voltage, sent a long way, and then stepped down again to usable levels. Direct current couldn't. So Westinghouse was able to build large generating stations a long way from cities and Edison wasn't. So Edison lost the electricity-supply battle. Still, he was already a multimillionaire, so what did he care.

In 1942 Edison's daughter-in-law (married to Charles Edison, then acting secretary of the navy) sponsored the launch of the giant, Iowa-class battleship USS *New Jersey*, which then went on to a distinguished fighting record in World War II, Korea, and Vietnam. In 1982 the ship had her final retrofit when she was provided with Harpoon and Tomahawk missiles.

Much of the success of the $467 million refurbishment was due to the marine engineer and naval architect involved, FRANK LEE.

CHAPTER FORTY

Carter Braxton

CARTER BRAXTON (VA) was thirty-nine. And drank. It was said his complexion "reflected the glow of good Madeira." He was a wealthy landowner and a reluctant rebel who described Independence as a "delusive bait." Braxton's father-in-law was a loyalist and Braxton was so certain a compromise with England would be reached he even borrowed money to hire more ships and buy more tobacco cargoes for the British market. In the end he lost everything either to privateers or the Royal Navy and ended up financially ruined. Then his wife made loyalist remarks and Braxton was removed from Congress immediately after signing.

Back in 1774 Braxton had hired a new graduate of St. Andrews University, Scotland, to come and teach his sons. Andrew Bell stayed till 1781 and when things got too hot returned to England to became a clergyman. In 1787 he left for India where he invented the Madras System school. Trays of sand and hanging pasteboard cards were used by older boys to teach younger boys. This and the use of discipline monitors (older boys) meant that two adult teachers could handle several hundred pupils. With no corporal punishment, no rote learning, and streaming by ability the system was a winner and caught on (all over the world) after Bell returned to England.

In 1803, when he was a curate in deepest Dorset, Bell took up the cause of Benjamin Jesty, local farmer. Who in 1774 had noticed that when his milkmaids caught (nonlethal) cowpox from infected cows' udders they could then nurse victims of (lethal) smallpox and not catch it. So Jesty used a needle to transfer pus from cowpox pustules into healthy arms. The vaccinated persons developed immunity to smallpox. This was thirty years before Edward Jenner got all the glory and ten thousand pounds government money for doing exactly what Jesty had done.

Andrew Bell's efforts brought Jesty recognition (but no money) in the form of a pair of mounted gold lancets and a portrait commissioned from Michael Sharp. In 1799 Sharp (father oboeist, mother actress) was a painter's assistant at Windsor Castle, caught the eye of George III, and in a few days had 140 commissions to paint the nobility. By 1801 he was exhibiting at the Royal Academy (theatrical themes). Then he started painting in and around the city of Norwich, where he made friends with the (much better) painter John Crome.

For ten years Crome painted the wooden signs that hung outside pubs, then went into picture dealing and landscape scenes. He founded the "Norwich School" of art (it made little impression) and did views of Norwich. About which no more need be said. In 1812 Crome was in debt to the nearby Gurney Bank (while giving painting lessons to some of the Gurney family). Hudson Gurney, rich, unwilling head of the bank, had only one ambition: to write "one good poem." Never happened. Instead, as he said, he moldered in the countryside, reading his fifteen-thousand-book library until finally he managed to buy a seat in Parliament, go to London, and entertain the rich and famous in his fancy town house. He then turned antiquarian, writing *Heads of Ancient History* (it'll give you catatonia) and becoming vice president of the Society of Antiquaries. Gurney was affable, argumentative, and dull.

His one bright moment was in 1802 when he left for the Grand Tour of the culture centers of Europe with his schoolmate George Gordon, fourth Earl of Aberdeen and cousin of the poet Byron. After visiting Paris (met Napoleon: "fatter than expected"), Florence, and Rome, Gurney went home. Gordon continued to Turkey and Greece, where he "picked up" ancient sculptures, then returned to join the Dilettanti Society (aristos who traveled) and organized their 1811 junket to the

Ionian islands. Meanwhile he also took his seat in the House of Lords and started a political career that ended with the prime ministership. Gordon was a natural scholar, and one of his publications criticized the location by his pal William Gell of the ancient city of Troy as being underneath the Turkish village of Bunabashi.

Gell was witty, eloquent, a dog lover, good company, and a great dinner host with guests ranging from earls to boxers. He was also permanently short of cash. After his Troy trip he wrote several articles on Greece and got them reviewed by Byron. Then came a spell as Queen Caroline's chamberlain, and in 1814 the queen gave him a small pension. This was enough to live on in Italy, where he spent the rest of his life excavating, entertaining, and writing letters to fellow enthusiasts about matters archeological and in particular the latest craze: Egyptology. Leading light of which was Gell's friend, Frenchman Jean-François Champollion.

At school Champollion had mastered Greek, Latin, Hebrew, Arabic, Syriac, and Coptic in preparation for his destiny. Which was to decipher Egyptian hieroglyphics. In 1808 a plaster copy of the Rosetta Stone, carrying an inscription in three scripts—hieroglyphs, demotic (a kind of hieroglyph shorthand), and Greek—arrived in Paris, and Champollion began to noodle. By 1822 he had worked out many of the hieroglyphs. In 1824 he was sent to Italy and in Turin came across *The Book of the Dead*, an Egyptian papyrus containing hieroglyph descriptions of religious rituals. With this extra material he cracked the hieroglyph code.

Looking for even more to decrypt, Champollion persuaded the French government to buy four thousand ancient Egyptian objects and drawings of inscriptions from Englishman Henry Salt. Who was U.K. consul-general in Egypt and had spent ten years "collecting" everything from amulets to saracophagi (and a giant bust of Rameses II), much of which he sold to the British Museum. Salt had also spent time in Abyssinia making friends with the king and collecting specimens of the local fauna for back-in-England Lord Stanley.

Stanley's day job was as member of Parliament, but most of his time was taken up by the menagerie he ran at his stately home, Knowsley Hall, near Liverpool. Spread over 170 acres, the zoo cost a fortune to run. Stanley filled daily diaries with his animals' behavior and when anything died he stuffed it. At one time Knowsley held no fewer than ninety-four species of mammal and 318 species of bird as well as the first Gambian lungfish ever seen in Britain. Stanley also managed the first successful breeding of Australian budgerigars. He even swapped samples with Queen Victoria.

In 1841 he hired young John MacGillivray on the grounds that his father had worked with the great American ornithologist J. J. Audubon. In 1842 Stanley sponsored MacGillivray as naturalist (and collector) on the survey ship HMS *Fly*'s trip to Australia. On the crossing, between Rio de Janeiro and Tasmania, MacGillivray kept the first-ever mid-oceanic records on sightings of albatrosses and petrels. In 1846 he set off again for another four-year trip to Australia on board HMS *Rattlesnake*, this time working for the Admiralty.

One of his fellow crew members was T. H. Huxley, the ship's assistant surgeon, with whom MacGillivray spent many happy hours ashore, peering about and picking up things on reefs and desert islands. Huxley's specialty was jellyfish and sea nettles (apart from surgery, for which he was only half-qualified, having had to quit medical school for lack of funds). The *Rattlesnake* voyage would make Huxley famous. When the Royal Society read his paper on how certain tissues in a jellyfish looked strangely like those in chicken embryos (and was this evidence of something general in all animal development?), they made him a fellow. When *Origin of Species* came out in 1859 Huxley became an immediate fan. After which he was known as "Darwin's bulldog" for the way he growled at people who disagreed with evolution.

Huxley was chronically short of cash and made money by writing about everything from slugs to philosophy and lecturing to full houses in the United States. In 1864 he started the X Club whose other eight members were with one exception scientists in the Royal Society. The exception was Herbert Spencer. Ex–railroad engineer turned philosopher, Spencer dabbled in head-bump-reading, then entered journalism, then began writing the books and lectures that made him famous. In 1850 his first publication, *Social Statics*, described a society working by natural laws and a state whose only function was to enforce those laws.

And, he asked, if natural laws brought a single cell to human adulthood in twenty years, couldn't nature go from a single cell to the entire human race over a million years? When Spencer read Darwin in 1859 it all made sense.

Spencer's argument was that every individual had equal freedom to survive and prosper, and that those who did were obeying the law that organisms which fit their environment best, survive best. This was music to the ears of entrepreneurial heavies like John D. Rockefeller. At a Sunday school class Rockefeller once said: "The American Beauty rose can be produced in splendor . . . only by sacrificing the early buds which grow up around it." Spencer's "Social Darwinism" gave big-time financiers a philosophical underpinning to their kill-or-be-killed approach to money-making. Rockefeller saw himself as living proof of Darwin's theory and died worth a billion dollars.

In 1905 Rockefeller hired a young Canadian college student, Cyrus Eaton, as a personal messenger. And then encouraged him to try a career in business. Eaton obliged. By 1913 he was a U.S. citizen and owned several utility companies. In 1938 he became chairman of the board of the Chesapeake and Ohio Railroad and went on to ownership of manufacturing companies as well as mountains of iron ore and coal. Ironically (given his capitalist beginnings), in the 1950s Eaton did business with the Soviet bloc and after the inevitable U.S. government surveillance famously accused the FBI of "creeping up on people."

Even more ironically, back in 1913 his railroad had built one of America's greatest hotels, the Greenbriar, in the Allegheny Mountains of West Virginia. The hotel would eventually become more famous as the site of the Cold War Congressional Emergency Relocation Bunker, buried deep beneath the hotel and top secret until exposed by the *Washington Post* in 1992.

After World War II the hotel was given a makeover by the country's premier interior decorator (referred to by Frank Lloyd Wright as "inferior desecrator") Dorothy Draper, who gave Greenbriar her special touch: black and white marble floor tiles, busts, chintz, and wallpaper with giant red cabbage flowers. Draper had her start at the Carlyle Hotel, in New York.

By 1968 the hotel included the Carlyle Café, where the resident entertainer was the talented singer and pianist Bobby Short, renowned for his interpretation of early twentieth century composers like Gershwin and Jerome Kern. Sadly, after thirty-five wonderful years at the café Short died of leukemia on March 21, 2005. The online Book of Remembrance, opened the next day, was soon full of electronic messages of appreciation and condolence from Short's admirers all over the country.

One message came from an Atlanta-based fan whose name was CARTER BRAXTON.

CHAPTER FORTY-ONE

Wm Hooper

WILLIAM HOOPER (NC) was thirty-four. Handsome, charming (a bit of a swell), the well-heeled lawyer had earlier taken the side of the royal governor in putting down a tax revolt and then tried hard for compromise instead of conflict, hoping till the very last minute for a reconciliation with the Brits. Even though in the end he went with the majority, he still wanted the U.S. government to be half-elected, half-appointed.

After the war Hooper lobbied for restoration of loyalist property. So did his good friend James Iredell, famous for having written the 1774 letter predicting Independence. Before the war Iredell had published articles suggesting the answer to the problem would be two independent governments ruled by the same monarch.

From 1777 Iredell was a North Carolina Superior Court judge, and he is today remembered for his 1787 opinion that no state legislature may pass an act contrary to the state constitution. The case in question regarded confiscated loyalist property. After the war a house, grounds, and wharf in New Bern, North Carolina, were owned by a certain Singleton, who had state deeds to prove it. The previous, loyalist owner, Elizabeth Bayard, petitioned for restitution. The judge decided to send the matter to a jury trial in spite of the fact that a North Carolina act stated that confiscated loyalist property could not be the subject of jury trial. Iredell ruled that the state constitution gave everybody the right to a jury trial, in every case, loyalist or not.

Iredell's cocounsel was William Davie. After a busy war (seriously wounded; commanded Andrew Jackson) the conservative, go-easy-on-loyalists Davie settled into local politics. Where he hassled fellow legislators about the need for a railroad and an up-to-date education system. He then persuaded the state to set up the University of North Carolina, got agreement for the Chapel Hill site (after serving "exhilarating beverages" at the committee meeting), wrote the university's charter, laid the cornerstone, organized the curriculum, made sure students wouldn't whisper in church, keep dogs, or be untidy, and hired the faculty.

One of whom was Joseph Caldwell, who arrived in 1796 as the second math professor, then became president in 1804. As well as publishing two major books on geometry, Caldwell was the South's premier astronomer and mathematician. In 1824 he persuaded legislators to give him six thousand bucks to go to Europe and buy astronomical instruments and books. When he got back with the bits and pieces in 1827 he built the university's observatory, the first in the United States designed for educational purposes.

No surprise, Caldwell was one of the three hundred-odd geeks subscribing to the *Mathematical Correspondent*, a very-limited-circulation journal catering to the tastes of math problem-solvers. One of the other subscribers (who ordered fifty copies) was English nerd Andrew Mackay. Who surveyed the exact position of Aberdeen, Scotland, wrote a major paper on how to do longitude (good stuff for sailors crossing the Atlantic), failed to get a Scots university job, and, annoyed, moved to London where he taught math, navigation, geography, architecture, engineering, "the sciences," and astronomy.

Mackay was a natural for reference book compilers on the lookout for material, and he wrote for the *Encyclopaedia Britannica*. And then contributed stuff on navigation for Abraham Rees's *Cyclopaedia*. Rees was a London-based Welsh Presbyterian minister (and charismatic preacher) who tutored in math, science, and Hebrew. In 1802 he started the *Cyclopaedia*. Published in 1820, it ran to over five hundred articles in thirty-nine volumes with plates and an atlas. Rees signed up more than a hundred contributors, most of them free-churchmen, others military, journalistic, or radical. One was Agnes C. Hall.

Agnes Hall's particular interests were botany and agriculture, and she wrote for several reference works besides Rees's. In her spare time she also wrote novels (pen name: Rosalie St. Clair), including *The Banker's Daughters of Bristol*. Give it a miss. Agnes's favorite activity was translating from French. Mainly the tourist guides of the period, mainly titled *Travels in . . .* One of her translations was *Travels in the African Seas* by French herbalist Bory Saint-Vincent, who had knocked around quite a bit and published a map showing the Atlantic location of Atlantis.

Early in life, after jumping ship in Mauritius during the French expedition to Australia, Saint-Vincent wandered round the local islands, then went home to join Napoleon's army and became so Bonapartist that for years after Napoleon had lost, Saint-Vincent was obliged to live in disguise. Finally, by 1820, memories had faded, so he came out from behind the beard. And his botanical work became known. In 1828 he was chosen to head the French (military-scientific) expedition to Morea in the Greek Peloponnese, which was Turkish but wanted to be Greek.

The Greeks there had been fighting Turkish occupation since 1821. By 1825 the Turks had brought in Egyptian troops, and nasty atrocities were piling up on both sides. The French, English, and Russians were keen to keep the anarchy from spreading, so in 1827 an allied fleet arrived and moved into the Bay of Navarino, where the Turkish-Egyptian fleet was anchored. At one point a Royal Navy frigate sent a boat to request that sorry chaps but could a Turkish fireship please be moved. Missing the point, the Turkish captain loosed off, killing several of the Brit boat crew. All hell broke loose. When it was over, three quarters of the Turkish-Egyptian fleet was sunk and the accidental battle of Navarino was over.

One of the Royal Navy ships was the *Talbot*, carrying fifteen-year-old William Neale, who later used his navy experiences in novels like *The Port Admiral*. Fellow writer and retired navy hero Frederick Marryat rubbished the book, and he and Neale ended up having a scuffle with walking sticks in Trafalgar Square. Marryat knew inventor Charles Babbage and was designer of a lifeboat. After a brilliant navy career he turned to writing (with more success than Neale) such classics as *Peter Simple* (1834) and *Mr. Midshipman Easy* (1836).

In 1837 he traveled for a year in Canada and the United States, where he met Eliphalet Nott, the controversial and innovative president of Union College in Schenectady, New York. Nott had dragged the college into modernity with lottery-sourced finance and a curriculum including science, medicine, and engineering, and as a result by 1820 the biggest graduating class in the United States. Nott was noisy on such subjects as slavery (anti), booze (anti), and religion (pro). He held over thirty patents for various efficient heating systems, including the "Nott stove," which successfully burned hard-to-burn smokeless anthracite.

As did the boiler of his new steamboat, the SS *Novelty*, built in 1826 at the Novelty shipyards on Fourteenth Street, New York City. After a number of ownership changes, in 1861 the Novelty Works were given the contract to manufacture the turret of the latest naval secret weapon, the ironclad semisubmersible USS *Monitor.* John Ericsson's revolutionary ship was designed to patrol shallow southern coastal waters and to enforce Lincoln's embargo on Confederate merchant shipping. This program was directed by Secretary of the Navy Gideon Welles, who at the start of the Civil War found himself with the job of building a Union navy virtually from scratch. So he recruited people like John Murray Forbes.

Forbes was already rich from early opium smuggling to China and then from speculative and very successful railroad investment. By this time he was also building ships, which, at Welles's suggestion, he sold to Congress for the U.S. Navy. And got even richer. Forbes also supported the black cause and on one occasion sheltered fugitive John Brown. Later in life he became involved in humanitarian work, financing Lifeboat Societies and Sailors' Retirement Homes. He also encouraged northerners to settle in Florida and wintered there himself.

In 1872 one of Forbes's Florida guests was the painter William Morris Hunt, who was recovering from the effects of the Boston Fire, which had destroyed all his paintings, including a portrait of Lincoln and five large works by the French artist Jean François Millet. With whom in 1851 Hunt had spent two years (of a twelve-year stay in Europe) at Barbizon, outside Paris, learning to paint in Millet's realistic style. While in Florida Hunt painted landscapes. One was *Rainbow Creek*. Five years later he was at work on two large murals for the Assembly Chamber of the New York State Capitol.

At one point back in 1859 Hunt had run a summer painting school attended by writer Henry James. Ten years later James was comfortably settled in Europe, writing novels about Americans in Europe (and full of the newly fashionable psychological realism). James went over famously with famous French and English writers, and when he settled in a small village in Sussex his local cronies included Kipling, Ford Madox Ford, and Joseph Conrad.

One of James's close friends was young American writer Edith Wharton, who came from the same upper-crust background as James. She wintered in Paris, summered in Newport, social-seasoned in New York, and spent her life writing about it all. Condemned to an unhappy marriage, she found brief sexual fulfillment in a secret affair with an American journalist. This may explain her admiration for a Romanian princess and writer for whom the same kind of satisfaction was a daily occurrence.

Sometimes referred to unkindly as the *grande horizontale*, Princess Marthe Bibesco was beautiful, talented, intelligent, and "knew" everybody in Europe from royals to politicos. Her books were greeted by Marcel Proust as masterpieces of style. At the same time Bibesco was also turning out bodice-rippers under the pen name Lucille Decaux. She spent her life traveling around Europe staying in palaces after losing her own in Romania. Above all (with a husband busy on innumerable love affairs), Bibesco was a man-eater. As in (at least): a German crown prince, a French president, a king of Spain, a French socialist MP, and a British prime minister. Whose air minister and "friend" of Bibesco was Lord Thomas of Cardington.

In 1924 Thomas had okayed the construction of two passenger-carrying airships, the R100 (to be built by a private company) and the R101 (government-built). Managing director of the R100 company was Charles Dennistoun Burney. After a successful transatlantic run by the R100 in June 1930, the future of airships ended with the catastrophic crash in France of the R101 later that year. After World War II the inventive Burney turned to development of stern-fishing trawlers, and in 1954 the first of these was off Newfoundland, soon to be joined by many others. By 1960 the Newfoundland Grand Banks cod were being fished in unsustainable numbers and the "factory-ship" trawlers were generating serious Canadian opposition.

The protests were led by longtime Newfoundland legislator Chesley Carter. Who later became a member of the Canadian Senate Committee on Science Policy and in 1975 helped found the Planetary Association for Clean Energy. By 1989 PACE had thirty-six hundred members in sixty countries and was a U.N.-recognized Nongovernment Organization. In 1983 the association conference on nonconventional power in Augusta, Georgia, heard a paper on the Earth's gravitational field as a source of energy.

The original experimental work for the paper had been done a few years earlier (before his death) by Berkeley physicist WILLIAM HOOPER.

CHAPTER FORTY-TWO

Joseph Hewes,

JOSEPH HEWES (NC) was forty-six. An experienced businessman with a fleet of ships plying Caribbean trade out of the North Carolina port of Edenton and with twenty years of commercial relations with the Brits, Hewes was a reluctant rebel. But in the end he became a revolutionary with the best of them. He never said much in Congress but worked twelve-hour days, without food, on anything Congress gave him to do, including the committee handling military provisions and materials. No-fool Hewes also rented ships to Congress for a healthy profit.

He was on the Committee of Secret Correspondence (the information network uniting the colonies) with another Edentonian, Samuel Johnston. About whom they said: "Johnston commanded respect but not love." He probably didn't care. Yale, landowning Johnston was no rabble-rouser, but he saw the way the wind was blowing. After the war he was three-time state governor and then U.S. senator, as well as the state's first Masonic grand master and member of the board of directors of the first Bank of the United States.

In 1791 the bank was given a twenty-year charter. Headquartered in Philadelphia, it had eight branches from Boston to New Orleans. The bank had been set up with $10 million seed capital (20 percent government, 80 percent private), and its main responsibilities were to protect the new paper currency, regulate the number of notes each state could issue, and handle the country's major borrowings (as in the case of the 1803 Louisiana Purchase). But when time came for the bank charter to be renewed in 1811 it wasn't. Because by that time the bank was 70 percent foreign-owned.

The bank's agent in London and the rest of Europe was Englishman Francis Baring, general merchant, then army supplier, then financial advisor to the American government, and finally international negotiator of loans and debts. And quite a salesman. By 1795 Baring had sold eight hundred thousand dollars' worth of U.S. bonds to finance deals with North African states and (in 1803) over $11 millions' worth to pay for Louisiana. He had also bought a million acres of American land. No surprise, his personal wealth was legendary.

Which was why he could afford to buy stately home Stratton Park from the Duke of Bedford and have it spruced up by architect George Dance the Younger, who gave Baring a Doric portico, an Ionic hall, and a Pompeian library (you get the feel). Dance's six years of study in Rome with the likes of Piranesi made him your man if you wanted the new "classical" look. And he changed the face of London with his buildings (temporarily, as most of them were later knocked down except, alas, Finsbury Circus). Dance also painted portraits, including one of famous actress and Prince of Wales's mistress, Mary Robinson the poet.

Whose meter in her "Haunted Beach" was copied by Wordsworth in one of his poems. While in another he celebrated Mary's namesake, contemporary, and another celeb, Mary Robinson the shepherdess. Hyped as a tourist attraction ("The Maid of Buttermere") by guidebooks on the Lake District (northeastern England and where Wordsworth lived). Mary the shepherdess became nationally famous in 1802 when the villainous John Hatfield entered her life. Hatfield was already married to the illegitimate daughter of a relation of the Duke of Rutland, who kept Hatfield financially afloat. After deserting the wife and children in America, Hatfield returned to more debts and forgeries in London and was jailed. Bailed by a woman he then bigamously married, made pregnant, and deserted, Hatfield headed north, amassing debts as he went.

Arriving in the Lake District and faking a name, he persuaded Mary the shepherdess to marry him. Exposed as a fraud, he fled, then was caught and hanged. Poor Mary thought she had married an army officer related to the Earl of Hopetoun and named Alexander Hope. No such luck. The real Hope was a happily married MP. By 1808 he was a major general, ahead of him a successful career as innovative commandant of the Royal Military College, Sandhurst, where he raised standards and modernized the curriculum.

Hope was also a friend of notorious American runaway Aaron Burr, recently acquitted of treason on a technicality and by now briefly in Scotland staying with such pals of Hope as eminent novelist Sir Walter Scott. Back in London Burr checked in at the home of all-purpose guru Jeremy Bentham, already world-renowned for his political and philo-sophical utterings. Bentham was the "father" of utilitarianism ("all acts should be judged by whether or not they bring the greatest happiness to the greatest number").

Bentham corresponded about these thoughts with Simón Bolívar, the tsar, the Duke of Wellington, John Quincy Adams, Madison, Jefferson, Mehmet Ali of Egypt, and many other world leaders. His work was translated into all the European languages. Bentham was both a social and political reformer, arguing for universal voting, women's rights, free trade, international law, and a world court. A workaholic who also played the violin and designed a new, more humane "panopticon" prison (adopted in the United States), Bentham still found time to sit for a bust by Peter Turnerelli.

The Belfast-born sculptor had trained in Italy and was influenced (like everybody) by the Italian sculptor Canova. By 1805, when Ben-tham sat, Turnerelli was already sculptor to the royal family, clay-modeling tutor to George III's daughters, and in consequence had an order book full of commissions for busts of aristos, social climbers, and majesties, including Louis XVIII of France. Turnerelli's most rewarding piece was his 1829 bust of Irishman Daniel O'Connell. Ten thousand copies were made and sold like hot cakes, earning Turnerelli fifty thou-sand pounds. Back then, a lot of bread.

1829 was the year of O'Connell's greatest triumph. Since 1799 he'd been a very successful lawyer in Ireland. A moderate reformer (he'd seen the French Revolution from close up and no thanks), his ultimate aim was independence for Ireland. But step one was political rights for Catholics. Ireland had a Parliament with a built-in Orange (pro-England, Protestant) majority. Catholics were barred from all government jobs. From 1812 onward O'Connell had regular run-ins with the Brit chief secretary for Ireland, Robert Peel, who felt that Catholics shouldn't be given rights because they owed allegiance to a foreign power, i.e.,the pope. However, O'Connell gradually mobilized the entire country and in the end wore the Brits down. In 1829 the Catholic Emancipation Act was passed, and O'Connell became an Irish folk hero with a Dublin Street named after him.

Eighteen twenty-nine was also a great year for Peel (O'Connell called him "Orange" Peel, and the pair nearly had two duels). By this time Peel was British home secretary (SecState) and responsible for law and order. He completely reorganized the criminal code, removing all or part of over five hundred outdated statutes, closing legal loopholes, and slashing the cobwebbed gobbledygook from legalese that in some cases hadn't changed for centuries. In 1829 Peel finally won his battle to establish the London Metropolitan Police Force. In recognition of his success the new officers of the law were referred to (after Robert Peel's name) as "bobbies," or in Ireland, as "peelers" (after ditto). They still are.

London was the second place to establish a police force, after Glasgow, Scotland, where they'd done it in 1800. By 1868 the Glasgow force included a clerk, William Mackintosh. In 1883 his son Charles Rennie Mackintosh began attending the Glasgow School of Art before taking up architecture. Over the next decades Mackintosh made his mark on Glasgow with his unique, eclectic style (love it or hate it). Mackintosh's work was kind of "art-nouveau-meets-fake-medieval" (at the time, faux Baronial was all the rage and Scotland filled up with imitation Sir Ivanhoe castles with turrets and crenellations and stuff now beloved of the Scottish Tourist Office). Mackintosh (and his wife) designed everything from the new Glasgow Art School to ladies' tea rooms and middle-class suburban houses.

One of their fellow students at the art school was Stansmore Dean, part of the group now known as the "Glasgow Girls." Glasgow women in art had recently made a statement by opening the Lady Artists' Club, known for its risqué habit of holding life classes (men not allowed). Stansmore would eventually have her own studio, paint à la Whistler, and exhibit as far afield as Buffalo, New York. First, however, she made it to Paris and the Colarossi studio, where in 1890 she studied (along with hundreds of others) under Gustave Courtois.

Temporary fellow student Henri Farman gave up classes with Courtois when it became a choice between art and cycle-racing. Henri had an obsession with things mechanical and after cycling came auto-racing. And then his dream: building, flying, and designing airplanes. In 1907 Farman bought the first airplane available for sale and modified it. In 1908 he did the first cross-country flight in Europe (seventeen miles in twenty minutes). Next came his introduction of ailerons (for stability) and finally the Farman Aviation Works, near Versailles, where he build the first (twelve-passenger) long-distance airliner (London-Paris) and turned out more than twelve thousand military biplanes for World War I.

In 1910 German Ernst Heinkel used a set of Farman plans to build his first machine. By 1922 he was making catapult-launched aircraft for the Japanese navy. By 1936 he had designed the twin-engined Heinkel 111, ordered by the Luftwaffe in 1936 and destined to become Germany's standard medium bomber in the early part of World War II. Fully loaded with bombs, it reached 250 mph at fifteen thousand feet. In 1938 the Heinkel 111 was used for drop-tests of an experimental wooden aircraft, the Heinkel 176, a rocket plane using hydrogen peroxide fuel in an engine designed by Hellmuth Walter. A demonstration in 1939 failed to rouse Hitler's interest and the test-dropping was dropped.

Walter moved on to U-boat submarine design. By 1943 his experimental wartime peroxide-fueled U-793 was twice as fast as the fastest submarine and faster than any surface ship. To handle the extra speed Walter changed the entire approach to submarine hull design, removing the sharp lines, stripping off the guns, and reducing the conning tower. Walter's new hull was rounder, blimp-shaped, and able to move through the water more easily at high speed. Walter's concept of a submarine that could remain submerged indefinitely was taken up after the war, and his hull design was incorporated in the first American ballistic missile submarine, the USS *George Washington*.

Which carried sixteen Polaris nuclear missiles and needed accurate navigational positioning in order to fire them accurately. No problem: In 1960 came the first Transit navigational satellites, superseded in 1989 when twenty-four Global Positioning Satellites were launched.

By the early twenty-first century GPS technology, with its ability to locate you to within a yard, was beginning to be used in the everyday world of automobiles, trucks, and buses. In 2004 the state of Virginia hosted a conference on Intelligent Transportation Systems. One of the conference delegates, the vice president of Routematch, Inc., gave a talk on the integration of Global Information Systems and information technology as an element of integrated transportation management.

The speaker's name was JOSEPH HEWES.

CHAPTER FORTY-THREE

John Penn

JOHN PENN (NC) was thirty-five. And spent more time at parties than in the chamber. A self-taught, successful back-country lawyer, Penn was unobtrusive, unassuming, and according to Benjamin Rush seldom spoke in debates but did a lot of whispering to the people next to him. Penn's otherwise quiet life was interrupted in 1778 by a near-duel with the Congress president, Henry Laurens. On the way to the duel, while giving a hand to the much older Laurens across a muddy street, Penn suggested they drop the whole thing and Laurens agreed.

Laurens had already been involved in at least three duels, each time taking fire but refusing to return it. Respected but not liked, he owned five plantations and before the war had made a ton of money selling the Brits indigo, rice, deerskin, and naval stores. In 1780 he was sent to negotiate a $10 million loan and a peace treaty with the Dutch. On the way, while passing Newfoundland, he was captured by a British warship. Laurens's papers (he dropped them overboard, they fished them out) revealed what he was up to and the Brits charged him with treason. Refusing to cop a plea bargain, Laurens ended up in the top person's jail, the Tower of London.

From which he was sprung in April 1782, exchanging for Lord Cornwallis, whose defeat at Yorktown had just ended the war. Cornwallis was a good general with a been-there done-that career behind him, loved by his men and let down by his political bosses. He thought Yorktown couldn't be defended without a lot of reinforcements. Which were promised and then didn't turn up. So on October 19, 1781, he surrendered. By 1786 he was governor-general of India, busy rooting out corruption and inefficiency, fighting Indian sultans and rajahs, and trying to work out a balance of power among them and between them and London. When his contract ended he found himself doing much the same thing again in Ireland, where things were a good deal less pleasant.

The country was close to civil war between loyalist Protestants (Cornwallis said their favorite pastime was murder) and Catholics. On August 22, 1798, the Catholics got the incompetent support of French general Humbert, who landed in Mayo with over a thousand men and cannon. Humbert skittered around the country for a month attracting Irish volunteers armed with shovels and scythes. Then, finally, faced seventeen thousand Brits, at which point it was hands-up time. Humbert left "with honor." All catchable Irishmen were executed on the spot. Humbert spent a few years kicking his heels back in France, then in 1812 set out for the United States. Two years later he was helping Jackson fight the Brits in New Orleans.

After which he was mysteriously involved in a mysterious plot that was supposed to involve snatching Napoleon from exile on St. Helena and installing him as emperor of Mexico (once the plotters had snatched Mexico from the Spanish). The plotters were a ragtag bunch of three hundred Napoleonic ex-army types headed by Napoleon's ex-general Lallemand, who in March 1818 left for Texas and set up an expedition staging post called *Champ d'Asile* ("The Field of Shelter") on Galveston Island. In September, after running out of food and ammunition, diseased and destitute, with their entire settlement flattened by a hurricane and a twelve-thousand-strong Spanish army on the way, the would-be conquerors of Mexico walked back to New Orleans. Humbert ferried a few.

Given the snail's pace at which news traveled back then, nobody in Paris knew about these catastrophic events, so helpful subscriptions were still being drummed up after the colony had already failed. Most of the drumming was being done by Benjamin Constant, overeducated politico and lover of the dreadful, self-obsessed author Germaine de Staël (and simultaneously many others). Constant also had two wives. Swiss-born liberal, indefatigable defender of press freedom, and in consequence frequently on the run, Constant finally switched sides after meeting Napoleon. When the Great Man was exiled to mid-Atlantic, Constant became misty-eyed about the Emperor's Guard now waiting for their hero and (he fondly imagined) growing their own food in distant Texas. So Constant decided to raise money for them through articles in his newspaper *Minerve*.

The cause was also helped by France's greatest art propagandist, Horace Vernet, who painted *Peace and War*, showing a veteran-turned-farmer leaning on his shovel. Real tear-jerker. In 1824 Vernet got two government commissions for more such iconic images and from then on could do no wrong. Gigantic canvases followed one another extolling the greatness of various aspects of French history. Some of it (the colonization of Algeria) quite recent. In 1828 Vernet was given every second-rate artist's dream, the directorship of the French Academy in Rome, where he hung around with real talent like Stendhal, Mendelssohn, and Berlioz.

At Vernet's leaving party in 1834 the guest of honor was Vernet's new friend Danish sculptor Bertel Thorwaldsen. By the time Vernet met him Thorwaldsen had been in Rome for over thirty years and was famous, on nodding terms with Bavarian and Danish royalty, and designer of the gigantic Lion of Lucerne carved into the cliff over the Swiss city. Thorwaldsen made pin money with portrait busts (Byron, Schiller, Sir Walter Scott, minor Russian aristos, etc.). This helped to finance his day job doing sculptures of primarily Classical themes with input from an archeology friend who kept him historically accurate. At his peak Thorwaldsen got the ultimate Roman accolade, a commission to do Pope Pius VII's monument.

In 1824 Thorwaldsen's friend the German diplomat Baron Bunsen introduced him to a young English aristo, Philip Pusey, who was in Rome with his new bride. In 1828 as Pusey was leaving he commissioned Thorwaldsen to do a relief on the pedestal of the font at the German Chapel. Pusey then returned to England and a life of farming.

Two years later he was a member of the Royal Society thanks to his new agricultural idea: using lush, early feed grown in watermeadows to fatten large flocks of ewes who then had early lambs. Pusey was an agrotech nerd and one of the first to use the new drainpipes to channel runoff water. He also helped set up the Royal Agricultural Society in 1840 and edited its journal, writing articles on fertilizer, sheep breeding, and farm machinery. In 1851 he was the first to test the McCormick reaper, newly arrived from the United States.

Cyrus Hall McCormick's patent for the reaper had just expired, and he was fighting imitators with the aid of high-profile lawyers like Abraham Lincoln, as well as boosting sales with mass production, advertising, demonstrations, guarantees, and consumer financing. It all worked. By the 1880s Cyrus was selling fifty thousand machines a year as far afield as Australia and Argentina.

In May 1886 during public demonstrations calling for an eight-hour-day strike workers outside the McCormick works in Chicago were shot at by police. Two days later a group of anarchists organized another protest rally and a bomb was thrown killing seven policemen. All known anarchists were rounded up and eventually seven were given the death penalty even though no evidence was produced that would have connected them to the bombing. When it was too late, in 1893 Illinois governor John Altgeld granted them full posthumous pardons.

In 1907 came the opening words of a new novel titled *The Bomb*: "My name is Rudolph Schnaubelt and I threw the bomb . . ." The novel's author was Frank Harris, "scoundrel and pornographer" (as one eminent biography puts it). In 1871 Harris had emigrated from Britain to the United States, qualified in law, and then returned to England in 1875. By 1883 he was editing the London *Evening News* and filling it with tabloid stories of aristocratic peccadilloes and stock-market scandals. In 1886 he moved to the *Fortnightly Review* where in his eight years he recruited George Bernard Shaw and Max Beerbohm as drama critics.

Harris's life was filled with boozy lunches, missed appointments, raucous shouting matches, and sex. He ran two mistresses and had two wives. He went on to ownership of the *Saturday Review* and *Vanity Fair* and built La Réserve super-luxury hotel in Beaulieu-sur-Mer on the

French Riviera (still there). In 1922 he spilled the beans in an immensely long, erotic-fantasy autobiographical work: *My Life and Loves*. In 1891, while editing the *Fortnightly Review*, Harris also discovered H. G. Wells, a quiet socialist teacher with several mistresses and dreams of a better world.

Wells was soon writing short stories and drama reviews. In 1895 he became instantly world famous with his first novel, *The Time Machine*. By 1902, with several major novels (including *War of the Worlds*) under his belt, Wells was being taken seriously enough to lecture at the Royal Institution ("The Discovery of the Future") and was foretelling the atomic bomb, world war, and tanks as well as generally holding forth about the future of society.

In 1904 Wells spoke at a London University evening meeting of the Sociology Society in response to a speech on eugenics by Francis Galton. Who was Darwin's cousin and had for some years also been obsessed with the cool new science of statistics. Galton, archnoodler, invented a small pocket ticker and used it to count the number of attractive women he passed during a long walk. He made a note of the frequency with which people fidgeted at boring scientific meetings. He analyzed biographical dictionaries to see how often eminent figures were related to other eminent figures. In one experiment he measured 9,337 people.

Galton's theory of eugenics reckoned that if marriage were limited to intelligent, energetic, hard-working, moral, good-looking people and denied to everybody else the human race would improve. After listening to Galton, Wells picked up on what he believed to be a flaw in the argument. What, asked Wells, about clever, hard-working crooks, and stupid, lazy aristocrats?

In 1890 E. R. Henry of the London Police Force asked about possible use of Galton's latest discovery, fingerprints, which Galton had discovered remained exactly the same in any individual all the way from birth to death and acted like an identification mark. Henry thought fingerprints might be useful in nailing criminals who'd left theirs behind at scenes of crime. Turned out to be right.

In honor of this, in 1915 Galton's right forefinger print was used as part of the logo for the new International Association for Criminal Identification (later they dropped the "Criminal"). No surprise, by the 1930s the IAI had developed a close working relationship with the FBI. In 1995 the FBI established the world's biggest computerized fingerprint facility (42 million prints) in Clarksville, West Virginia.

In 1998 they signed an agreement with nearby West Virginia University as a result of which the university opened the world's first degree course in forensic and investigative sciences. Three majors were offered: forensic examiner, forensic biology, and forensic chemistry.

Majors in forensic chemistry were taught by the chemistry faculty, which in 2006 included associate professor JOHN PENN.

CHAPTER FORTY-FOUR

Edward Rutledge J.

EDWARD RUTLEDGE (SC) was twenty-six. And worried that independence would put power in the hands of the "cunning" northerners with their hard-left, "leveling" (egalitarian) ideas. He was a London-trained lawyer, a member of the South Carolina elite, and reluctant to go to war, favoring a deal that would give America autonomy within the British Empire. As late as June 1776 he was still lobbying (he got references to slavery removed from the Declaration).

On September 6 that year, together with "leveler" John Adams and middle-of-the-road Ben Franklin, the conservative Rutledge stepped off a barge at British military headquarters on Staten Island to be met by a guard of honor and the leader of the Brit negotiating team, Admiral Richard Howe (known from his swarthy complexion as "Black Dick"). Howe asked for the Declaration to be withdrawn. The Americans said no. After three hours it was over and war was inevitable. Two days later the Brits took New York.

Howe was known to be generally sympathetic to the American cause, and for this reason parliamentary hard-liners in London worked behind his back to make things difficult. Once hostilities were official Howe did his best with his mission to blockade the American coastline and prevent French supplies from getting in. But the ships and backup he needed never materialized. Unable to trust his own government, in

1778 Howe resigned and went home, where he was attacked in the press and put out to grass.

Five years later a new government gave him command again and he nursed the Royal Navy through an outbreak of peace (no jobs). Things warmed up as the Anglo-French situation turned scary. In 1790 there were rumors of an imminent French invasion and Howe was put in charge of the Channel Fleet. The same year he cleaned up the chaotic naval messaging system (an invitation to dinner was often signaled by hanging a tablecloth over the side and signals could only be sent to all ships at once). Howe introduced the idea of using flags to represent a numerical code.

Thirteen years later Admiral Home Popham took signaling reform all the way and published *Telegraphic Signals.* Popham's system used flags to represent the numbers 0–9. Flying two 1's meant "10+1." Flying three 1's meant "100+10+1." Numbers indicated by flags could then be checked off against a code book where each number represented a word or phrase. By 1813 Popham's signalers were able to choose from six thousand phrases and sixty thousand words. Popham was also an entreprenurial type. Back in 1787 when peacetime naval jobs were few and far between he'd bought a ship and gone into Far Eastern trade. When war with the French looked likely he got back in service. In 1804 he was asked to take a look at a new high-tech idea being offered to the Admiralty by an American inventor. It was a "submarine bomb" (a floating mine).

Inventor Robert Fulton had been back and forth between the French and English, playing them off against each other for his new terror weapon. Tactic didn't work. After the Brits turned him down in 1797 Fulton spent time in Paris being number *trois* in a *ménage à trois* with the American Joel Barlow and wife. He also built his *Nautilus.* The twenty-foot wooden boat was crewed by two men cranking a handle to turn a propeller and sunk to their shoulders in the water. The aim was to creep, unseen, up-current of a target ship and release the mines. The current would then do the rest (wooden cask, a hundred pounds of gunpowder, cork float, flintlock mechanism on top, gizmo eventually bumps into ship's hull, bang). This time the Brits paid Fulton just to stay away from the French.

Fulton's most successful scheme was for a paddle-wheel steamboat. In the long run, with financial help from rich American partner and U.S. minister to France Robert Livingston, Fulton returned to the States and by 1807 had a working prototype steaming up and down the Hudson. Fulton may have had the steamboat idea from an early working acquaintance with the English Lord Stanhope, who was interested in building a canal back in the days when Fulton was also in that business. Stanhope already had a steamboat patent and was a serious spare-time geek.

During the day he was in the House of Lords haranguing the government on liberal issues, including parliamentary reform, the French Revolution (he called himself "Citizen Stanhope"), freedom of the press, and the activities of radical activist friends who were being dumped in the Australian penal colony. In his other spare time Stanhope invented a printing press, a pyrometer, fireproofing (his demo involved burning the ground floor while interested parties ate ice cream on the upper floor, unscathed), a multiplying-and-dividing machine, and a floating mine (before Fulton).

Stanhope was also impossible to live with, subsisting as he did on soup and sweetened barley water. Members of his family left him as soon as they could. One such early absconder was Stanhope's daughter Hester. From 1803 to 1806 she played hostess for her bachelor uncle William Pitt (prime minister). In 1810 she went to Gibraltar, then Malta (where she took a lover), then (with lover) Istanbul, Cairo (where the viceroy entertained her lavishly and she responded in like style), Palestine, Lebanon, Syria, and finally Lebanon again. Lady Hester threw money about and shocked locals by wearing Turkish male clothing.

In 1813 while they were in Syria Hester's lover went back to England when his father cracked the whip. A year later Hester was back in Lebanon, alone, settling into a house in the hills behind Sidon and later moving deeper into the hills to a ruin at Dar Jun. Where she rebuilt, refurbished, set out a garden, and, surrounded by her thirty cats, servants, and slaves, held lavish court for visiting European and local bigwigs. Gradually her debts grew unmanageable. Finally, when her pension back home was diverted to pay the creditors, Hester wrote a complaining letter to Queen Victoria, took to her bed, and died.

In 1816 one of Hester's more eccentric visitors was William Bankes. Who dressed like an Arab, sported a bushy beard, and stayed with Hester for three weeks before leaving after an argument. At the time Bankes (recently rich from an inheritance) was on his first trip around the Middle East "collecting" antiques, sketching, writing reams of descriptive scribble, drawing maps, and copying hieroglyphs. On his second trip, in 1818 (financed by an even bigger inheritance), Bankes excavated, "collected," even more Egyptian bits, and barged back to England an obelisk, which he erected on his estate at Kingston Lacy, Dorset, in front of the house. This was a modest brick residence that Bankes was now able to afford to upgrade (after yet another inheritance) with the help of a young English architect he'd met in Syria and who was now doing home-improvement jobs for the gentry. In 1835 Charles Barry encased Kingston Lacy in stone and called it "Italianate."

Barry was on the verge of greatness. The previous year he'd watched the Houses of Parliament become a smoldering heap of ashes and was now waiting to hear who was going to get the rebuilding job. He did. And it took him the rest of his life. Barry's coworker on what is perhaps the most famous piece of pseudo in architectural history was A. W. N. Pugin, who in 1841 got so caught up in Gothic he wrote *The True Principles of Pointed or Christian Architecture*, all about how medieval buildings were good for you and we all needed more of them.

Music to the ears of a new young immigrant in New York. In a country short of architects, cabinetmaker Richard Upjohn drew houses so well people asked him to build for them. He eventually produced a how-to book of church designs, which was copied all over the country as far west as Wisconsin. In New York he entirely rebuilt Trinity Church in Pugin's style, and when it was finished in 1846 it kicked off the American Gothic Revival and church fathers regarded it as the bee's knees.

Not so sculptor Horatio Greenough, who thought it was dreadful and said so. He might have been having a bad day, since much the same remarks had been recently passed regarding his own monumental statue of George Washington. Intended for the new Capitol Rotunda, it showed G.W. naked with a cloak over his knees and pointing to the sky.

Critics made noises about "getting into the bath." Then the statue turned out too heavy and became the target of pigeons outside for sixty years. Ended up in the Smithsonian. Greenough's other customers seemed happy enough with his "portrait busts" of such as Adams, Lafayette, Fenimore Cooper, and Sam Morse.

From 1861 on, when Morse wasn't inventing the telegraph or being a professor of design or the American agent for Daguerre's new camera, he was on the charter board of Vassar College. Matthew Vassar was a very successful brewer with interests in banking, whaling, and other enterprises in Poughkeepsie. He decided to do something philanthropic with his money and after seven years' planning got the go-ahead for a women's college. The project benefited from the attentions of a major promoter of women's causes, Sarah J. Hale, editor of *Godey's Lady's Magazine*, in which she agitated (among many other causes) for the completion of the Bunker Hill Monument, Liberian colonization, the renovation of Mount Vernon, the end of tight lacing in women's dress, and the use of anesthetic during childbirth.

Sarah also made Matthew drop the "Female" from the college name. And she made sure the faculty included women. So when Vassar opened in 1865 Maria Mitchell was the first female professor of astronomy in America. A self-taught amateur (higher education wasn't available to women at the time), Mitchell was a formidable woman, active in promoting women's education, organizing Women's Clubs all over the country, first woman member of the American Academy of Arts and Sciences, and the discoverer of a comet ("Miss Mitchell's Comet"). And her students loved her.

One of the stars to come out of the department soon after Mitchell's retirement in 1888 was Phoebe Waterman, who went on to become one of the first two women to take a Ph.D. at Berkeley. In 1913 Phoebe was offered a job at the National Observatory in Cordova, Argentina, and boarded ship for Buenos Aires. After an on-board romance she returned to the United States almost immediately and a year later was married to chemist Otto Haas. When the two met, Haas had been heading for South America with some of his firm's new product. Haas and his partner Otto Rohm ran a chemical company. Later, in 1920, Rohm returned to the subject of his German doctorate (acrylic chemistry) and developed polymethyl methacrylate (PMMA). Which by 1936 was on the market as "Plexiglas."

By the 1950s PMMA was being used as a mold (key attribute: it didn't stick) by surgeons making templates for pieces of a person's bone they were going to replace with prostheses. By 2002 the Zimmer Corporation was using PMMA to service the orthopedic market and giving five hundred thousand dollars to the education and outreach program of the American Orthopedic Foot and Ankle Society.

In 2005 one of the society's major figures was orthopedic surgeon EDWARD RUTLEDGE.

CHAPTER FORTY-FIVE

Thos Heyward Junr

THOMAS HEYWARD, JR. (SC) was thirty. And hoped till the very last minute that the war would be canceled. Patrician, handsome, London-trained lawyer and member of a rich, plantation-owning family, after two years in Congress in 1778 Heyward returned to Charleston and military service as commander of an artillery company. He had an active war, was wounded and then captured when the Brits took Charleston in 1780 and stuck him in a Florida prison until he was prisoner-exchanged a year later.

Fellow prisoner (in 1782 exchanged for General "Gentleman Johnny" Burgoyne) was Heyward's commander during the Charleston defense, General William Moultrie. Who back in 1776 had fought off a British attack on the Sullivan's Island fort in Charleston Harbor. For which Moultrie was a hero and Congress gave him his rank. In 1783 Moultrie went into politics and became state governor. That year he was also the first president of the Society of the Cincinnati (named after the Roman hero), a vet organization lobbying to get Congress to settle the up-to-four-years' back pay owed to many officers. Society members got a fancy badge. Membership was (and still is) hereditary, raising Ben Franklin's eyebrows for being unrepublican.

One of the Cincinnati founder members was French military engineer and architect Pierre L'Enfant, pal of and courier for George Washington. It was L'Enfant's idea to set aside a piece of malaria-infested swampland for common use by all the states and build a capital city there. In 1784 L'Enfant got the contract to design Washington, D.C. By 1792, after disagreements with the federal commissioners about who was in charge, L'Enfant got the boot. And joined Alexander Hamilton's Society for Establishing Useful Manufactures. This included designing a new city (Paterson, New Jersey). When L'Enfant's grid plan ignored minor inconveniences like hills and valleys he was once again fired.

S.E.U.M. president was William Duer, who speculated with the shareholders' money and was also sacked. Duer was a recent immigrant from his estates in the Caribbean, an active revolutionary from 1776, and spent two years in Congress. Then went back to business. Highly placed friends put him in the way of lucrative contracts to supply the army. He moved on to trade in stocks and bonds. You know where this is going. An insider-dealing scandal forced him out of the market in 1790 but he wouldn't give up. In 1792 Duer got an inside tip that the Bank of the United States was going to buy the Bank of New York, so he used other people's money to buy a zillion shares. When the tip turned out to be a dud, hundreds of investors were ruined, the market nearly collapsed, and Duer went to jail.

One of Duer's unfortunate clients was Alexander Macomb, who'd just bought 3,670,715 acres of upstate New York. So after the bank-share debacle Macomb had to unload, and 210,000 acres went to Frenchman Pierre Chassanis, whose scheme was to bring aristos over from revolutionary France and start a "New France" in what he described fancifully as "Castorland." Backers went bankrupt, the small print was of the worst kind, and the whole scheme went down the *toilette*. Chassanis had to sell most of the land to James Donatien Le Ray de Chaumont. Who was an old family friend of Franklin from his Paris days and on first-name terms with everybody American who mattered.

In 1812 the commissioners of the Erie Canal Board sent Le Ray to Europe to raise $6 million, but with another war with England looking closer than was comfortable the bankers wouldn't play. Eventually the canal (363 miles long, forty feet wide, and four feet deep) was built with $7,143,789.86 of state money. One of the commissioners was Stephen

Van Rensselaer II, among the richest men in New York state and owner of a twelve-thousand-square-mile spread with three thousand tenants. To whom Van Rensselaer gave perpetuity leases and charged low rents so the tenants had spare money to invest in improving the land. Van Rensselaer also failed twice to be elected state governor and made a hash of invading Canada in 1812, surrendering a thousand men and losing his general's rank.

In 1824 Van Rensselaer hired Amos Eaton to do a geological survey of the land alongside the canal. Eaton (itinerant teacher and ex-jailbird) asked Van Rensselaer for three hundred bucks to open a school to teach practical science and the two became involved in setting up what was eventually known as Rensselaer Polytechnic Institute. As its first senior professor in 1825 Eaton began a long and successful teaching career with a floating summer geology camp. Students were housed, fed, and taught on canal boats.

One of the floating learners was Joseph Henry, who would go on to fame: inventor of the electromagnet, discoverer (simultaneously with Faraday) of how to turn magnetism into electricity, helper of Sam Morse (Henry told him about how an electromagnet would cause a switch to operate at the other end of a wire because he'd had already done it), major educational reformer, first secretary of the Smithsonian, and president of the National Academy of Science.

And in 1842 supporter of a young English Jewish academic, J. J. Sylvester, in his (failed) attempt to get a math job at Columbia. Sylvester had already resigned from University College, London, and the University of Virginia, so after the New York rejection he returned to London, took singing lessons from Gounod, taught Florence Nightingale, and studied law. And then met math prodigy Arthur Cayley. The two of them changed the world of algebra. Sylvester's major advances in the discipline meshed with Cayley's work on a theory of invariants and quantics. Don't ask. Cayley wrote a thousand math papers and ended up the United Kingdom's leading mathematician. Mathematicians (and only mathematicians) say his work was famous for its clarity. Not a term that would describe the thinking of his brother Charles.

Bald, shortsighted, untidily dressed, Charles Cayley was the absent-minded professor in spades. Apart from translating the Gospels into Iroquois, Charles studied Italian at King's College, London, under Gabriele Rossetti and in 1855 while doing a major translation of Dante's *Divina Commedia* met the Rossetti family and fell hard for daughter Christina. Who called him her "special mole" and turned him down because he was agnostic. But she wrote poems to him.

Early in life Christina became what her brother called a "fountain sealed." Repressed and hypochondriac, prone to depression, angina, abscesses, and not too attractive, she fell three times: The first she left when he turned Catholic, the second was the special mole, and the third was a painter she kept secret. Unrequited was Christina's middle name, giving rise to verses like: "Hug me, kiss me, suck my juices." Surrounded by suicidal Pre-Raphaelite Brotherhood artists (her brother Dante Gabriel was a leading light in the brotherhood and Christina posed for them twice as the Virgin Mary), Christina ended her days religious and writing the Christmas carol "In the Bleak Midwinter."

One of Christina's close friends was not surprisingly a vicar, Charles Dodgson (aka Lewis Carroll). He was tall and slim with long hair and a stammer, deaf in the right ear, and everybody liked him. He was also an accomplished mathematician (crazy for Euclid) and as well as holding a fellowship at Oxford taught in local schools and gave private lessons. After a mysterious incident with the eleven-year-old daughter of his college dean, Dodgson wrote *Alice in Wonderland* and then the weird books and poems that changed the nature of children's literature. Dodgson's passion was for photography and prepubescent girls, many of whom he photographed (some *"sans habillements,"* as he put it). Arguments still rage as to whether he was a repressed pedophile. His other on-camera sitters were the famous (painters Millais and Rossetti; Queen Victoria's youngest son) and the not-so-famous (Edward Hill, honorary canon of St. Alban's Cathedral from 1872).

In 1878 Edward's cathedral began to suffer damage (aka "restoration") at the hands of amateur architect and "pompous bully" Lord Grimthorpe, a parliamentary lawyer famous for his controversial statements on virtually everything and who paid £120,000 of his own money for the privilege of "improving" St. Alban's. Grimthorpe redesigned the cathedral front (trashing the great medieval window) and rebuilt naves, cloisters, turrets, and vaulting the way he thought they should be. Unmitigated disaster.

Grimthorpe did a little better designing the clock for the tower of the Houses of Parliament (the clock is often wrongly called "Big Ben," which is the bell). When Grimthorpe died with no children his aristo title went to his nephew Ernest Beckett. Who was probably the father of Violet Trefusis (the mother was Alice Keppel, King Edward VII's mistress). Violet had a magic childhood (frequent visits to Buckingham Palace and letters from Edward VII signed "Kingy"), then two love affairs during World War I, then started the greatest scandal of the period, a passionate lesbian relationship with her old school friend Vita Sackville-West.

Vita played a man, often cross-dressing and calling herself "Julian" on the frequent occasions when the pair were either abroad or in English hotels. Violet's mother insisted she get married so she did, on the understanding that there would be no sexual relationship. Then she went back to Vita. In 1920 the two eloped to France, chased in a small plane by both husbands (lesbian Vita was now married to gay Harold Nicolson). In the end to avoid even greater scandal Violet and hubby Denys left England for Paris.

Where Violet was the *n*th lover of Winnaretta Singer, sewing-machine heiress, immensely wealthy, and married to the gay Prince Edmond de Polignac. Singer went in for riding boots and spankings. She and the prince also ran a salon for the intellectual and artistic demimonde, specializing in composers (Edmond was a talentless amateur). Winnaretta was a great patron and among others supported Horowitz, Rubinstein, and Nadia Boulanger, the legendary composer and piano teacher.

From 1921 Boulanger taught at the American Conservatory in Paris. After several visits to the United States, she became the first woman regularly to conduct the Boston Symphony. During World War II she taught at the Longy School in Cambridge, Massachusetts, and the Juilliard in New York before returning to Paris. Her long teaching career included big-name pupils like Aaron Copland and Leonard Bernstein.

In 1941 (in Boston) and again in 1950 (in Paris) Boulanger taught a young American composer, Robert Middleton. After Paris he returned to the United States and in 1953 joined the music faculty at Vassar (where he was head of department in 1973). To commemorate Vassar's hundredth anniversary the college commissioned Middleton to write an opera-concerto, *Command Performance*, which debuted at Poughkeepsie in 1961.

One of the cast was Metropolitan Opera tenor THOMAS HEY-WARD.

CHAPTER FORTY-SIX

Thomas Lynch Jun

THOMAS LYNCH, JR. (SC), was twenty-six and the youngest signer. And either "uncouth and tedious" (Adams) or "sensible and well-spoken" (Benjamin Rush). Lynch dropped out of London law school, then as a member of the South Carolina planter elite he dutifully went into public service and in 1776 was sent to Congress to look after his sick congressman dad (who had a stroke, was unable to sign the Declaration, and died). Thomas got there just in time for the vote. He'd earlier picked up malaria during his brief military service and doctors advised the health-giving properties of the Caribbean. So Lynch and wife set sail in 1779. The ship went down and they drowned.

Lynch senior had been highly regarded by all as an experienced politico, although he was a moderate who favored colonial autonomy within the British Empire. Because of this he was involved in the cliffhanger 1775 New York negotiations with Lord Drummond. Over a month, the sides came close to agreement on two key issues: England had no right to tax the colonies and America would obey the trading restrictions imposed by Britain. Things were looking good. It seemed as if the moderate southern proreconciliation majority would tip the balance against the radical, proindependence North. Then suddenly Drummond's secret letters to his government (about the talks) were leaked to

Congress. At which point everything hit the fan and any hope of a deal went out the window.

None of this bothered Drummond's relative Henry, son of a viscount and head of the bank acting as paymaster to the U.K. troops in North America. With over ten thousand men to pay, the contract made Henry's bank rich. There were also eighteen U.K. regiments on the books, and average annual profits were healthy enough for Henry to be able to lend Prime Minister Lord North the modern equivalent of $4 million for an election campaign.

Like all young men in the world of finance then and now Henry worked hard and played hard. Particularly at the "boisterous" twelve-member dining club known as "The Gang" (of aristos, financiers, and politicos). A fellow club drunk was ex–wine merchant Thomas Harley, son of an earl and after 1770 Henry's partner in supplying clothing and blankets to the troops in America. Harley had been sheriff of London and was an MP. He was also a mover and shaker in the London financial district. No surprise, Harley was very rich and spent his money (as most of them did) conspicuously. In his case on stately-home real-estate at Berrington Hall, Hertfordshire. In 1778 he refurbished the place (as most of them did) in the latest Neoclassical style. Which usually meant having a colossal Ionic portico stuck on the front of whatever you owned, a posh marble staircase added inside, and (sometimes) a library.

The Berrington Hall refurbishment was done by a father-and-son-in-law team. The grounds were done by the father, Lancelot "Capability" Brown, the greatest landscape gardener in England and famous for creating parks and gardens using natural features to embellish the buildings they surrounded. Brown's best trick was the "ha-ha," a sunken trench that prevented livestock (decorously placed, in a particular setting) from entering another, different setting in which they would not be so decorous. The surprise when visitors came across this hidden feature caused them to exclaim "Ha-ha!" (Or else that's all nonsense and the expression came from the Old English word for hole: *hoeh*.)

Brown's son-in-law, Henry Holland, Jr., reworked the Berrington Hall buildings. Holland's first big job in his own right was Brooks's Club in London. Then he went on to built brick terraces (Sloan Street, Cadogan Place), which became must-haves for the socially aspirant. The star in Holland's architectural crown was Carlton House, London, which he did for the Prince Regent. Holland also embellished many country seats for such as the Althorps, Princess Diana's ancestors. And he renovated the Drury Lane and Covent Garden theaters in London.

While busy on Carlton House Holland saw the work of a young draughtsman, C. H. Tatham, and hired him. By 1793 Tatham was in Rome, drawing, making plaster casts, and picking up bits of ancient ruins for Holland. Over two years he met all the English expats and a couple of U.K. princes having fun. One of the royals was "excavating" with an Irish painter-dealer-spy and social climber, Robert Fagan. The purpose of Fagan's archeology was to find hidden treasures and then sneak them out of Italy to London where they would sell for a fortune. Same went for artworks belonging to Italian princes, panic-stricken in 1796 by the imminent arrival of the invading French and selling heirlooms to people like Fagan at knock-down prices (Titians, Lorrains, etc). Fagan bricked up the loot until such time as the French had gone and in the meantime moved off to Florence to spy for London. When the invaders had gone Fagan unbricked his ill-gotten gains and carried on where he'd left off.

One of Fagan's buyers was Thomas Hope, collector, furniture designer, esthete, and stinking rich because his family was in banking (the Hope Bank helped the United States to buy Louisiana). Hope collected over fifteen hundred ancient vases during his eight years touring the Mediterranean, Turkey, and Egypt, where he also caught the bug for things Pharaonic. Returning to London as the best-informed person on canopic vases, sphinxes, heads of Ra, mummies, and other such Nilotic arcana, Hope then blew away the art world when he opened his Egyptian "Black Room" and issued visitors' passes to the discerning and well-heeled.

Hope was inspired to all this by an 1802 book, *Journey in Upper and Lower Egypt*, written by French diplomat-turned-historian Jean-Dominique Vivant Denon, who'd gone with the scholarly commission that accompanied Napoleon's abortive invasion of Egypt in 1798 (main aim, which failed: cut the Brits off from India). Denon and pals grabbed all they could carry and sketched or measured the rest. When they got home Egyptomania gripped France, where stylish builders added lion-headed, winged everything to everything. Denon later traveled with Napoleon and told him what art to snatch on the way past in Austria, Poland, Italy, Spain, and Germany. Then returned to Paris to be director of imperial museums (i.e., organize the booty).

In 1824 young American ex–military engineer and canal designer Loammi Baldwin II turned up to inspect the fashionable Denon-inspired French monuments and then went back to the States to suggest Bunker Hill ought to be an obelisk. Baldwin had also taken a look at the Antwerp docks. This stood him in good stead when in 1827 he moved on to his magnum opus: the first granite-built, steam-pumped dry docks in America at Charlestown, Massachusetts, and Norfolk, Virginia. Capable of handling the biggest ships in the American fleet.

Baldwin got the job from Secretary to the Navy Samuel L. Southard, a New Jersey lawyer and congressman who might have done an efficient and effective job except for the fact that his plans to enlarge the navy were thwarted by a penny-pinching Congress. As were his plans to send the United States Exploring Expedition to the South Pacific to improve navigational knowledge of the area and draw charts and maps, in response to pressure from businessmen who wanted their cargoes not to hit rocks.

Finally, in 1838 the expedition was approved. Four ships moved off under the command of Charles Wilkes and spent four years sailing down the Pacific, along the Antarctic coastline, and up through the Atlantic. The big event of the trip happened on July 19, 1840, when Wilkes made the discovery of the Antarctic land mass. The flotilla carried 82 officers, 9 scientists and artists, and 342 sailors. It returned with 100,000 artifacts and specimens. Many of which were badly labeled, damaged, or lost in transit to the Smithsonian.

Not good news for the trip's organizer of materials, Charles Pickering, probably the best naturalist in the United States and busiest member of the science team on the expedition. After he'd finished saving and logging what he could (of the badly labeled, damaged, etc.), Pickering set off on his own great mission "to enumerate all the races of man." In October 1843 he visited Egypt, East Africa, Arabia, and India. In 1848 he produced *The Races of Man*. There were, said Pickering, eleven races. The big question (for people who believed biblical chronology): Where had Adam lived (Africa?)? And how had the races separated into eleven over the (too short?) biblical time span? Pickering fudged the issue, probably because of religious pressure.

Not so his friend Samuel Morton. From 1830 Morton began collecting skulls (by mail) from all over the world and came to the conclusion that the human races had multiple origins. Then he went a step further. He said black skulls were the smallest, North American native skulls were midsized, and Caucasian (white) skulls were biggest. And that these measures related to stages of development. Caucasians were therefore superior. Which meant slavery was okay and so was colonialization. Skulls also convinced Morton that black and white were separate species.

Morton picked up his craniology from George Combe, a phrenologist who believed the brain housed all the organs of character. And if one organ were extra-well-developed there'd be a bump on the skull just above the organ (of "benevolence," "criminality," "amativeness," etc.). This bump could be identified by feeling the head. Great lovers had a bump behind the left ear, in case you want to check. Once a bump had been located its size could be precisely measured and the strength of that particular characteristic known. Combe made this flim-flam popular in the United Kingdom (even Queen Victoria went for it), and in 1838 he lecture-toured America where the theory was already being huckstered by brothers Lorenzo and Orson Fowler.

By 1842 the Fowlers had New York City offices where they would measure your head and analyze your problems. The aim of both Combe and the Fowlers was primarily social reform. If head bumps could identify an individual's shortcomings then maybe something could be done to lengthen the odds. As in the case of rehabilitating criminals or improving the condition of new immigrants. In the second half of the nineteenth century head-bump-reading fed straight into the welfare work of the American Progressivists, who were addressing the problem of overcrowded cities (immigration), bad working conditions (industrialization), and local government (corruption).

In 1897 a Columbia-educated Progressive, Charles Sprague Smith, set up the People's Institute in New York. Aim: arrange lectures to educate the workers, the poor, and the newly immigrant in matters such as the political process, science, literature, and history. Smith's lectures were held anywhere rooms could be found in schools and colleges after the end of the working day. At one point the hall at Cooper Union was used. In 1923, W. W. Norton suggested printing the "Cooper Union Lectures" and founded the People's Institute Publishing Company to do so. This job soon became full-time. Norton changed the firm's name to W. W. Norton Publishing Co., Inc., and started turning it into a proper printing house. It did well.

By the late twentieth century well-known Norton authors included physicist Richard Feynman, economist Paul Krugman, and paleontologist Stephen Jay Gould. In 1997 the company published *The Undertaking—Life Studies from the Dismal Trade*, a chronicle of small-town life and death by a poet-undertaker from Milford, Michigan.

His name was THOMAS LYNCH.

CHAPTER FORTY-SEVEN

ARTHUR MIDDLETON (SC) was thirty-four. Owner of fifty thousand acres of plantation and eight hundred slaves, with a Cambridge (England) education and cultural Grand Tour of Europe behind him (and then a second similar tour, with bride), Arthur's plan had been to continue to enjoy the life of the well-endowed. Unfortunately, his father took sick in Congress and Arthur was sent to replace him. During which, the Declaration.

In 1780 Arthur fought in the defense of Charleston, was captured, and spent a year on the Brit prison ship *Jersey*. Prisoner-exchanged, he was understandably anti-Brit and advocated tarring and feathering all loyalists. After the war he toned down a little and became a trustee of Charleston College. As was his schoolmate and cousin by marriage the *really* rich Ralph Izard. Who achieved what Arthur had wanted: time off in Europe. Before the war he enjoyed four years there of fun and frolic (with wife), until things Anglo-American turned nasty and the Izards settled in temporarily neutral Paris. Whereupon Congress made Ralph U.S. commissioner to the Grand Duchy of Tuscany. On the grounds of dangerous Italian roads, Ralph did the job by mail.

In 1778 he got involved with "Commodore" Alexander Gillon, top man in the (as yet nonexistent) South Carolina Navy, who was in Paris to buy a ship. The five-hundred-crew frigate *L'Indien* had been commissioned by the United States but had turned out too expensive, so it had been passed on to the king of France, who passed it on to the duke of Luxembourg. Who did a three-year-lease-and-share-of-prize-money deal with Gillon, thus miffing John Paul Jones, who had recently arrived fully expecting to take command of the ship himself. After a complex financing deal was worked out, Gillon set sail in the now-renamed *South Carolina*. Brief fame and fortune as the biggest ship in the U.S. Navy was followed by sixty years of lawsuits from creditors, crew members, investors, and governments over who owed whom what.

Gillon's other helper in the wheeling-and-dealing had been French Minister for Marine Gabriel de Sartine. Famous for having introduced roulette to Paris, Sartine had also been the Paris chief of police when he had the pleasure of questioning Giacomo Casanova on one of the famous seducer's many Paris sojourns. Casanova (who left every major European city one step ahead of the sheriff) claimed to have made love to more than a thousand women, treating each of them, he said, with love, understanding, and above all as an equal. Casanova knew such major players as Madame de Pompadour, the pope, Catherine the Great, Frederick the Great, Voltaire, Franklin, George III, Rousseau, and Mozart. And many other lesser lights.

Casanova was at various times businessman, spy, writer, soldier, philosopher, magician, priest, and violinist, and suffered from gambling and venereal disease. His very readable memoirs of a life spent traveling and meeting the period's movers and shakers bring the eighteenth century vividly to life. One of Casanova's pals visited the same cities and knew the same people. Prince Joseph de Ligne was a megarich aristo (with vast estates in the Low Countries), a famous wit, gardening freak, and soldier (fought in many battles, became field marshal in both Austria and Russia). He also wrote, and in his book on military matters he suggested setting up an international academy of war where generals could be judged.

After losing his estates to the invading Napoleonic French in 1793 the prince retired to a life of relative luxury as a friend of the emperor in Vienna. Where he got to know a colorful Scotsman. At the time Quintin Craufurd was keeping out of the way of the French Revolution because he'd been close to the recently guillotined Queen Marie Antoinette. After an early career in India (where he got very rich by siphoning off some of the oodles of boodle being paid as tribute by local princes and nabobs to the British government) Craufurd had returned home with a Mrs. Sullivan, ex–trapeze artiste, ex-mistress of a German duke, and mother of illegitimate children with titles.

After checking out Europe, the couple settled into a posh house and art collection in Paris. Where Craufurd then met Marie Antoinette and Mrs. Sullivan loaned a fortune to pay for the (abortive) French royal escape. At which point Craufurd and Mrs. S. speedily left for Vienna and Casanova. Revolution over, it was back to Paris. After Craufurd died in 1819, Mrs. Craufurd (by this time they'd married) sold the art collection and rented part of the house to Earl and Countess Blessington.

The countess spent it faster than the earl could mortgage estates for her and, after his death, to earn pin money she began to write. At first polite essays, later novels. Most of the royalties went on furnishings, food, and booze for the countess's extravagant London literary salon, at which the elite would meet and exchange badinage.

One of the regulars was the man who first discovered Blessington's talent for scribbling, William Jerdan, editor of the *Literary Gazette*. Over the years Jerdan mixed with the great, the good, and the average. As illustrated by those in his 1866 memoirs, *Men I Have Known*, which included Sir Walter Scott, Wordsworth, Sheridan, Coleridge, and Galt ("The Scottish Dickens"), as well as long-forgotten stars like Dibdin and Douce. In addition to editing, Jerdan did sterling work helping to verify sixteenth-century documents.

He also discovered Laetitia Elizabeth Landon, poet and then (this was not generally known at the time, given that Jerdan already had two wives) mother of his three children. Ms. Landon was Jerdan's London neighbor in 1820 when the *Literary Gazette* published her poem "Rome" and then several more that year. She soon became a regular contributor and reviewer. Her initials, "L.E.L." (this was, no kidding, the time of the "Initial" school of literature), raised wild speculation about everything from was she a woman to her eye color to how many affairs she was having. Laetitia wrote more than three hundred poems for the *Gazette*. Most of them were about love and were of generally greeting-card quality. In 1838 Laetitia met George Maclean, married him, and left for Africa where he was governor of a bit of Ghana. Two months after they arrived she was found slumped against her bedroom door with an empty bottle of prussic acid in her hand. No autopsy was performed. She died the mystery she had lived.

One of Laetitia's confidantes was one of the first professional women historians, Agnes Strickland. Agnes and her sister formed a partnership famous for writing about women. And doing extensive work in the field. Since they wrote about royalty and churchmen "field" tended to be castles and cathedrals in Britain and France. Subjects included queens of England followed by queens of Scotland then bachelor kings of England then seven bishops then Tudor princesses. Research kept the two women constantly on the road. Arriving in Oxford on one occasion they were greeted by the undergraduates with the cry: "The Queens!"

On one trip (to France) they consulted Prime Minister François Guizot, who also happened to be the country's premier historian and a Sorbonne professor. Strangely, Guizot's sense of history failed him when to his cost he ignored the tide of French affairs. Maybe because of a love affair with England, Guizot supported the (increasingly unpopular) monarchy in France. Even Guizot's reforming work setting up France's primary education system (thirteen thousand new schools, new teachers' training colleges, new boards of education) was not enough to save him from public discontent with royalty. In 1848 the street barricades went up, the revolution happened, and Guizot was back to being a history professor. After a year in England he returned to France and in 1851 met James Russell Lowell, asking him the famous question: "How long do you think the American Republic will endure?" Lowell's answer: "As long as the ideas of its founders continue to be dominant." Both men must have been expecting to be quoted.

Lowell was from an elite New England family. After Harvard (and then giving up on law), he settled for second-rate poetry that got good crits because in the 1840s there wasn't much else literary-and-American to crit. Then for three months Lowell's *Pioneer* magazine enjoyed contributions from Hawthorne and Poe before it went out of business.

Lowell moved on to political analysis: antislavery, -church, -Constitution, even -Union, and political satire (for those who care, try *The Bigelow Papers*). After Lowell's trip to Europe (when he met Guizot), Harvard offered him the chair in modern languages. Requirement: that he spend a year in Europe to learn some. There followed editorship of the new *Atlantic Monthly*, editorship of the new *North American Review*, then essays on Dante, Spenser, et al. At last Lowell was a recognized man of letters.

Joining the Harvard faculty at the same time as Lowell (in 1854) was mathematician and chemist Charles Eliot, who found himself more interested in education than educating. After a year visiting the European systems (especially the German), he returned to a professorship at MIT and then in 1869 presidency of Harvard. Which he proceeded to drag, protesting, into the nineteenth century. Eliot gave students freedom of choice of subject, a broader curriculum, and written exams. He gave faculty more money. Result: He turned Harvard from a small academic backwater into a major world university. Then he ruined every student's life by laying the groundwork for SATs.

In 1909 Eliot rashly claimed that a five-foot shelf of the classics ought to give anybody a good education. The Collier publishing house challenged him to put his volumes where his mouth was, and he produced what became known as the "Harvard Classics" (fifty books, ranging from Shakespeare to Franklin to Descartes to Sophocles to Shelley). Collier sold 350,000 sets over the following twenty years.

In 1952 Collier produced the twenty-volume *Collier's Encyclopedia*. The 1982 edition included portraits of the presidents. These inspired an amateur artist from Seymour, Tennessee, to paint his own thirty-nine presidential portraits. In acrylic.

The artist was ARTHUR MIDDLETON.

CHAPTER FORTY-EIGHT

Button Gwinnett

BUTTON GWINNETT (GA) was forty-one. An immigrant from England, he failed at business and farming so went into local Georgia politics, organizing the left-wing back-country vote. After signing in Philadelphia Gwinnett went home and got embroiled in rows about who ran the military. Of which there were two kinds: continental troops and Georgia militia.

Gwinnett's political archrival Lachlan Macintosh commanded the troops and Gwinnett the militia. In 1777, while Gwinnett was president of Georgia, an attack was mounted on British Florida and Gwinnett took political control of all troops. The attack failed, Macintosh blamed Gwinnett, and they dueled. Gwinnett died from his wounds. The following year another unsuccessful attack was mounted. The Brits took Savannah and other bits of Georgia.

On this occasion the Brits were led by General Augustine Prevost, whose brother was also a general but not so good at it. After a period in the Caribbean (governing various islands), in 1811 George Prevost became commander-in-chief, British forces in North America. So when 1812 happened it was his job to invade the United States. He made two attempts and failed both times (earning from his troops the nickname: "our little nincompoop").

Back in the Caribbean one of Prevost's personal staff had been army officer Colquhoun Grant. By 1811 Grant was in Spain where the Duke of Wellington was fighting Napoleon. Grant was a brilliant linguist whose job was to get behind enemy lines and relay intel back to Wellington. When he was captured and taken to Salamanca he escaped and was able to get to Paris by masquerading as an American officer. Finally he made it back to his boss, who promoted him head of Intel.

Grant's escape from Salamanca had been facilitated by Patrick Curtis, rector of the Irish College in Salamanca, another of Wellington's spies and professor of astronomy at the local university. In 1817 he retired to Dublin, where in 1818 he put his name forward for the vacant Catholic archbishopric of Armagh and was astonished when the pope said yes. In 1823 Curtis's Protestant counterpart in Armagh (the primate of the Church of Ireland) appointed a new director of the Armagh Observatory. The Reverend Romney Robinson had started as a child prodigy at Belfast Academy, then (aged twelve) went to Trinity College, Dublin, where he was elected a fellow at eighteen. Once in position at Armagh he did a 5,345-star catalog and generally kept busy for fifty-nine years (longest observatory directorship in history). He also invented the (now-standard) cup-anemometer for measuring wind speed and generally re-equipped the observatory with the help of Dubliner Thomas Grubb.

Whose experience as a cast-iron billiard-table-maker gave him a flair for the heavyweight, so he made particularly good large telescopes. In Armagh's case a fifteen-inch reflector with a clock drive (it moved the telescope four degrees a minute so it could follow the same star while the Earth turned). Telescopy paid badly, so Grubb's day job was at the Irish Bank making machines for designing, printing, and numbering banknotes.

In 1837 Grubb also turned out twenty sets of magnetometers for the Trinity College prof. of science, Humphrey Lloyd. Whose plan was to set up a network of magnetic stations on British colonial sites around the empire. In 1839 Lloyd spent the summer training a young army lieutenant in magnetic matters. John Lefroy (evangelical, Sunday school teacher in his spare time) set off to measure magnetism on the mid-Atlantic island of St. Helena (the circuitous route via the Canaries,

Cape Verde, and Trinidad took them three months). Two years going nowhere on St. Helena were followed by a spectacular 5,475-mile trip in Canada (by canoe and snowshoe) taking 314 magnetic observations along the way.

While he was on St. Helena Lefroy was able to watch the disinterment of one of history's more magnetic personalities. On October 8, 1840, two French warships arrived carrying Prince de Joinville (French King Louis-Philippe's son) and various harrumphs, everyone in full dress and medals. Over the next few days they and the Brits running St. Helena argued about how many guns' salute the about-to-be-dug-up Napoleon would get (French: "103"; British: "21"). At midnight on October 15, they started excavating. At 9:00 A.M., they hauled up the box and opened it. The emperor (in perfect condition) was transferred to an ebony coffin inside an oak sarcophagus and hauled down to the harbor. Commemorative gifts were handed out all round (except, for some reason, to Lefroy) and the ships made off, throwing much of their furniture and equipment overboard to make better speed. By the way: twenty-one guns.

Back home the revolution of 1848 then sent Prince de Joinville off to exile in England. In 1861 he arrived at the White House asking if there was anything a French prince could do to help. In 1862 he found himself witnessing the first successful Union Balloon Corps flights at the battle of the Chicahominy when "Professor" Thaddeus Lowe got to a thousand feet and reported on what he could see of Confederate movements (including useful stuff like where the enemy artillery was and in which direction to fire).

This happened because Lincoln had earlier been impressed by Lowe's hovering five hundred feet above Washington, D.C., and sending telegraph messages down a wire. The man who arranged Lowe's presidential demo was Salmon Chase. A radical abolitionist campaigner who had spent a number of years earning the name "Attorney General of Fugitive Slaves," Chase's view was that the Constitution left slavery up to the individual states, so blacks were only slaves in slave states. In 1861 Lincoln appointed Chase secretary of the Treasury. In order to finance the war, Chase established paper money as legal tender (the first "greenbacks") and set up a national banking system. He then added insult to injury with a new "Internal Revenue Service" set up to collect the first "income tax."

Part of Chase's mandate was to deal with Confederate estates abandoned by their proprietors. On the South Carolina Sea Islands the local plantation owners had fled the scene, quitting their land and ten thousand now-unemployed not-free-not-slave blacks. Seeing the opportunity for a rehearsal of postwar Reconstruction, in 1862 Chase set up the Port Royal Experiment, designed to educate and prepare freed slaves for life after Union victory. Hospitals and schools were set up on the islands and land was offered to those who'd worked it, at twenty-five cents an acre. Once Lincoln was gone the price was hiked to eleven bucks. No freed slave could afford that price, the entire scheme fizzled, and by 1865 most of the original owners were back in place, paying slave wages to their now-free workers.

Disappointed Port Royal Experiment volunteers included Charlotte Grimke, who'd volunteered to teach in the scheme and spent a year there before ill health forced her resignation. Grimke was a rarity for 1862: a woman who was well-educated, literate, intelligent, cultured, multilingual, and black. In 1864 her account of the Experiment appeared in *Atlantic Monthly*. Five years later came her translation of the French play *Madame Thérèse*, written by a duo from Alsace, France. Emile Erckmann wrote and Charles Alexandre Chartrain arranged the publishing. They produced more than twenty novels and short stories under the pseudonym Erckmann-Chartrain. One of their plays (*Le Juif Polonais*) was to establish the career of Britain's premier Victorian actor, after being translated by a nondescript ex-lawyer named Leopold Lewis and titled *The Bells*.

Today the the play is stock for student and amateur drama groups because it requires little skill and less subtlety (tavern-keeper in debt welcomes rich Jewish overnight guest, murders him for his money, then dies of horror at hearing the merchant's ghostly sleigh bells). In 1871 when a new young actor named Henry Irving went into melodramatic overdrive in the lead role at the Lyceum Theater, London, he became an overnight sensation. And never looked back. Irving played every role to excess. And in an era of amazing new electricity he kept the old-fashioned gas and limelight for maximum dramatic effect. In 1878 he and new acting partner Ellen Terry did Shakespeare from A to Z.

Including four tours in America, where in 1885 they played *Much Ado* to full houses at the Columbia Theater, Chicago. Watched from the front stalls by Marshall Field and son. Field was dry goods from the age of seventeen. Arriving in Chicago in 1856 he worked his way up (in dry goods) to a partnership. Bought his partner out. Set up Marshall Field and Company in 1881. Went from dry goods to retail, the first store with an overseas buying office (in Manchester, England), and one of the first with fixed prices and full refund. Field got very rich and gave lots of it away to the University of Chicago, the Academy of Fine Arts, and the Field Museum. He also spent over eight hundred thousand dollars on his new Chicago store. One of the finest examples (they say) of "Richardsonian Romanesque."

H. H. Richardson had a thing for the eleventh-century Romanesque architecture of southern France (massive walls, semicircular arches). He set the style for a Romanesque Revival in the United States with his Trinity Church, in Boston. Loved or hated. Never ignored. Richardson influenced people like Frank Lloyd Wright and Fenimore C. Bate, whose pièce de résistance (in more ways than one) was a Disney-before-Disney castle on Bolivar Street, Cleveland. The Grays' Armory was supposed to be an arsenal and drill hall but soon turned into a social center (Sousa, boxing matches, proms). In 1918 the armory hosted the opening night of the new Cleveland Orchestra.

Six years later the orchestra took on press agent James Thurber, who'd just spent four years as reviewer for the Columbus *Evening Dispatch*. By 1926 Thurber was writing for the *New Yorker* and on his way to fame, especially for his delicious cartoons of aggressive women, bewildered men, and amorphous dogs. He is best remembered for *The Secret Life of Walter Mitty*, filmed in 1947 and starring Danny Kaye. A year later Kaye was at the London Palladium for the first of four tours of the United Kingdom, where he was a sensation, especially with the royals.

In 1952 Kaye took with him an English pop group, the Beverley Sisters, who were in the States at the time. Thanks to Kaye, their Palladium debut began a singing career that was still going strong in 2005. In 1958 Joy Beverley married Billy Wright, soccer star of Wolverhampton Wanderers. Wright became a national hero, playing for England 105 times and captaining the national team ninety times (including three World Cup finals). In 1994 he died, and his funeral at St. Peter's Church, Wolverhampton, brought the city to a standstill.

In the church births-marriages-and-deaths register, together with Wright's name there are baptismal records for three eighteenth-century girl babies. The first (Amelia) was christened in 1758, the second (Ann) in 1759, and the third (Elizabeth) in 1762, just before the family left for America with their father, whose marriage is also recorded in St. Peter's parish register.

The little girls' father was BUTTON GWINNETT.

CHAPTER FORTY-NINE

Lyman Hall

LYMAN HALL (GA) was fifty-two. Yale. Fired for "moral" matters from his Connecticut church. Moved south and after an attempt at rice-planting in Georgia went into local politics. Georgia was so conservative that at one point the revolutionary Hall tried to get his parish to secede to South Carolina (the state turned him down). In 1783 as one-year state governor, Hall pushed through legislation for a state university and then persuaded Abraham Baldwin to join the board of trustees. Lawyer Baldwin (another Yalie) arrived the following year and helped to write the charter for the University of Georgia (then called Franklin College). It took twenty years for the school to open.

Baldwin's colleague John Milledge provided the campus acreage. In 1802, when the federal government opened all western lands to settlement "once a reasonable price had been peacefully agreed with the Indians," Milledge and Baldwin were asked to review Georgia's treaties with the tribes. The review triggered one of the darkest episodes in American history.

The Georgians wanted the land that in 1791 had been guaranteed to the local Native Americans in perpetuity. The Cherokees, seeing which way things were headed, began a policy (it lasted twenty years) of acculturation to white customs, replacing hunting with agriculture, setting up schools and a legislative assembly, a police force, a newspaper, then writing a constitution and applying for U.S. citizenship. In spite of all this, in 1838 they were to be forced at gunpoint to leave for Oklahoma on the Trail of Tears. Four thousand of them would die on the way.

Meanwhile, in 1803, Cherokee schooling was in the hands of Gideon Blackburn, a fiery Tennessee Presbyterian preacher (and whiskey distiller) who traveled the country raising money for education. By 1810 he was a reformed drunk and lecturing on the evils of booze. Spent the War of 1812 as a chaplain. After which his revivalist meetings became so famous his portrait was painted by second-rate painter Richard Street, whose output was prolific and who usually specialized in portraits of people already dead. In 1815 Street exhibited at the Philadelphia Academy of Fine Arts, where he met the academy's founder, Charles W. Peale.

Who was a first-rate painter. And *really* prolific. After spending two years in London watching the by-then-famous American Benjamin West at work, Peale took classes, met the painterly elite, and in 1769 went back home to a life of art and science. Peale painted over a thousand miniatures as well as landscapes, still lifes, and history paintings. In 1785 he opened the first American Natural History Museum (eventually renting Independence Hall for the purpose) where everything was exhibited in its natural setting. Stars of the show in 1802 were two mastodon skeletons from the Hudson Valley. About which Baron Cuvier got very excited.

Cuvier (French science big cheese) founded the study of paleontology with his idea that muscles made impressions on bones and that all animal parts were exactly related to their function: e.g., a carnivore needed intestines, powerful jaws, sharp teeth, claws on flexible toes, and musculature to move fast enough to catch food. Putting all these comparative anatomy clues together, Cuvier could reconstruct long-vanished prehistoric animals from the evidence of a single bone. Which he did with one of Peale's mastodons (and gave the animal its name). He went on to run French education and write the definitive textbook on zoology.

This was the heyday of French research, led by major noodlers such as Arago, Biot, St. Hilaire, and Buffon. All of whom fell for the beauty and intellectual charms of Mary Somerville, over from London in 1817 with her Royal Society husband (whom she outshone then and since). Somerville (the Oxford College is named after her) was fluent in geology, mineralogy, botany, Greek, and math. She made her name with a series of books popularizing science. And the "read-this-first" preface to her translation of Laplace's math-dense *Celestial Mechanics* became a standard higher-math course paper. All this done without a degree because women weren't allowed into university.

In Britain Mary hobnobbed with the intelligentsia, including (a particular fan of hers) Great Historical Novelist Sir Walter Scott. Who created the genre and helped to invent Disney Scotland replete with kilts (invented by an Englishman), sword dances (taken from French ballet), and baronial halls (fake). Scott spent so much money turning himself into a Scottish nobleman with residence to match that it took every penny of a fortune in royalties to pay off his debts. Between 1814 and 1832 Scott churned out twenty-three novels.

One of them, *Quentin Durward* (a tale set in 1465), was reproduced with only the names changed by Alfred de Vigny, French Romantic poet and big fan of Scott. De Vigny's plagiarized-Scott opus was *Cinq Mars*, considered by the French to be the greatest French historical novel. No comment. The impression you get is that De Vigny was a bit of a sad sack. His poetic output was small-and-Romantic just as Romanticism was going off the boil. Unhappily married to a sickly Englishwoman and with a mistress (actress Marie Dorval) who gave him nothing but grief, Vigny retired hurt to a country estate. His friend Sainte-Beuve coined the phrase "ivory tower" to describe De Vigny's situation there.

While the English wife was still ambulatory, on a trip to London De Vigny made friends with one of the sharpest tongues in criticism, Henry Fothergill Chorley. A measure of Chorley's acerbity was his description of *dernier cri* Verdi as "noisy and vulgar." Between 1833 and 1868 Chorley wrote more than twenty-five hundred go-for-the-throat book reviews, but saved his best work for musicians. Among whom he was a power to be reckoned with. He introduced Gounod and Meyerbeer to the Brits, loved Rossini and Mendelssohn unreservedly, and from 1862 onward did all he could to promote the career of new composer ("so young an artist, so full of promise") Arthur Sullivan.

Sullivan might have surfaced unnoticed in the sea of Victorian chorales and songs-for-the-drawing-room had it not been for his partnership with W. S. Gilbert and the operettas they wrote together: *Trial by Jury*, *H.M.S. Pinafore*, and *Mikado*, to name but three of the witty, satirical takes on British social customs. Gilbert did the clever words and Sullivan the whistleable music. Audiences went wild. Between 1875 and 1889 the pair made and squandered a fortune and Sullivan was made Sir by Queen Victoria, who asked if he would please return to serious music. In 1889, after a row with Gilbert, he did. And never succeeded again.

The operettas had all been the idea of impresario Richard D'Oyly Carte, who commissioned *Jury*. In 1888 he married his secretary Helen who then turned into the greatest businesswoman of the age. Helen was a workaholic. She criss-crossed the Atlantic fixing productions and tours and organized the staging, finance, and management of everything. She was also a big pal of American painter James Whistler, who painted her London apartment yellow (his favorite color).

Whistler did experimental work that took a while to make its mark. His insistence on titles such as *Arrangement in Grey and Black* (portrait of his mother) and *Arrangement in Grey and Black No 2* (portrait of writer Thomas Carlyle) gave the critics a field day. For years they razzed him. In a famous lecture in 1885 (organized by Helen Carte) he razzed back, arguing that art had nothing to do with politics or morals or social change or education or anything. Art was for art's sake. The critics razzed the lecture. But in the end Whistler won through and became an international art celeb. In 1898 he was made president of the International Society (mission statement: "Art has nothing to do with nationality").

After him came the man who carved Whistler's monument, French sculptor Auguste Rodin. Whose work unnerved most critics and exhibition organizers. Following twenty years on the fringe, in 1880 Rodin was finally commissioned to do the monumental doors for the new Paris Museum of Decorative Arts. He chose as a theme Dante's *Inferno*. The museum never happened but his pieces lived on as single works, including *The Thinker* (first named *The Poet* and representing Dante) and *The Kiss*. Rodin worked with amateur sitters such as street musicians, acrobats, or dancers and made "notes in clay" as they moved around. His public commissions (Hugo sexually aroused and Balzac naked with nymphs) shocked everybody. An exhibition of his many erotic drawings caused a major scandal in Germany.

In 1890 Rodin taught Gutzon Borglum, the Danish-American mountain-shaper. The first mountain happened in 1915 when Borglum was commissioned to carve (out of Stone Mountain, Georgia) a view of Lee, Jackson, and Davis with a troop of artillery "coming round the hill." After arguments with the backers (who included the Ku Klux Klan), Borglum destroyed the work and moved on to bigger things at Mount Rushmore. Begun in 1927 and finished after his death in 1941, the piece included sixty-foot-high faces of Washington, Jefferson, Lincoln, and Teddy Roosevelt. It was said Borglum's dynamiters could work with four-inch accuracy.

In 1922 Borglum told a young apprentice he'd never be a sculptor, so Japanese-American Isamu Noguchi took up medicine. Then dropped it for a brilliant life in sculpture: abstract pieces in New York, sculptural gardens for UNESCO in Paris, and the National Museum in Jerusalem, as well as portrait heads of inventor Buckminster Fuller and dancer Martha Graham. Who introduced Noguchi to George Balanchine, one of the greatest of twentieth-century choreographers. In 1948 Noguchi designed the set of Balanchine's *Orpheus*.

Balanchine had defected from the U.S.S.R. in 1924, then choreographed ten ballets for Diaghilev's Ballets Russes and in 1933 arrived in the United States. Where he formed the American Ballet. *Orpheus* earned his company a permanent home as the New York City Ballet and Balanchine went on to change the art of dance with extraordinary innovations in step, posture, and movement, working to music ranging from Bach to Gershwin.

In 1954 Balanchine's *Nutcracker Suite* became a long-running national phenomenon with a giant Christmas tree, an on-stage blizzard, and dozens of children including (as the Nutcracker Prince) twelve-year-old Eliot Feld. In 1974 (when he was already a major choreographer), Feld set up the Eliot Feld Dance Company and recruited as a principal dancer the son of Houston's Jazz Ballet director Patsy Swayze.

Patrick Swayze, who made Hollywood stardom in 1987 with the hit movie *Dirty Dancing*, had initially headed toward a dance career via an athletic scholarship at San Jacinto College. Where, in 2004, the College Dance Show was taped by Houston MediaSource.

The video producer was LYMAN HALL.

CHAPTER FIFTY

GeoWalton.

GEORGE WALTON (GA) was thirty-five. He did well, rising from apprentice carpenter to self-educated lawyer to member of Congress and state governor (twice) as well as becoming chief justice of Georgia and member of the University of Georgia Board of Trustees (in spite of involvement in a high-profile forgery case and general political skull-duggery). Walton also browbeat conservative Georgia into support for Independence.

In 1778 at the battle of Savannah Walton was wounded and interned by the Brits, commanded that day by Sir Archibald Campbell, Scottish military engineer with service in the Caribbean and then administration experience in India, where like everybody he made a fortune. Some of which he used to buy a seat in Parliament and a posh estate. In 1776 he raised a Highland regiment and went off to Boston. Oops, nobody told him it had already fallen to the American rebels, so Archie ended up in Concord jail. From which he was prisoner-exchanged in 1778, then headed for Savannah and Walton.

Congress might later have regretted the Campbell exchange deal. It freed Ethan Allen, who'd been captured by the Brits during his attack on Canada in 1775 and held for three years. Allen had been a congressional nuisance since 1771 when he'd founded the Green Mountain Boys to fight for Vermont independence from New York. Congress wouldn't play, so in 1778 Allen declared Vermont an independent republic and started talking to the Brits in Canada about maybe Vermont becoming an autonomous Canadian province. For five years he played each side off against the other. In the end, Congress recognized the real possibility of losing Vermont and agreed to a fourteenth state.

Up north, the man Allen had been courting was General Frederick Haldimand, Swiss-born ex–Prussian army, ex–Dutch army, and by 1778 governor of Quebec. Haldimand didn't trust Allen farther than he could throw him so the congressional decision pulled Haldimand's Vermont chestnuts out of the fire. Just as well, since he had other chestnuts (Native Americans and loyalists agitating for land to live on). The Iroquois were fussing because they'd been forced out of the Mohawk Valley by New York settlers. The loyalists were up in arms because since being chased out of America they had nowhere to go.

Haldimand got his local Canadian natives to agree to take money in return for giving the Iroquois some real estate on the north shore of Lake Ontario. The four thousand loyalists headed for the (uninhabited) north shore of the St. Lawrence. Haldimand even bought sneak American provisions to feed them. Alas, all this expenditure put the good burghers of Quebec in so much hock Haldimand was fired.

The man who did Haldimand's Native American and Loyalist land surveys was Surveyor General Samuel Hollandt. In Canada with the Royal American Regiment since 1756, two years later Hollandt was surveying Cape Breton, where he met Captain Cook and taught him how to take a proper sighting. In 1764 Hollandt became surveyor general and did major surveys of the coastline from Cape Cod to New London, adding valuable data to the overall coastal survey put together later by his assistant and constant war companion, Joseph Des Barres (who also taught Cook trigonometry).

In 1763 Des Barres had been ordered to prepare a map of the entire Atlantic coastline. After twenty years' hard graft his "Atlantic Neptune" ended up as the definitive high-tech navigational aid, detailing the American coastline all the way from Labrador to the Florida panhandle and including every creek and hazard. Just what the British navy needed for the war (the ink was hardly dry on some of the charts).

Des Barres did much of his last-minute work on board HMS *Haer-lem*, commanded by John Knight. In 1780 Knight joined the *Barfleur*, flagship of Admiral Hood, and then saw action in Martinique and in the Chesapeake Bay just before Cornwallis's surrender. In 1782, when *Barfleur* was anchored off Staten Island, a seventeen-year-old midshipman joined the crew from New York, where he'd been having too much of a good time for his father's liking. The father (George III) asked for Prince William Henry to be given a taste of discipline. For the next six months Knight taught William math and made him a good enough officer to get his own command and have a successful navy career. Until 1788, when George's madness caused his recall home.

With little to do in London except be a royal, after innumerable nights on the town Prince William finally found happiness in the arms of England's best actress, Dorothy Jordan. The pair set up unofficial home in a royal residence and lived happily for twenty years as if they were man and wife. Jordan went on acting. Her best stuff was "breeches" parts (women acting men's roles and showing off their legs). Meanwhile, the prince was on his last legs financially. In 1811 Jordan was on tour when she got a letter from him explaining awfully sorry but they had to separate because he needed to marry a rich woman. Within six years Jordan was dead, poverty-stricken in Paris, leaving behind her ten royal bastards.

One of whom was George Augustus Frederick FitzClarence (the family name of all ten of Jordan's kids, because their princely father had also been Duke of Clarence and because "Fitz" meant "illegitimate child of"). George went into the army and did a good job during the Napoleonic Wars. In 1814 he was sent to India and did well there, too. After his return in 1817 he wrote up the trip and then became a bit of a noodler, joining the Royal Society as well as the Societies of Antiquaries, Geography, Geology, and Astronomy. In 1841 he also became president of the Asiatic Society. In 1842 (after Queen Victoria denied him the throne he thought was rightfully his), George Augustus shot himself. Leaving unfinished a paper on the history of Muslim mercenaries in Christian armies, half-written by his secretary, Dr. Aloys Sprenger, a Tyrolean doctor with a penchant for the East.

Now out of work, in 1843 Sprenger moved to India, and in 1845 was made president of the new Delhi College (where students were taught in Urdu), published the first Urdu weekly mag, and spent several years editing Arabic, Persian, and Indian texts. By 1850 he was head of a madrassa in Calcutta and translating for the government of India. In 1856 he went back to Europe, where he gained fame as a major authority on all things Oriental. Sprenger had been fighting a losing battle in India thanks to the efforts of missionaries who reckoned his idea of teaching Indians in Urdu was Not A Good Thing. The issue had come to a head in 1835 when the governor general of India published his personal views: Indian knowledge was rubbish (geography with seas of treacle and butter, astronomy that would "raise laughter in an English girls' school"); best thing would be to teach the Indians European literature and science in English because English was rapidly becoming the language of the empire.

So when Alexander Duff turned up in Calcutta how could he fail? Duff (Scots missionary who believed the English language had civilized Scotland) took lodgings just up the road from Sprenger, editing the English-language *Calcutta Review* (himself writing stuff about Indian infanticide of unwanted girl babies) and running a seven-hundred-pupil college (classes in English). The Indians got the point. English was going to be the *lingua franca* for any subcontinental wannabe. Duff went back and forth between Scotland and India. On one trip he became moderator of the Free Church of Scotland and helped draw up U.K. government plans for British-style Indian universities and schools (and in 1857 would end up running the new University of Calcutta).

Meanwhile, in 1854 his impressive public-speaking skills got him invited to visit Canada and the United States where he met President Pierce, got as far west as St. Louis, and went north to Quebec. Duff's American invitation ("we want to be stirred up here") came from George Hay Stuart, a Philadelphia businessman who opened the Philadelphia YMCA in 1856. Five years later came the Civil War and Stuart was made director of the Christian Commission, put together from the fifteen Ys existing at the time. The commission's job was to provide support and spiritual help to Union military personnel (and their POWs) by providing libraries, canteens, emergency hospitals, gyms, food and clothing, writing materials, and postal services, as well as giving inspirational lectures on temperance and Sunday Observance. The commission ran five thousand field agents and distributed 40 million tracts, over one million Bibles, one million hymn books, and 18 million copies of Christian newspapers.

In 1858 Stuart's director of the Philadelphia Y was John Wanamaker. Two weeks before the outbreak of war he resigned and set up a men's and boys' clothing store, which then signed government contracts to make uniforms. By 1858 Wanamaker had a second store and the first one-price, cash-payment, full-refund policy. By 1879 he had invented one-stop shopping and introduced the first in-store elevators, electric lighting, and restaurant. Wanamaker's greatest idea was that shopping ought to be an "experience" so the rotunda of his new "Grand Depot" store (he bought the old Philadelphia railroad depot) featured musical selections played on an orchestrion. This was a perforated-roll-driven automated organ and looked like an upright piano with a stained-glass-windowed chinaware cupboard on top (this bit housed the pipes).

Orchestrions (sometimes known as "nickelodeons" because one version operated by a coin-in-the-slot system) and other such musical gizmos were comprehensively catalogued in the 1972 *Encyclopedia of Automated Musical Instruments* produced by Q. David Bowers. By 1980 Bowers, also a lifelong coin buff, was partnered with Raymond Merena in a numismatic business and then became involved in the Great 1913 Liberty Head Nickel Mystery. Back in 1912 the U.S. Mint had decided to withdraw the Liberty Head nickel and replace it with the Buffalo nickel. After the withdrawal deadline in 1913 five Liberty Heads were illegally minted. By 2000 four of these coins were worth at least a million dollars each. The fifth coin had been lost. Bowers and Merena offered a million for its rediscovery (and ten grand for the first chance to view it). The coin suddenly reappeared.

The owners had thought the nickel was a fake so it had been kept in a closet after the original collector-owner had been killed in 1962 in a car crash. In 2003 his relatives brought the coin to a meeting in Baltimore where the coin was identified as the true fifth nickel.

The name of the coin's owner (victim of the 1962 crash) was GEORGE WALTON.

Fall 1776
and Later

CHAPTER FIFTY-ONE

George Wythe

GEORGE WYTHE (VA) was about fifty. He signed on August 27, because he'd been away with the army. Wythe was a quiet lawyer and neither an effective speaker nor a great debater. And since he burned his papers there's not much to say about him. Except to wonder why he burned them.

Wythe had been a local Virginia politico since 1753, was a lifelong friend of Thomas Jefferson (he taught T.J. law), and had been attorney general under the royal governor. After Independence he rose to chancellor of Virginia. In 1779 he was the first U.S. professor of law (at William and Mary). In the end he came to an unfortunate end, poisoned by his grandnephew over the inheritance Wythe wasn't going to leave him.

While on the Board of Visitors at William and Mary he met professor of natural history (aka science) William Small, a temporary (six-year) visitor to the United States who in 1764 returned to Birmingham, England, to set up his doctor's practice and become rich. As a founding member of the geek talking-shop Lunar Society (membership included such tech buffs as doctor Erasmus Darwin, potter Josiah Wedgwood, and buckle-maker Matthew Boulton), Small was also an early supporter and helper of James Watt, a close friend of oxygen discoverer Joseph Priestley, and was active in geology, optics, metallurgy, chemistry, and gunnery. He also developed a new lead pencil. Busy guy.

When Small died in 1775, Darwin wrote to Dr. William Withering about the job opportunity and Withering came to take over Small's practice. And become rich. Withering's wife sketched nature, so Withering went looking for plants for her, developed an obsession with botany, and wrote a three-volume standard text on English vegetables. In 1785 he published the result of ten years' work on foxglove. After hearing about its curative properties from an old woman (he said), Withering experimented on 173 cases of dropsy (swelling) and found that an infusion of the foxglove leaves caused vomiting, diarrhea, and urinating (it was a powerful diuretic) and reduced the swelling. The plant was also effective in cases of cardiac failure. By 1785 Withering's infusion (now called digitalis) was in general use.

Four years later Withering's *other* other work (in geology) was recognized in Germany, where in 1796 a new mineral was named "witherite" by Abraham Werner. Major mineralogist and theorizer on the origins of rocks, Werner taught at the famous Freiberg School of Mines, where he lectured on his theory that rocks had been originally deposited as sediments in an ancient sea and that the kind of rocks produced in this process varied with the weather at the time. Over a million years, he said, five different climates and sea states had created five sets of rock type. He was wrong.

One of Werner's pupils was Henrik Steffens, a Norwegian physicist who fell for German Romantic nature philosophy ("everything in nature is one") and came up with a complex system of "fours" (four elements, four temperaments, four cardinal points of the compass, four continents, and four races: Mongolian, American, Negroid, and Malaysian). Steffens's writing was at best an opaque, bombastic, gobbledygook mixture of science and speculation. At the lovely Rahel Varnhagen's Berlin salon (where the Romantic Movement German elite met), any time Steffens held forth on anything (too often) Rahel's husband, Karl August, described the experience as "torture."

Karl August Varnhagen was a biographer of queens and field marshals, though most of his writing took the form of letters to Rahel (well worth the read). In 1804 he joint-edited a short-lived literary mag with poet and traveler Adalbert von Chamisso. Who first described the Californian poppy and several Mexican trees and ran the Berlin Botanical Garden. Chamisso also wrote a novel about a man who sold his soul (see elsewhere).

Chamisso's pal Baron Friedrich de La Motte-Fouqué churned out plays, novels, and poems full of nationalist, Teutonic waffle: much medieval chivalry and northern mythology. No surprise, he influenced Wagner. Fouqué's only generally remembered piece is about a Germanic mermaid with no soul, *Undine*. Full of fairies, goblins, an enchanted wood, and a knight who falls for the mermaid but marries a woman with legs, so Undine kills him with a kiss. When the book was translated into English in 1818 it was a runaway bestseller.

The translator was the son of distinguished architect Sir John Soane. George Soane was disinherited by his father for laziness, jail sentences for debt and fraud, and not least for getting his sister-in-law pregnant. George turned to writing and produced plays, poems, novels, and translations, all now mercifully forgotten. One of George's operas, *The Innkeeper's Daughter*, was a vehicle for actor Tom Cooke, who'd had a colorful life to that date. Starting as an errand boy, Cooke then joined the navy and saw action and shipwreck. Then came a traveling circus and finally a life on the stage. Where he was known for three major roles: 265 performances as the (silent) monster in *Frankenstein*, 562 performances as a coxswain, and 785 performances as a sailor dancing the hornpipe. In 1817 he appeared in Soane's *Innkeeper* at Drury Lane the same year the theater switched to gas lighting.

Top London figure in gas at the time was German immigrant Friedrich Accum, who wrote a "how-to-make-gas" book and in 1810 became a director of the Gas Light and Coke Company of London, soon supplying gas for seventy-five thousand London lights (among them, those at Drury Lane Theater). Accum was associated with Rudolph Ackermann (another German immigrant) whose weekly *conversazioni* were held in his (gaslit, of course) Great Room in the Strand. Ackermann produced a monthly mag on literature and the arts and in 1826 sent his son George to Mexico City to open up the South American market. The firm soon had outlets in Buenos Aires, Lima, and Caracas. And a letter of appreciation from no less a figure than Simón Bolívar.

Back in London George and his brothers eventually set up a publishing company, Ackermann & Co., doing prints as well as art and travel books. In 1862 George, wife, and family emigrated to North America. The ship was aiming for Portland, Maine, but because of storms ended up in Quebec. So the Ackermanns settled in Belleville, Ontario, where George illustrated over four hundred botanical studies in *Wild Flowers of Upper Canada* by the botanist Asa Gray.

Originally qualified as a doctor, Gray spent eight years working in botany research before becoming (1842) professor of natural history at Harvard and the first professional botanist in the United States. His 1848 *Manual of Botany of the Northern United States* became a definitive work and over the years Gray produced textbooks on plants for every school grade from little kids to college level. Gray was also Darwin's champion in America and helped get the theory of evolution accepted.

One of Gray's colleagues at Harvard was professor of Spanish Henry W. Longfellow, who was to make his own international name in 1855 with the Native American (or not) epic poem *Hiawatha* (see elsewhere). Fifty-four years later the poem inspired German immigrant Carl Laemmle, who had tried working in a department store, then in 1906 had bought a nickelodeon theater (the White Front Theater) in Chicago, then realized that the best way to be sure of having a steady supply of films was to make them.

In 1909 Laemmle moved to New York City, set up the Independent Motion Picture Company, and made his first one-reeler: *Hiawatha*. Over the next few years he developed stars like Mary Pickford who were attracted to work for Laemmle because he gave them film credits when nobody else would. By 1915 Laemmle was in Hollywood, his company was called Universal Studios, and he was well on the way to dominating the industry with such greats as *Hunchback of Notre Dame* (1923) and *Phantom of the Opera* (1925).

In 1929 Laemmle's son Carl Jr. took over and started a string of successful horror movies including *Frankenstein*, *Dracula*, and *The Mummy*. By 1935 he was "Universal Pictures" and one-quarter owned by Brit entrepreneur J. Arthur Rank. Who had come into films because as a devout Methodist and Sunday School Society president he was bothered by the low moral quality of American movies. He said: "I am in films because of the Holy Spirit."

Things went so well that in 1934 Rank and two partners set up Pinewood Studios outside London (and the rest is British film history). One of the partners was the flamboyant Lady Henrietta Yule. Widow (at £13 million the richest in England) of a jute tycoon, Lady Yule was a horse enthusiast who kept penguins and wallabies on her estate and opened a home for ill-treated animals in the south of France decades before Brigitte Bardot. In 1929 she also commissioned John Brown shipbuilders in Clydeside, Scotland, to build one of the last great steam yachts to be launched in Britain. The *Nahlin* had a crew of fifty-eight and was a floating gin palace.

In the summer of 1936 the ship was chartered for a rather special cruise down the Adriatic to Istanbul. On board (and followed by the world's press) were King Edward VIII of Great Britain and his American mistress Wallace Simpson, wife of a businessman based in London. Edward had given up his other mistresses for Simpson and was hopelessly infatuated with her. In spite of government and church warnings from the prime minister and archbishop of Canterbury that as king he could not marry a divorcée, Edward continued the affair. In December 1936 things came to a head and Edward abdicated so that they could tie the knot.

The new king was George VI. In 1941 he sent a prayer book to commemorate the two hundredth anniversary of the Episcopal Church of St. John in Richmond, Virginia.

In St. John's graveyard lies the mother of Edgar Allan Poe. And GEORGE WYTHE.

CHAPTER FIFTY-TWO

Elbridge Gerry

ELBRIDGE GERRY (MA) was thirty-two. He signed on September 3, having missed the August signing because he was at home recovering from overwork. He was a tiny, nervous, birdlike figure with a stammer. Gerry had started business life in Marblehead, Massachusetts, exporting fish to Spain and Portugal. Which stood him in good stead during the war, when he switched from salt cod to military logistics. In the revolution everybody was an amateur.

At the 1787 Constitutional Congress Gerry was always on his feet "objecting to everything he did not propose," especially when he thought anybody was getting in the way of his political baby: a Bill of Rights. Gerry also went into the language. At the end of his second term as Massachusetts governor his involvement in redistricting a salamander-shaped area of the state (to make sure his party, the Democrat-Republicans, would hang on to it) caused the coining of the word "gerrymandering."

Gerry's wife, Ann Thompson (who refused to live in Marblehead because of the smell of his business), was said to be the most beautiful woman in America. She was Irish-born and was unfortunate enough to have two brothers in the British army. Her sister Catherine married Isaac Coles, a colleague of Gerry's. A militia colonel during the war, Coles was an elegant, smoothie raconteur and whisked the lovely

Catherine off to live on his large estates in Pittsylvania County. Not that Catherine missed Washington much. At the time, the place was like early Brasilia, without cultural life or amusements, a nowhere swamp, populated only when bureaucrats turned up to occupy dirty boarding-houses for as long as Congress was in session and then left the place deserted again.

Except for when Isaac's famous cousin was giving one of her evening entertainments where so many people gate-crashed that the affairs were known as "squeezes." Dolley Madison was the original hostess with the mostest. To the reps and senators in their muddy boots and grubby shirts Dolley's décolletage, feathers, turbans, and ready wit were the epitome of sophisticated social whirl. And her ice cream, macaroons, pecans, and caraway-seed cakes dunked in brandy were to die for. Dolley made the white house "The White House," a presidential palace full of high-style American furniture and great conversation. Everybody loved her because, as she said, she loved everybody. The reason her husband got his second term? Dolley.

Who lacked only black and white stockings, gloves, headdresses, and such "pritty" stuff (as she wrote, when asking her pal Ruth Barlow to send frippery back from Paris). Ruth's husband, Joel Barlow, had begun life with one ambition: to become the American National Poet. So in 1787 he wrote a turgid nine volumes of doggerel (the can't-pick-it-up *Vision of Columbus*) before heading for Europe to sell Ohio land for his partners in Scioto Associates. Turned out Scioto was a megascam but Barlow was later cleared. The Barlows stayed away for seventeen years, flitting back and forth between Britain and France, getting more and more involved in murky revolutionary matters and meeting dangerous pro-American radicals like poet William Blake and oxygen discoverer Joseph Priestley.

In 1794 the couple left Parisian political perils behind and headed for Hamburg, where they had a fun time making lots of money running a transport business. And meeting Friedrich Klopstock. By this time Klopstock was seventy and revered because he'd written the first giant German epic poem (*Messiah*), proving to most of his chip-on-shoulder conationals that you didn't have to be French to be cultured. Klopstock failed to persuade Goethe, whose opinion of the piece was: "sentimen-tal" (in one of Goethe's novels two young lovers gaze at a beautiful scene, the boy whispers, "Klopstock!" and they both burst into tears).

Sentimental or not, Klopstock was the grand old man of new Ro-manticism, so Brit poet and Romantic wannabe Samuel T. Coleridge was desperate to check him out and in 1798 turned up in Hamburg. And was disappointed by the uninspiring performance of the toothless old guy with his swollen legs and bad English. Coleridge himself was noth-ing to write home about, already well into his "reverie" mode (i.e., high on opium most of the time). And regretting the hare-brained scheme cooked up by his fellow poet Southey to set up a utopian commune on the banks of the Susquehanna. Fortunately for Coleridge it failed be-cause they couldn't get the money or the volunteer women.

Thanks to an annual remittance from industrialist admirer and pot-tery king Josiah Wedgwood, Coleridge was in Germany (with the boring Wordsworths) to learn German and then sop up the latest German thinking on such cutting-edge stuff as biblical analysis or the new-wave idea that "humans and nature were all of a piece." On that score, when Coleridge got to Göttingen in 1799 (and before returning to London, more opium, and fame) he was also able to sit at the feet of the great J. C. Blumenbach. Which is also where the German anthropology guru put his skulls.

Blumenbach's idea was to place the skull between your feet, view it in this "Blumenbach position," and from its shape identify the race of the skull's original owner. Blumenbach invented the concept of race: Cau-casian, Malaysian, American, and Ethiopian. White was first and best. Everybody else was degenerate descendant. Blumenbach was the first to regard humans as part of nature ("the perfect domesticated animal") and his book *Human Diversity* established scientific anthropology and became the must-have for people watchers almost till today.

Blumenbach's ideas blew the socks off Prince Alexander Philipp Max-imilian zu Wied-Neuwied. After thirteen army years ending as a major general (as princes did), Max went off to Brazil in 1815 on an expedition dedicated to Blumenbach-type studies of local tribes and their skulls. Then returned and in 1832 left again for America. Max's two-year trip to check out the Native Americans took him three thousand miles up the Missouri to Fort McKenzie (in modern Montana). Everywhere he went he wrote about the tribes he met: their culture, customs, physical appearance, and language. Before white settler smallpox wiped them out, Max recorded the lives of the Mandans, Arikara, and Hidatsa and the world they inhabited. In obsessive, Blumenbachian, anthropological detail.

This may be why the paintings by his Swiss artist companion and sidekick Karl Bodmer are so knock-out realistic. Before the days of the camera, Max would check out Bodmer's sketches and make sure they were accurate. Bodmer's paintings of the Native Americans are extraordinarily beautiful and poignant, showing a pristine America and a culture that were both about to disappear forever. Back home, the book of the trip and its eighty-one illustrations took both men ten years to finish and never made a profit. Four hundred and twenty-seven other Bodmer works remained lost in Max's castle library till they were found after World War II.

In 1849 Bodmer left the prince for a more affordable life in the woods outside Paris with a group of painters known (after the name of the village) as the "Barbizon" school. One of whom was Jean-François Millet, who'd left Paris to escape cholera and who, like all of them, was poverty-stricken because his work didn't sell. In Millet's case because before the 1848 revolution his laboring-peasant paintings looked like dangerous working-class propaganda (*The Winnower, The Gleaners, Man with a Hoe, The Potato Planters*).

Although Millet would eventually die destitute, for a brief time after the revolution things went fractionally better for him. "Fractionally" meant the sale of *The Winnower* to the new mayor of Paris, Ledru Rollin, a rich lawyer who defended the rights of the proletariat. Socialist Rollin had been a major player in the 1848 revolution and as minister of the interior in the new provisional government he introduced secret ballots. Trouble started when he came out in opposition to the new president, an ex-exile Bonaparte who then became Emperor Napoleon III. Accused of imperial assassination plans, Rollin skedaddled to London, where he mixed with other like-minded types, including the American consul (self-styled, because so far the Senate hadn't confirmed him), the dubious George Sanders.

After an early career as a Kentucky horsetrader (in more senses than one), Sanders then advanced to leading light of the free-trade-and-invade-Mexico "Young America" movement (it got nowhere). Once in London Sanders promised (without authority to do so) American money for Euro-revolutionaries of all stripes. The Brits thought him "too stupid to do real mischief." Congress eventually nixed his appointment. After which he returned to the United States and was made a southern commissioner at the fiasco known as the 1864 Niagara Peace Conference.

The whole Niagara event was rigged by the South as an attempt to blow Lincoln's chances of re-election. The plan was to make him look antipeace because he was bound to insist on emancipation and refuse to cut a deal with the Confederacy and in this way could be blamed for extending the war. This neat trick failed. Lincoln's "To Whom it May Concern" letter called southern bluff and ended the so-called conference. It was delivered by his assistant secretary John Hay.

By 1870 Hay was U.S. Legation secretary in Madrid, doing little but culture and writing poems in praise of democrats like the first Spanish Republic's fourth-in-one-year president Emilio Castelar y Ripoll. Ex–university prof., novelist, and historian Castelar had a complicated presidential time (September 1873–January 1874) at the end of which a military coup returned Spain to her more traditional ways. For a while, though, it looked as if American backing might save Castelar's skin. Until, right in the middle of his brief term of office, on October 30, 1873, the *Virginius* affair scuppered his chances.

The *Virginius* was a paddle steamer on her clandestine way to (Spanish) Cuba with a cargo of arms, ammunition, and revolutionaries when she was stopped in international waters by a Spanish warship and towed to Cuba. On November 4, the four on-board revolutionary leaders were executed. Three days later the captain and thirty-four crew, including U.S. and U.K. citizens, were shot. On November 8, twelve more revolutionaries bit the dust. By which time the U.K. government was going crazy, Congress was talking war, and a British navy frigate, HMS *Niobe*, was in the Cuban harbor calling for hands up all round. Castelar stopped the firing squads.

The *Niobe* skipper was Lambton Loraine. Whose son Percy took a similarly international career as a diplomat, with a life like a travelogue. From 1904: Istanbul, Teheran, Rome, Beijing, Paris, Madrid, Warsaw, Teheran, Athens, Cairo, Ankara, Rome. In Ankara he gave full Brit support to Turkish modernizer Kemal Ataturk and in Rome did very little about Mussolini. Which may be why Churchill passed him over for promotion during World War II.

After the war Loraine became a horse owner and hired Noel Murless to train his stable. By 1948 Murless was working for such other notables as King George VI and the Dewar whiskey family as British champion trainer (three Derby winners, five Oaks winners). Murless had started his career outside at Thirsk in Yorkshire where in 1612 on the Hambleton Hills the first horse races had taken place under the patronage of King James I. In 1794 one of the greatest thoroughbreds of all time was named after the place: "Hambletonian."

In 1849 the name was used again for the stallion that went on to become the foundation sire of all great American trotters and then in turn gave its name to the annual American harness-racing event: "The Hambletonian." For some years after 1951 the venue for the race was Goshen, New York, where the sport established the Hambletonian Racing Museum and Hall of Fame.

From 1976 to 1992 the museum director was ELBRIDGE GERRY.

CHAPTER FIFTY-THREE

Richard Henry Lee

RICHARD HENRY LEE (VA) was forty-four. Scion of one of Virginia's first families. Patrician, redheaded, slim, and elegant, Lee was a great speaker and although he referred to politics as "the science of fraud" he was a consummate politico. It was Lee's idea to set up the network of correspondence among the colonies so that they could stay in touch about British troop activity. Incredibly, Lee found time to work on about a hundred revolutionary committees. In Congress, a month or so before signing, Lee uttered the immortal (Brit: infamous) words: "Resolved: that these united colonies, are, and of right ought to be, free and independent states."

While he was sixth President of the United States (in Congress Assembled), Lee extended the contract of the (one and only) geographer of the United States, Thomas Hutchins. Who had earlier spent years surveying and mapping for the Brits (from Minnesota to New Orleans), during which time he had three mistresses and three illegitimate kids, billed his employers for every hour of overtime, and was tried for and acquitted of treason. And invented the great Public Land Survey System using the grid system (six-mile squares, each containing thirty-six one-mile squares, each containing 640 acres) later adopted by all but the first thirteen states. Hutchins's sidekick in this activity was David Rittenhouse, by 1785 one of America's greatest scientists and in 1792 first director of the U.S. Mint. Self-taught astronomical- and surveying-instrument-maker, Rittenhouse built an observatory in Philadelphia and his night-work soon became known in Europe. Where from 1787 he was published by Charles Dilly.

Dilly was famous for his dinner parties (any visiting American was welcome) and for feeding starving authors at all times of day. Dilly had visited Philadelphia in 1764 and was a paid-up member of the American Independence cause. On both sides of the Atlantic he was well-connected. Friends included Dr. Johnson and Boswell as well as Ben Franklin and Benjamin Rush (who described Dilly's salon, where scribblers met to argue, as a "coffee house for writers.") In 1781 Dilly published *Rimes* by an arrogant creep named John Pinkerton.

In 1783 Pinkerton produced *Selected Scottish Ballads* (many of which were in fact written by himself). Then in 1787 came his essay arguing that the Celts were an inferior race. Then Pinkerton committed bigamy. Then ran away to a poverty-stricken life in Paris. Little else to say. Pinkerton's great enemy was Joseph Ritson, real estate agent who spotted the fake Scottish ballads. Ritson was also an antiquary with a penchant for the medieval and a fascination with forgery. He also exposed a counterfeit Shakespeare play and was an early collector of (real) folk ballads. In 1795 he wrote the definitive work on Robin Hood (inspiring his admirer Sir Walter Scott to write *Ivanhoe*) and a work on vegetarianism (he was one), and before going nuts became fast friends with fellow left-winger John Thelwall.

Thelwall was the radical's role model. Certain that a British revolution was on the way, he lectured on this topic until the government (certain that a British revolution was *not* on the way) shut down his Society for Free Debate and suspended habeas corpus. Then arrested Thelwall and his agitating pals and put them in the Tower of London for seven months. At Thelwall's trial for treason he was acquitted and returned to the lecture circuit, this time giving talks on "Classical History" (geddit?), attended as ever by government spies.

Another (slightly less) revolutionary colleague was Dr. John Parkinson, who was hauled before the Privy Council to give evidence about the (failed) conspiracy to kill George III with a poisoned dart (the "Pop-

gun Plot"). After which, Parkinson wisely kept out of politics and returned to medicine, publishing several volumes of medical advice for
the general public. He then developed a passion for fossils, which he believed offered evidence of the life forms that had been present on the
planet before the biblical Flood wiped them all out. But it was his publication in 1817 of *Essay on the Shaking Palsy* that put him in the history
books. It was the first description of what is now known, after him, as
Parkinson's disease.

Meanwhile the Pop-gun Plot went to trial and one of the accused (a
friend of Parkinson's) was successfully defended by legal whiz John
Gurney. Who in 1816 really hit the headlines when he led for the prosecution in the case of the great "Napoleon is dead!" Stock Exchange
scam. On February 21, 1814, a man claiming to be the aide-de-camp to
Britain's ambassador to Russia disembarked at the English port of
Dover and sent a message to the governor of the local garrison that
Napoleon had been defeated in battle and was dead. Thick fog prevented this extraordinary message from being semaphored to London.
By noon the aide had galloped hard and was in London spreading the
word. The idea that the war might be over sent government stocks
rocketing up the charts. Then it was discovered that a massive buy-low-
and-sell-high transaction had just taken place on the Stock Exchange.
The previous week £1.1 million worth of stocks had been bought. On
the day of the Napoleonic-death news the stocks were sold for mucho
profit. Investigations revealed that the "ambassador's aide" was a fake.
Even his admitted identity was fake ("Baron" Random de Berenger was
no baron).

The whole operation had been masterminded by an aristo scoundrel
named Cochrane-Johnson. Wife-beater and defrauder of women,
Cochrane-Johnson was up to his ears in mistresses and debt, suspected
of smuggling, and involved in a recent international scam selling mus-
kets, which didn't work, to Spain in return for Spanish sheep, which
died en route to America. In the hullabaloo following the discovery of
the Napoleon swindle, Cochrane-Johnson skipped town and was never
seen again. De Berenger, rifleman, explosives expert, and in debt, was
caught trying to flee the country two weeks later. He eventually avoided

prison by claiming he'd been only a hired hand. By 1831 he was back in the gun business publishing *How to Protect Life and Property* and running a shooting club in Cremorne House, Chelsea.

In 1845 the lease on the property passed to Thomas Simpson, owner of the North and South America Coffeehouse, who turned the grounds of Cremorne House into a pleasure garden with puppet theater, grotto, hermit's cave, circus, and (at night) music and dancing (and hookers). In 1861 Simpson retired and E. Tyrrel Smith took over. Son of an admiral, Smith had a reputation for doing everything but not for long. He was a kind of English lesser P. T. Barnum. After brief employment in the police, his activities included restaurateur, land agent, picture dealer, *Sunday Times* owner, producer of the first flying-trapeze artistes, and (in 1849) proprietor of a pub, The Coal Hole. Where in 1851 he dressed the barmaids in the latest fashion craze from America, bloomers.

Amelia Bloomer lived in Seneca Falls, New York, and began her rise to fame by writing anonymous local-paper articles about women's rights. In 1848 the town hosted a women's rights convention and a year later Amelia founded *Lily*, a women's mag dedicated to promoting the women's vote as well as women's education, jobs, short hair, and dress reform. This last included popularizing the new style: a short skirt worn with full Turkish trousers. The outfit soon became known as "bloomers" although it was a pal of Amelia's, Elizabeth Smith Miller, who originally designed and wore them.

Miller's cousin (and friend of Amelia) Elizabeth Cady Stanton was the real power in the women's rights movement and it was she who had organized the Seneca Falls Convention. Stanton started out in the anti-slavery movement and then through her social contacts with legislators and lawyers in Albany, New York, began to lobby for the women's suffrage issue. Her demands were simple: votes for women ("no taxation without representation"), establishment of any individual woman's rights in marriage as well as equal rights in child custody, and reassessment of the laws on marriage and divorce. At first Stanton had the support of the New York *Tribune* but then its owner, Horace Greeley, decided Stanton's stance on marriage was a bit too "free love" and came out against her. Greeley's paper was tough on slavery, aristocracy, capital punishment, infidelity, and booze. And soft on vegetarianism, peace movements, and labor rights.

Greeley turned the *Tribune* into a great national daily and used it to promote one of his catchy slogans: "Go West, young man." In 1859 Greeley himself criss-crossed the country, filing reports on American life as he went. Eventually he was nominated by the Democrats as presidential candidate in 1872 but failed to win election. Much of the *Trib's* success was due to the efforts of Greeley's left-leaning managing editor Charles Dana. Who during a visit to Europe in 1848 (to cover the numerous revolutions that year) succeeded in recruiting Karl Marx as the paper's European affairs correspondent. It was also Dana who remarked, " 'Dog bites man' isn't news. News is: 'Man bites dog.' " In 1862 Dana and Greeley fell out over how the Civil War was being fought and Dana left the paper.

One of Dana's spare-time activities back in 1858 had been his involvement with the sixteen-volume *New American Cyclopaedia* produced by his friend William Henry Appleton. Who turned his book company into one of America's greats, publishing travel, poetry, fiction, and biography. Appleton also produced the memoirs of Ulysses S. Grant as well as the first American editions of *Alice in Wonderland* and *Origin of Species*.

One of Appleton's contributors to the *New American Cyclopaedia* was the Astor Library librarian, Willard Fiske, recently returned from two years at Sweden's Uppsala University where he had studied Scandinavian languages. About which he wrote for Appleton. After another year in Europe Fiske became professor of northern European languages (his collection of Icelandic literature was the biggest outside Reykjavik), teaching Danish, German, Swedish, and Icelandic. He also got the job of librarian at the recently opened Cornell University. Where he extended library hours from two to nine hours a day, a first in the United States.

In 1880 Fiske married the tubercular Jennie McGraw, heiress to the McGraw lumber fortune, and when she died a year later Fiske got into a legal battle with the university over her will (he won). Eventually McGraw's father's partner Henry Sage fulfilled what he believed Jennie had originally had in mind for the university, funding the construction of a bell tower now known as McGraw Tower. In which a set of nineteen bells is rung three times a day by a chimemaster who climbs the 161 steps to do so.

In 1941 the Cornell chimemaster was RICHARD HENRY LEE.

CHAPTER FIFTY-FOUR

Oliver Wolcott

OLIVER WOLCOTT (CT) was forty-nine. He signed on October 1, because he'd been sick in August. Described by a congressional colleague as "not having much political knowledge," Wolcott was one of three generations of Connecticut governors (his father, himself in 1796, and his son). Wolcott (Yale, judge, business) had a pretty quiet time in Congress, joining only the Committee on Army Accounts. In 1776 he transported the torn-down metal statue of George III from New York City to his hometown of Litchfield, where he had it turned into 42,022 bullets.

In 1795 his son Oliver Wolcott, Jr. (lawyer, Federalist), became secretary of the Treasury after Alexander Hamilton. Whom he also helped in setting up the First Bank of the United States and the Bank of America. In 1803 Oliver moved from Litchfield to New York, where he got together with four other guys (the Litchfield China Trading Co.) and started an export-import business.

One of Oliver's partners, Colonel Ben Tallmadge, had spent an exciting war. In 1778 Washington had made him head of intelligence, so with a few childhood friends Tallmadge set up the "Culpeper spy ring." They used invisible ink, a numerical code (711 was George Washington), dead-letter drops in a field, and a laundry-line signal system (a black petticoat meant a message was waiting, the number of handkerchiefs indicated which Long Island cove was being used by the messenger). The spy ring was amazingly successful in bluffing and counterbluffing the Brits.

In 1780 Tallmadge came across three militiamen who had just caught a British spy, Major John André, and were about to send him for questioning to General Benedict Arnold at nearby West Point. In fact, traitor Arnold had just given André the Point's defensive plans. Tallmadge thought there was something suspicious about Arnold so he got the prisoner redirected to Tappan. Where he was tried and sentenced to hang in spite of his protestations that he was a military officer and ought to be shot. Everybody liked André but George Washington gave them no choice.

On October 2 André went to the gallows, gallant and respected by foe and friend alike. And the subject of later vociferous complaints from English poet Anna Seward, known as the "Swan of Litchfield" (in England), who wrote: "Remorseless Washington! The day shall come / Of deep repentance for this barb'rous doom." Washington sent Seward a messenger to say sorry but he hadn't had any choice.

Anna Seward knew André because he had been jilted by her adopted sister Honora (with whom Seward herself had a more-than-close relationship). Although Seward was propositioned (to no avail) by no less than Dr. Johnson's amanuensis James Boswell, her relationships with men remained intellectual and epistolary (she wrote back to everybody who wrote). And she had limited fun with family friend Erasmus Darwin, who lived in Litchfield. Seward's books and poems did well (if you liked that kind of high-flown stuff).

Later in life the nails of Seward's fingers and toes fell off, and she developed severe arthritis and spent time looking for healthy places to stay. One such was a beauty spot in North Wales where Seward made the acquaintance of the local "Ladies of Llangollen" aka Lady Eleanor Butler and Sarah Ponsonby. Who had first met each other in 1805 when Eleanor was thirty and Sarah fifteen, then eloped in men's clothing and carrying pistols, were caught, eloped again, and finally made it to their Welsh cottage. Where they lived "the most celebrated virgins in Europe" with their dog Sappho. Lesbian or not, their relationship and dress were ambiguous enough to attract the interest of such as Queen Caroline and a visit from such famous faces as the Duke of Wellington, Edmund Burke, and a distant cousin of Sarah's, Lady Caroline Lamb.

Lamb was the great scandal of the day. Marriage at a young age in 1805 had introduced her to what (she hinted) were Sir William Lamb's unnameable perversions. And it was all downhill from there. Two still-borns and one autistic child later, in 1812 she met poet and lecher Lord Byron, already a world figure. The club-foot voluptuary gave her the full treatment and over two months their behavior shocked London. Caroline was high on passion and violent arguments in public, mad with jealousy, ostracized by society, and burned her boats at one point by trying to stab herself to death. Inevitably, Byron became bored and moved off to other adventures in adultery, incest, and pederasty. In 1815 he married somebody else. Caroline went right off the rails and took to drink. And the famous dinner party when *soupe du jour* was Caroline naked in the tureen.

A year later Byron left his new wife and hightailed it for foreign parts accompanied by his best man, the faithful John Hobhouse. The two had met at Cambridge and had already traveled the Eastern Mediterranean, where they had nearly been mugged. Byron had also swum the Hellespont and had affairs of every kind. In 1816 on a second trip Hobhouse caught up with Byron at a villa near Geneva, where, according to Hobhouse, Byron, Shelley, Mary Shelley, and her cousin Claire Clairmont were having an incestuous *ménage à quatre*.

After tours of the Alps, Hobhouse and Lord B. headed for Milan. There they met Silvio Pellico and (in five days) Hobhouse translated Pellico's latest tragedy, *Francesca da Rimini*. Then it was off again to Venice and Rome. After which Hobhouse went home and Byron hit the high spots of Greece. Pellico fared less well. Four years later he was arrested by the Austrian occupying powers and sentenced to death for "reformist activities." Death was eventually commuted to ten years' prison in an underground cell in Moravia. In 1832 Pellico emerged, blinking, to write his only great work: *My Imprisonments*. Translated a year later by Englishman Thomas Roscoe.

Whose languages weren't up to some of the more complex stuff he

tackled (eleven volumes of assorted Italian, Spanish, and German novelists). Roscoe did better with his travel books, producing one a year for a
collection known as the *Landscape Annual*. A particularly good Roscoe
piece described the fall of the fifteenth-century Moorish kingdom of
Granada and included a prediction that religion would hold Spain back
for centuries. David Roberts did the illustrations.

Roberts had started life in Scotland as a scene painter and moved on
to interior décor. In 1823 he arrived in London with a contract to work
at the Drury Lane Theater and was soon getting rave reviews for his oils
(he did well enough eventually to be commissioned by Queen Victoria
to paint the opening of the great 1851 Crystal Palace Exhibition). In
1832 he became the first British artist to travel through Spain (producing the work that would feature in Roscoe's book), and in 1838 he
ranged as far as southern Egypt (in Arab dress) and all over the eastern
Mediterranean, bringing back 272 sketches.

In 1846 the historical descriptions for Roberts's paintings of Palestine
were provided by William Brockedon. Who had started out as an
Alpine-pass devotee, in 1821 following Hannibal's trail and also checking out fifty-nine other ways of getting over the mountains, sketching as
he went. But Brockedon's real talent lay in invention: rubber stoppers,
oblique-slit pen nibs, wadding for cartridges, wire-drawing machinery.
He also suggested the use of gas to heat rooms and the development of
rubber gizmos for milking cows. In 1843, fed up with brittle pencil
leads, he developed a way to compress the graphite.

Then he turned the compression machine into one that would make
medicine pills. By 1854 compressed pills were in the United States, and
by 1877 the method was the subject of a dissertation at the Philadelphia
College of Pharmacy by one Silas Burroughs. Who made friends with a
fellow student from Wisconsin, Henry Wellcome. The two opened a
business selling the pills ("tabloids") and became millionaires almost
overnight. Wellcome, convinced that the sun never set on the British
market, moved to London, set up the Burroughs Wellcome drug company, and started giving tabloid medical chests to everybody from royalty to African explorers.

In 1901 at the age of forty-eight Wellcome married the strikingly beautiful twenty-one-year-old Syrie Barnardo (daughter of the orphan-children-organization founder). Syrie soon found that raincoats and whips weren't her preferred bedroom accoutrements and started sleeping elsewhere. In 1913 one of the beds belonged to already-renowned playwright Somerset Maugham, whose *Of Human Bondage* was just about to make him the greatest living playwright (although he said of himself, "I am in the very front rank of the second-raters"). Alas for Syrie, after they had had a child and then married, Maugham turned out to be homosexual. And left for pastures greener among the Literary Ambulance Drivers of World War I.

His codrivers included such as John Dos Passos, Dashiell Hammett, e.e. cummings, and Ernest Hemingway. Whose life read like his notes. War wounded. Reporter, Toronto *Star*. In 1922: living, reporting, and writing in Paris in the company of Gertude Stein and Ezra Pound. Marriage. Toronto again. Paris again. By 1929 four major novels. Divorced. Remarried. In 1930: living in Key West. In 1937: Madrid and the Spanish Civil War.

The year before Madrid, Hemingway had begun an affair with a leggy blonde writer named Martha Gellhorn who was about to become a great war correspondent. When they met Gellhorn had just written *The Trouble I've Seen* (foreword by H. G. Wells), a New-Reportage-style set of four novellas based on the experiences she'd had while checking out the effectiveness of Federal Emergency Relief Administration projects in industrial cities.

Her boss at FERA was Harry Hopkins, who'd already had more than ten years' experience in welfare administration. In 1933 when Roosevelt became president he appointed Hopkins to FERA with a $500 million budget. Half of the money went in matching grants to states and half was to be given out as discretionary funding. It was a trough waiting for the pigs. A year later Hopkins was embroiled in the affairs of Ohio, whose new governor, Martin Davey, had taken over an administration in desperate straits, with bankrupt local government, closed schools, defunct banks, and massive unemployment.

Davey attacked Roosevelt for "wasteful" use of federal funds and Roosevelt replied by quoting something Harry Hopkins had said about corruption. Davey swore out a warrant for the arrest of Hopkins if he ever set foot in Ohio. Meanwhile, as a prominent and successful local businessman, Davey had recently bought his hometown's newspaper, the Kent *Courier-Tribune*.

Sports editor was ex–football star OLIVER WOLCOTT.

CHAPTER FIFTY-FIVE

Matthew Thornton

MATTHEW THORNTON (MA) was sixty. He signed on November 4, the day he first entered Congress. Six feet tall and a great storyteller, Thornton was an Irish-born New Hampshire doctor-turned-politician and then (with no legal training) judge. He made money speculating in land, helped write the constitution of New Hampshire (it was the first state to do so), wrote newspaper articles, produced an unpublished treatise on sin, and bought the confiscated estate of runaway loyalist Edward Lutwych.

Lutwych had been involved (on the government side) in the great 1772 Weare, New Hampshire, Pine Tree Riot, a Tea Party before the Tea Party. Back then if the Brits discovered New England sawmills cutting down white-pine trees whose trunks were over twelve inches in diameter the mill owners were fined and the mills shut down. Twelve-inch-plus-diameter trees were strictly booked for use as British ship masts. However, given the local terrain and with only half a dozen enforcement officers, the law was hard to enforce. Finally, however, the increasing number of absent trees triggered a real crackdown. Some perpetrators were identified and threatened with jail or worse. Twenty of them blacked their faces and ran the sheriff out of town. Lutwych helped bring them to justice, since he represented the king's law in those parts. But the way things were going, not for long.

The white pine became yet another great revolutionary reminder of the repressive rule of the Brits and was fittingly chosen to appear on the first flag flown by the first U.S. Navy ships. The new flag and the new navy were both thought up by Joseph Reed, Washington's confidential secretary and the man who wrote most of the letters Washington signed (including the one to Canada saying come join us). Before things went warlike, Reed got a Brit back-channel offer of half a million and a top government job if he would agree to persuade Congress to back down and call off the fight. He spurned the offer and blabbed about it to everybody who would listen.

Reed's wife did her bit for the war effort, too. Society queen, hostess of lavish dinner parties, in 1778 First Lady of Pennsylvania Esther Reed decided to pitch in and in 1780 persuaded thirty-nine other patriotic women to go round knocking on more than sixteen hundred doors. They raised three hundred thousand dollars and Esther proposed to give every soldier a two-dollar bonus. Washington said not to do that because the guys would spend it on booze, so Esther bought linen and all her women sewed twenty-two hundred shirts.

The project enjoyed the enthusiastic support of the Marquis Barbe-Marbois, secretary to the French Legation and head of not-so-secret French support operations throughout the war. After he returned to France the aristocratic Marbois managed to survive French revolutionary exile to French Guyana, and when things settled down again he was released and appointed minister of Finance under Napoleon. For whom in 1803 he handled the Louisiana Purchase. With which the United States doubled its territory at a stroke and forever blocked French ambitions in America.

During the behind-closed-doors Purchase chicanery (see elsewhere), there was a strange one-month period during which (a) the Spanish gave Louisiana to the French (in return for a kingdom in Italy) and then (b) the French passed it on to the United States for $15 million. Involved on the ground in New Orleans during (a) was Cuban-based Spanish Louisiana military governor Sebastian de Casa Calvo. Whose brother Nicholas, doctor of theology at the Pontifical University in Havana, was an early volunteer in the Royal Economic Society of Friends of the Country, a group of liberals dedicated to modernizing Cuba's agriculture, education, science, and anything else that needed it (i.e., everything).

In 1803 Nicholas got the high-powered assistance of a passing German explorer, Alexander von Humboldt, who was about to astonish the world with his South American sketches, maps, measurements, descriptions, and sixty thousand plant specimens. For five years Humboldt walked, canoed, rode, and climbed all over Venezuela, Colombia, Ecuador, Mexico, and Peru and wrote about their climate, geology, oceanography, magnetism, zoology, ecology (he invented the science), and ethnography in a giant thirty-four-volume work that took him another twenty-five years.

He also brought back some interesting Peruvian bird droppings. Guano (for such it was) saved the overcrowded European industrial city populations from starvation because it was full of nitrogen that quadrupled the crop yield. In England guano made the Gibbs family (a small trading outfit) very rich. By 1841 they had the Peruvian export monopoly, buying guano at five bucks a ton and selling at fifteen. On a good year: three hundred thousand tons. And they did this for forty years. Work it out.

With money like that a humble merchant like William Gibbs could build himself an enormous pseudo-Gothic palace complete with domes, chapel, library, conservatory, turrets, and towers. Inside he had everything from gold mosaics to stained glass, carved oak flowers, Japanese screens, Oriental porcelain, and Old Masters by the yard. And that was just the ground floor.

Gibbs's Tyntesfield Hall near Bristol was the work of architect John Norton, who did everything to excess. In the case of another such new startup (Elvedon Hall, Suffolk), Norton razed to the ground what was there and built a brick imitation Italian Renaissance piece with Indian interiors copied from photographs and drawings provided by his client, the exiled maharajah of Punjab, Duleep Singh. Who in 1863 obligingly left for a honeymoon in Egypt and Scotland and let Norton get on with it.

Duleep was the guy who is said to have picked out from his baubles the gigantic Koh-I-Noor diamond to give to Queen Victoria. In fact back home in India the conquering British military had persuaded Duleep to do so. The diamond (its name meant "Mountain of Light") went from 186 carats down to a recut 105 under the guiding eye of hottest-mineralogist-of-the-day James Tennant and finally ended up sparkling in the crown of Queen Elizabeth II's mother.

The other famous thing Tennant did was invite Garibaldi to the London Zoo. During the Great Italian's brief London visit in 1864 the country closed down for three days and crowds lined the streets. Garibaldi was already so famous that a U.K. biscuit and a U.S. fish were named after him. In 1861 Lincoln had even offered Garibaldi general-ship of the Union armies (no, thanks). After heroic behavior in South America (fighter for Brazilian independence from Portugal and then head of the microscopically small Uruguayan navy against Argentina), Garibaldi, the revolutionary's pin-up, was back in Europe. Where he kept coming out of retirement for yet another shot at invading Rome. At the time of his London banquet-in-honor-of he still had one more shot to come. That one didn't work, either. Still, he helped unify Italy, and today there's a street or square named after him in every single Ital-ian town and village.

Presiding at Garibaldi's London sit-down was one of those typically British types: an aristocrat (dukes, marquesses, and earls in the family) who becomes a social reformer. Robert Grosvenor (first Baron Ebury, Eton, Cambridge, silver spoon) was vice president of the Incorporated Society for Improving the Condition of the Labouring Classes, tried (but failed) to get shops closed on Sundays, and became member of Par-liament for Chester (where his father was "influential"). In 1868 he suf-fered the ignominy of losing the election for the London borough of Westminster to a man who had spent four times more on getting out the vote than Grosvenor.

Rumors of pre-election bribery were probably just that, given the winner's stolid, middle-class, God-fearing character (he was described later by Queen Victoria as "modest and simple"). William Henry Smith had begun life the son of an impoverished newspaper distributor who had the bright idea of using the new trains to deliver the news. In 1854

W.H. followed up by getting the book-selling monopoly on all railroad lines in the country. Soon his bookstalls adorned every station, carrying enlivening and uplifting out-of-copyright (cheap) texts with which to while away the journey.

Inevitably W.H. (whose company is today billion-dollar, worldwide) went into politics and made it to leader of the House of Commons. Not bad for a nobody. He also gave others of a similar background similar opportunities. In 1873 a ten-year-old delivered W.H.'s newspapers from Clapham Junction train station in London and then went into railroad engineering, machine tools, and electrical equipment. Finally in 1903 the kid (name of Henry Royce) bought a secondhand car that was such a wreck he decided to build his own. When he showed the finished product to an aristo car salesman named Rolls the result made history in the form of the 1906 Silver Ghost. About which it was said that if you had to ask the price, you couldn't afford it. At top speed the only noise you could hear was the ticking clock.

By World War II Rolls-Royce engines were in Spitfires, Hurricanes, Mustangs, and more. By 1960 their Pegasus jet engine was using clever swiveling nozzles to power the prototype of what would eventually become the Harrier vertical takeoff attack fighter, favored by the U.S. Marines for its ability to jump up out of the bushes and spoil the other person's day. NASA also used the airplane as a research vehicle. In the 1970s NASA had dreams of sending unmanned reconnaissance spacecraft to Mars where they would hover here and there to take pictures. So the subject of vectored thrust (like that of the Harrier) was in the air, so to speak.

U.S. governmental reality checks altered these blue-yonder matters somewhat, but NASA pressed ahead with scaled-down plans for Rovers and Orbiters and such. In 1999 they commissioned a simulation study (of future exploration and colonization of the Red Planet) by a company whose previous experience had been in Sim games.

The company's Mars project producer was MATTHEW THORN-TON.

CHAPTER FIFTY-SIX

THOMAS McKEAN (DE) was forty-two. He was the last signer, on January 18, 1777, having been absent in the army the previous August. Lawyer McKean began public life as a justice of the peace and collector of excise for the Brits. In 1773 his revolutionary views took him to Philadelphia. In spite of his ego, bad temper, and small-mindedness McKean did good work for the cause. Later problems occurred when he was governor of Pennsylvania (he appointed more than a dozen relatives to public positions and impeachment proceedings were started).

In 1781 McKean was elected the second president of the United States (in Congress Assembled). He also ran simultaneous jobs working for several states and cities and was a member of the Society for the Promotion of Agriculture, where one of his friends was a young doctor from Long Island, Sam Mitchill. Who qualified in Edinburgh and then took the cultural Grand Tour of Europe.

By 1791 Mitchill was in the New York Legislature, and a year later he started a fifteen-year term as professor of chemistry, natural history, and agriculture at Columbia College. In 1797 he cofounded the first American medical journal. He also spent six years in the House and another four in the Senate. Mitchill wrote over two hundred articles on everything from Galapagos tortoises to Spanish chestnuts, Hudson Valley geology, politics, Native American culture, biography, and zoology and earned the nickname "chaos of knowledge." In the course of all this he corresponded with contemporary American scientists including Constantine Rafinesque.

Brought up in Marseilles, France, Rafinesque arrived in America in 1798 to learn business and then traveled the country collecting botanical specimens. In 1805 he was appointed secretary to the American consul in Palermo, Sicily, where he wrote a book about Sicilian natural history (1810) and started the first Sicilian science journal (1814). On the way back to the United States he lost everything in a shipwreck. In 1817 he produced a list of sixty-seven hundred plant names arranged by morphology (the idea was attacked on all sides as "crack-brained" but later became standard practice). Darwin said of Rafinesque, "He saw evolution before me." Rafinesque then moved to Kentucky where he wrote on Mayan glyphs and the Hebrew Bible and peddled a quack cure for tuberculosis.

Back in his Palermo days Rafinesque had met a British ex-army shell collector and artist, the stammering William Swainson. In 1817 Swainson shot off to Brazil to collect he knew not what and sent a grower in Scotland a new flower, now well known at every modern prom as the "corsage orchid." Alas, Swainson forgot to say where he had found the flower (Pernambuco), so it took another seventy-one years for it to be rediscovered. Meanwhile Swainson made a name for his beautiful lithographs of birds and shells and in 1833 signed a contract to write fourteen volumes (three a month) on natural history for the great science popularizer Dionysius Lardner.

By 1817 Lardner was already a celeb. His lectures on you-name-it science and technology were standing-room-only. His book, rivetingly titled *The Steam Engine Familiarly Explained*, went into dozens of editions and four foreign languages. Before his life went down the toilet thanks to elopement with an army officer's wife (the guy flogged him) followed by a messy trial, Lardner's proudest moment was the 144-volume *Cabinet Cyclopedia*. Published between 1830 and 1844, it covered an encyclopedic range of subjects. Lardner managed to get all the big names to contribute, including Sir Walter Scott on Scottish history, David Brewster on optics, Mary Shelley for biographies, and Thomas Moore on the history of Ireland.

By this time Moore had published his sensational best-seller oriental romance (full of exotic sensualism) *Lalla Rookh*. Also various political diatribes, a few (dead-duck) plays, and numerous essays. But what made Moore a star by 1821 was *Irish Melodies* (including the still-remembered "Last Rose of Summer" and "The Minstrel Boy"), whistled in every street in Britain and America. At the fashionable London salons (where even the Prince Regent turned up), Moore laid 'em in the aisles with his own rendering of the *Melodies*, accompanying himself on the guitar. Even Henri Bayle (aka the author Stendhal) referred to Moore as one of only two singers in Britain worth listening to. Bayle didn't name the other one.

Bayle was the archetypal Romantic: innumerable love affairs, dangerous political tendencies, passions of all kinds, excesses ditto, and a tendency to hallucinate. He was the dilettante's generalist. By 1802 he was in Paris determined to be a writer and meeting actresses. Through an aristo cousin Bayle wangled an army commissary job in Germany and then took his pen name (Stendhal) from a nearby German town. In 1830 came his first major novel, *The Red and the Black* (liberalism versus reactionary church). After this Bayle spent eleven years as French consul in "an abominable hole" (the rather pleasant coastal town of Civitavecchia, Italy), during which he wrote his masterpiece, *The Charterhouse of Parma*.

The Civitavecchia consulship had been arranged as a punishment for Bayle's liberal views by Prince Metternich, the man who invented *realpolitik*. And who had been a diplomatic genius since an early age. Austro-Hungarian Empire ambassador to Berlin at thirty and then minister in Paris (where he gained a reputation for determined womanizing), in 1818 Metternich was pulling the strings at the post–Napoleonic Wars Congress of Vienna. His main aim was to keep kings on thrones and revolutionaries in jails. But the liberal tide was rising fast. In 1840 Metternich recognized he couldn't prevent Hungarian independence from Austria and freed Budapest tough guy Lajos Kossuth.

By 1848 the European continent was high on independence mania and Kossuth was Hungarian minister of finance, issuing Hungarian banknotes and talking extravagant republican stuff about secession from the Austrian Empire. So with Russian military help Kossuth was stopped in his tracks and, voting with his feet, skipped the country, ending up with others of his ilk in London. Where in 1851 he negotiated jobs for fellow Hungarian exiles at the gunpowder factory of William Hale.

Hale had tried and failed to get a jet-powered ship engine off the drawing board and then switched to rocket development, replacing the stabilizing sticks on the old Congreve rockets ("red glare" in 1812) with a system inspired by the way rifling made bullets spin. Gas-exhaust holes drilled at a tangent in the side of the rocket caused it to rotate and made it more accurate. In 1846 Hale sold the manufacturing rights to the U.S. Army. A year later his rockets were being fired at Mexicans by General David Twiggs.

By 1861 Twiggs was in charge of the Texas Department. When the South seceded, as a southerner he felt obliged to hand over power to a Confederate officer. So he was charged with treason. Twiggs's eventual Texas replacement was Confederate general Octave Hebert, first in his class of 1840 at West Point and by now recent Louisiana governor. Before the war Hebert had been president of the New Orleans Metairie Jockey Club. In 1862, when New Orleans was occupied by Union forces, thoroughbred horses were stolen and moved north where they were sold at auction.

One of the buyers was George Wilkes, editor of the New York horse-racing mag *Spirit of the Times*. One of Wilkes's reporters (he filed dispatches from the Mexican War) was Englishman and great raconteur Mayne Reid, who had spent a lot of time in America, where he met ornithologist J. J. Audubon and novelist Edgar Allan Poe. Reid also wrote boys' adventure novels like *The Headless Horseman* but didn't do too well, and in 1866 was saved from bankrupty only by a contract from the Tinsley publishing company.

Tinsley was a gamekeeper's son from deepest bucolic nowhere. He walked to London, took odd jobs in the book trade, and in 1854 started his own imprint. In 1862 the blockbuster *Lady Audley's Secret* made him rich. In 1871 against general opinion he took on an unknown writer named Thomas Hardy and published his first two novels, *Disreputable*

Remedies and *Under the Greenwood Tree*. Tinsley's list eventually included Trollope and Meredith. One of his great friends was writer Harriet Martineau.

Deaf (ear trumpet) by age twenty-eight, Martineau was a formidable woman. From the time of her first essay, written when she was eighteen, Martineau went for the most extreme liberal causes: electoral reform, abolition of slavery, free education. She was also a "necessitarian," denying free will in favor of the controlling effect of social and educational contitions. Which, she argued, could and should be improved. She was also into mesmerism and head-bump-reading (in revealing an individual's character, bump-reading gave a clue to what could be done to improve the person). Between 1852 and 1860 Martineau wrote sixteen hundred leading articles on social topics of the day for the London *Daily News*. In addition to major writers like George Eliot and Matthew Arnold, her circle included the "ponderous and verbose" Alexander Bain.

Who made psychology more or less scientific. In 1876 Bain founded the first psychology journal, *Mind*. Bain's obsession was the link between mind and body. For him physical sensations played a vital role in mental processes. Bain wrote the classic but unreadable *Emotions and the Will* and introduced the concept of "trial-and-error" learning. After a number of years teaching in London and befriending such VIPs as George Eliot, John Stuart Mill, Herbert Spencer, and the equally ponderous Thomas Carlyle, in 1870 Bain was awarded the chair of logic at Aberdeen University, Scotland. Where in 1872 he taught Gavin Greig.

After graduation the musical Greig ran a local school and introduced folk song to the curriculum. In 1902 he was persuaded by an Aberdeen historical society to rescue what might be left of northeastern Scots folk song and poetry. With a Carnegie grant he collected material non stop until 1911 when he published *Folk-songs of the Northeast*. By this time Greig had assembled a collection of thirty-five hundred texts and thirty-one hundred tunes. After his death in 1914 this mass of barely understandable material in a Scots dialect known as "Doric" was left ignored until late in the century. Then, in 1995, the University of Aberdeen set up the Elphinstone Society, dedicated to the recovery and support of the Doric culture.

In 2004 the head of the Archive and Research Gaelic Section at the institute, responsible for oral tradition, songs, and ballads, was THOMAS McKEAN.

SELECT BIBLIOGRAPHY

SIGNERS

Alexander, John K. *Samuel Adams: America's revolutionary politician*. New York: Rowman & Littlefiend, 2002.

Barthelmas, Della Gray. *The signers of the Declaration of Independence: A biographical and genealogical reference*. Jefferson, NC: McFarland, 1997.

Bellesiles, Michael A. *Revolutionary outlaws : Ethan Allen and the struggle for independence on the early American frontier*. Charlottesville, VA: University Press of Virginia, 1993.

Billias, George Athan. *Elbridge Gerry, founding father and republican statesman*. New York: McGraw-Hill, 1976.

Bland, James E. *The Oliver Wolcotts of Connecticut: The national experience, 1775-1800* (Ph.D. diss., Harvard University, 1970).

Bogin, Ruth. *Abraham Clark and the quest for equality in the revolutionary era, 1774-1794*. Rutherford, NJ: Fairleigh Dickinson University Press, 1982.

Bridges, Edwin C. *George Walton: A political biography* (Ph.D. diss., University of Chicago, 1981).

Brown, Imogen E. *American Aristides: A biography of George Wythe*. Rutherford, NJ: Fairleigh Dickinson University Press., 1981.

Carter, W. C., and Glossbrenner, A. J. *History of York County from its erection to the present time, 1729-1834* (1834); new ed., with additions, ed. A. Monroe Aurand, 1975.

Clark, Ronald W. *Benjamin Franklin*. London: Weidenfeld and Nicholson, 1983.

Cole, Jayne. *Who declared in 1776?* Hartpury, England: J.F. Cole, 2000.

Coleman, John M. *Thomas McKean, forgotten leader of the revolution*. Rockaway, NJ: American Faculty Press, 1975.

Collier, Christopher. *Roger Sherman's Connecticut: Yankee politics and the American revolution*. Middletown, CT: Wesleyan University Press, 1971.

Collins, Varnum L. *President Witherspoon*. Princeton, NJ: Princeton University Press, 1925.

Cunningham, Mary E. "The Case of the Active," *Pennsylvania History*, 13 (1946).

Delafield, Julia. *Biographies of Francis Lewis and Morgan Lewis*. New York: Andson D.F. Randolph & Co., 1877.

Dill, Alonzo T. *Francis Lightfoot Lee, the incomparable signer*. Lanham, MD: University Press of America, 1977.

————*Carter Braxton, Virginia signer: A conservative in revolt*. Lanham, MD: University Press of America, 1983.

Elsmere, Jane S. *Justice Samuel Chase*. Muncie, IN: Janevar, 1980.

Ely, Warren S. *George Taylor, signer of the Declaration of Independence*. Bucks County Historical Society Publications 5 (1926).

Fehrenbach, Theodore R. *Greatness to spare: The heroic sacrifices of the men who signed the Declaration of Independence*. Princeton, NJ: D. Van Nostrand Co., 1968.

Foster, Joseph. "William Whipple," *Granite Monthly* 43 (1911).

Gifford, George E., Jr., ed. *Physician signers of the Declaration of Independence*. New York: Science History Publications, 1976.

Goodrich, Rev. Charles A. *Lives of the signers to the Declaration of Independence*. New York: William Reed & Co., 1856.

Hammond, Cleon E. *John Hart: The biography of a signer of the Declaration of Independence*. Newfane, VT: Pioneer Press, 1977.

Hanley, Thomas O'Brien. *Revolutionary statesman: Charles Carroll and the war*. Chicago: Loyola University Press, 1983.

Hanson, Edward W. *"A Sense of Honor and Duty": Robert Treat Paine (1731-1814) of Massachusetts and the New Nation* (Ph.D. diss., Boston College, 1992).

Hastings, George E. *The life and works of Francis Hopkinson*. Chicago: University Press, 1926.

Haw, James. *John and Edward Rutledge of South Carolina*. Athens, GA: University of Georgia Press, 1997.

Hawke, David F. *Benjamin Rush, revolutionary gadfly*. New York: Bobbs-Merrill, 1971.

————*Honorable treason: the Declaration of Independence and the men who signed it*. New York: Viking Press, 1976.

Jenkins, C. F. *Button Gwinnett*. New York: Doubleday, Page & Co., 1926.

Kneip, Robert C. *William Hooper, 1742-1790, misunderstood patriot* (Ph.D. diss., Tulane University, 1980).

Lee, Nell Moore. *Patriot above profit: A portrait of Thomas Nelson, Jr., who supported the American revolution with his purse and sword*. Nashville, TN: Rutledge Hill Press, 1988.

Lovejoy, David S. *Rhode Island politics and the American revolution, 1760-1776*. Providence, RI: Brown University Press, 1958.

McCullough, David G. *John Adams*. New York: Simon & Schuster, 2001.

McGaughy, J. K. *Richard Henry Lee of Virginia: A portrait of an American revolutionary*. Lanham, MD: Rowman & Littlefield Publishers, 2004.

Onuf, Peter S., ed. *Jeffersonian legacies*. Charlottesville, VA: University Press of Virginia, 1993.

Quinn, C. Edward. *The signers of the Declaration of Independence*. Bronx, NY: Bronx County Historical Society, 1988.

Read, William T. *Life and correspondence of George Read, signer of the Declaration of Independence*. Philadelphia, PA, 1870.

Scott, Jane H. *A gentleman as well as a Whig : Caesar Rodney and the American revolution*. Newark, NJ: University of Delaware Press, 2000.

Smith, Charles Page. *James Wilson, founding father 1742-1798*. Chapel Hill, NC: University of North Carolina Press,1956.

Stark, Bruce P. *Connecticut signer: William Williams*. Chester, CT: The Pequot Press, 1975.

Stiverson, Gregory A, and Jacobsen, Phebe R. *William Paca, a biography*. Baltimore: Maryland Historical Society, 1976.

Unger, Harlow G. *John Hancock: Merchant king and American patriot*. New York: John Wiley & Sons, 2000.

Ver Steeg, Clarence L. *Robert Morris, revolutionary financier; with an analysis of his earlier career*. Philadelphia: University of Pennsylvania Press, 1954.

Wearmouth, John M., and Wearmouth, Roberta J. *Thomas Stone: Elusive Maryland signer*. Port Tobacco, MD: Stones Throw Publishers, 2002.

Woodbury, C. H. "Matthew Thornton." *Proceedings of the New Hampshire Historical Society* 3, 1896.

THE REST

"Dr. Emma Phoebe Waterman." *Astronomical Society of the Pacific*. Vol. 25, June 1913.

Ackroyd, Peter. *J. M. W. Turner*. London: Chatto & Windus, 2005.

Alberts, C. *The golden voyage: The life and times of William Bingham, 1752-1804*. Boston: Houghton Mifflin, 1969.

Alexander, Michael, and Anand, Sushila. *Queen Victoria's Maharajah, Duleep Sing, 1838-93*. London: Phoenix Press, 2001.

Alger, John. *Englishmen in the French Revolution*. London: Sampson Low, Marston, Searle & Rivington, Ltd., 1889.

Allars, K. G. "Barron Field: His association with New South Wales," *Journal of the Royal Australian Historical Society*, Vol. 53, Pt. 3, 1967. Sydney: Royal Australian Historical Society, 1968.

Altick, R. D. *The Shows of London*. Cambridge, MA: The Belknap Press of Harvard University Press, 1978.

Anderson, James. *Sir Walter Scott and history*. Edinburgh: The Edina Press, 1981.

Anderson, R.D. *Education and opportunity in Victorian Scotland*. Edinburgh: Edinburgh University Press, 1983.

Andrew, John A. III. *From revivals to removal*. Athens, GA: University of Georgia Press, 1992.

Appleton, William W. *Madame Vestris and the London stage*. New York: Columbia University Press, 1974.

Ashton, Dore. *Rosa Bonheur*. London: Secker & Warburg, 1981.

Astin, Marjorie. *Mary Russell Mitford, her circle and her books*. London: Noel Douglas, 1930.

Atholl, J. *Chronicles of the Atholl and Tullibardine families, collected and arranged by John, seventh Duke of Atholl, KT*. Edinburgh: Ballantyne Press, 1908.

Baker, Carlos. *Ernest Hemingway: A life story*. New York: Scribner's, 1969.

Barman, R. J. *Citizen emperor: Pedro II and the making of Brazil, 1825-1891*. Stanford, CA: Stanford University Press, 1999.

Bechert, H. *Wilhelm Geiger: His life and works*. Colombo: Gunasena, 1977.

Beechey, Captain F. W. *A voyage of discovery towards the North Pole, performed in His Majesty's ships* Dorothea *and* Trent, *under the command of Captain David Buchan, R.N., 1818*. London: Richard Bentley, 1843.

Bellesiles, Michael A. *Revolutionary outlaws : Ethan Allen and the struggle for independence on the early American frontier*. Charlottesville,VA : University Press of Virginia, 1993.

Bennett, J. A. *Church, state and astronomy in Ireland, 200 years of Armagh Observatory*. Belfast: The Armagh Observatory, 1990.

Benyowsky, M. A. *Memoirs and travels*. London: Kegan, Paul, Trench, Trubner & Co., 1904.

Bergonzi, Bernard. *A Victorian wanderer. The life of Thomas Arnold the Younger*. Oxford: Oxford University Press, 2003.

Berry, Paul. *By royal appointment. A Biography of Mary Ann Clarke, mistress of the Duke of York*. London: Femina Books, 1970.

Bing, Rudolf. *5000 nights*. New York: Doubleday, 1972.

Birkner, Michael. *Samuel L. Southard: Jeffersonian Whig*. Rutherford, NJ: Fairleigh Dickinson University Press, 1984.

Blackburn, Julia. *Charles Waterton, traveller and conservationist*. London: Century, 1989.

Boydell, C. *The architect of floors: modernism, art and Marion Dorn designs*. Coggeshall: Schoeser, in association with the British Architectural Library, Royal Institute of British Architects, 1996.

Boyne, Walter J. *Beyond the horizons: The Lockheed story.* London: St. Martin's Press, 1998.

Bradford, R. H. *The Virginius affair.* Boulder, CO: Colorado Associated University Press, 1980.

Brady, James Edward. *Wyoming: A study of John Franklin and the Connecticut settlement in Pennsylvania.* Syracuse, NY: Syracuse University Press, 1973.

Brewer, David. *The flame of freedom: The Greek war of independence, 1821-1833.* London: John Murray, 2001.

Brightfield, Myron F. *John Wilson Croker.* Berkeley, CA: University of California Press, 1940.

Brockett, Oscar G. *History of the theatre.* Boston: Allyn and Bacon, 1977.

Bronson, Bertrand H. *Joseph Ritson, scholar-at-arms.* Berkeley, CA: University of California Press, 1938.

Buist, Marten G. *At Spes.* The Hague: Martinus Kijdhof, 1974.

Butler, E. M. *The tempestuous prince: Hermann Puckler-Muskau.* London: Longmans, 1929.

Butler, Marylin. *Maria Edgeworth, a literary biography.* Oxford: Clarendon Press, 1972.

Cerutti, T. *Antonio Gallenga: An Italian writer in Victorian England.* London: Oxford University Press for the University of Hull, 1974.

Chandler, Michael. *The life and work of John Mason Neale.* Leominster, Herefordshire: Gracewing Books, 1995.

Chitty, Susan. *Playing the game: A biography of Sir Henry Newbolt.* London: Quartet Books, 1997.

Clark, Aylwin. *An enlightened Scot, Hugh Cleghorn, 1752-1837.* Duns, Scotland: Black Ace Books, 1992.

Clifford, Derek, and Clifford, Timothy. *John Crome.* London: Faber and Faber, 1968.

Clymer, Kenton. *John Hay: The gentleman as diplomat.* Ann Arbor, MI: University of Michigan Press, 1975.

Collins, J. H., ed. *A catalogue of the works of Robert Were Fox, F.R.S., with notes and extracts and a sketch of his life.* Truro: Lake and Lake, 1878.

Cook, Trevor M. *Samuel Hahnemann, the founder of homeopathic medicine.* Northamptonshire: Thorsons Publishers Ltd., 1981.

Cooke, Alan, and Holland, Clive. *The exploration of northern Canada, 500 to 1920, a chronology.* Ontario: The Arctic History Press, 1978.

Cortada, J. W., ed. *Spain in the nineteenth century.* London: Greenwood Press, 1994.

Cowden, Gerald Steffins. *The Randolphs of Turkey Island: A prosopography of the first three generations, 1650-1806* (Ph.D. diss., College of William and Mary, 1977).

Cox, C. *The enigma of the age. The strange story of the Chevalier d'Eon.* London: Longmans, 1966.

Cross, A. G. *The Caledonian phalanx: Scots in Russia.* Edinburgh: National Library of Scotland, 1987.

Cunnington, Robert H. *From antiquary to archaeologist, a biography of William Cunnington.* Aylesbury, Buckinghamshire: Shire Publications Ltd., 1975.

Curl, J. S. *Egyptomania: The Egyptian revival: A recurring theme in the history of taste.* Manchester: Manchester University Press, 1994.

Dillon, Dorothy Rita. *The New York Triumvirate: A study of the legal and political careers of William Livingston, John Morin Scott, William Smith, Jr.* New York: AMS Press, 1968.

Edith, Marchioness of Londonderry. *Frances Anne. The life and times of Frances Anne Marchioness of Londonderry and her husband Charles third Marquess of Londonderry.* London: Macmillan & Co. Ltd., 1958.

Ernst, Robert. *Rufus King, American Federalist.* Chapel Hill, NC: University of North Carolina Press, 1968.

Eyman, Scott. *Ernst Lubitsch: Laughter in paradise.* New York: Simon & Schuster, 1993.

Fleming, Thomas. *The Louisiana Purchase.* London: John Wiley & Sons, 2003.

Florence Nightingale and the Crimea, 1854-55. London: The Stationery Office, 2000.

Flower, Milton E. *John Dickinson: Conservative revolutionary.* Charlottesville, VA: University Press of Virginia, 1983.

Ford, John. *Ackermann, 1783-1983, the business of art.* London: Ackermann, 1983.

Fowler, W. B. *British-American relations, 1917-1918. The role of Sir William Wiseman.* Princeton, NJ: Princeton University Press, 1969.

Francis, Basil. *Fanny Kelly of Drury Lane.* London: Rockcliff, 1950.

Frear, Ned. *The Whiskey Rebellion.* Bedford, PA: Frear Publications, 1999.

Freedland, Michael. *The secret life of Danny Kaye.* London: W.H. Allen, 1985.

Galbraith, John S. *The Little Emperor, Governor Simpson of the Hudson's Bay Company.* Toronto: Macmillan of Canada, 1976.

Gauld, Alan. *A history of hypnotism.* Cambridge: Cambridge University Press, 1992.

Gernsheim, Herbert and Alison. *The history of photography.* London: Thames & Hudson, 1969.

Gilmartin, John. "Peter Turnerelli, Sculptor 1774-1839." *Quarterly Bulletin of the Irish Georgian Society,* Vol. 10, No. 4, October-December 1967. Dublin.

Glass, Ian S. *Victorian telescope makers, the lives and letters of Thomas and Howard Grubb.* Bristol: Institute of Physics Publishing, 1997.

Gough, Barry M., ed. *To the Pacific and Arctic with Beechey, the journal of Lt.*

George Peard of HMS Blossom, *1825-1828*. Cambridge: Cambridge University Press for the Hakluyt Society, 1973.

Grant, Sir Allan. *Steel & ships: the history of John Brown's*. London: Michael Joseph, 1950.

Graustein, Jeannette E. *Thomas Nuttall, naturalist*. Cambridge, MA: Harvard University Press, 1967.

Gray, Edwyn. *The devil's device: Robert Whitehead and the history of the torpedo*. Annapolis, MD: Naval Institute Press, 1991.

Grubb, Sarah. *Some account of the life and religious labours of Sarah Grubb*. London: W. Darton & Son, 1837.

Gruber, Ira D. *The Howe brothers and the American revolution*. New York: Atheneum, 1972.

Guest, I. F. *Fanny Elssler*. London: Adam & Charles Black, 1970.

Haining, Peter. *The Hashish Club: An anthology of drug literature*. London: Peter Owen Ltd., 1975.

Hamburger, L. and J. *Contemplating adultery: the secret life of a Victorian woman*. New York: Fawcett Columbine, 1991.

Haslip, Joan. *Madame du Barry: The wages of beauty*. London: Weidenfeld & Nicolson, 1991.

Hawes, Frances. *Henry Brougham*. London: Jonathan Cape, 1957.

Healey, Edna. *Coutts & Co. 1692-1992. The portrait of a private bank*. London: Hodder & Stoughton, 1992.

Heyde, C. C., and Seneta, E., eds. *Statisticians of the centuries*. New York: Springer-Verlag, 2001.

Hidy, R. W. *The House of Baring in American trade and finance, 1763-1861*. Cambridge, MA: Harvard University Press, 1949.

Higham, C. "Francis Barthelemon," *Biographical Tracts*. London, 1896.

Hodgson, J. E. *The history of aeronautics in Great Britain*. London: Oxford University Press, 1924.

Holmes, Jack D. L. "The Marquás de Casa-Calvo, Nicolás de Finiels, and the 1805 Spanish expedition through East Texas and Louisiana," *Southwestern Historical Quarterly* 69, January 1966.

Hughes, Thomas P. *Elmer Sperry: Inventor and engineer*. Baltimore: Johns Hopkins University Press, 1994.

Hunter, James M. *Perspective on Ratzel's political geography*. New York: University Press of America, 1983.

Irvine, Valerie. *The king's wife, George IV and Mrs Fitzherbert*. London: Hambledon & London, 2004.

James, Robert Rhodes. *Henry Wellcome*. London: Hodder & Stoughton, 1994.

Johnson, W. B. *The English prison hulks, etc*. London: Christopher Johnson, 1957.

Jones, Robert F. *"The King of the Alley": William Duer; politician, entrepreneur and speculator, 1768-1799*. Philadelphia: American Philosophical Society, 1992.

Juxon, John. *Lewis and Lewis*. London: Collins, 1983.

Kahan, S. *Music's modern muse: A life of Winnaretta Singer, princesse de Polignac*. Rochester, NY: University of Rochester Press, 2003.

Kauffman, C. M. *John Varley, 1778-1842*. London: B. T. Batsford, Ltd., 1984.

Kinross, John. "Jervois and the defence of Britain, 1860," *The Historian*, No. 47, Autumn 1995. London: The Historical Association.

Kirby, R. S. *The noble stockjobber*. London: R.S. Kirby, 1816.

Kybett, Susan Maclean. *Bonnie Prince Charlie : A biography of Charles Edward Stuart* . New York: Dodd, Mead, 1988.

Lefroy, Sir John Henry. *Autobiography of General Sir John Henry Lefroy*. London: printed for private circulation only, 1889.

Leopold, R. W. *Robert Dale Owen, a biography*. Cambridge, MA: Harvard University Press, 1940.

Lerski, H. H. *William Jay: Itinerant English architect 1792–1837*. Lanham, NY: University Press of America, 1983.

Lewis, James A. *Neptune's militia: The frigate* South Carolina *during the American revolution*. Kent, OH: Kent State University Press, 1999.

Linder, A. *The Swiss Regiment Meuron at the Cape and afterwards, 1781-1816*. Cape Town: Castle Military Museum, 2000.

Lomask, Milton. *Aaron Burr: The conspiracy and years of exile, 1805-1836*. New York: Farrar, Straus, Giroux, 1982.

Mackerras, Catherine. *The Hebrew melodist. A life of Isaac Nathan*. Sydney: Currawong Publishing Co., 1963.

MacNish, Robert. *The modern Pythagorean. A Series of tales, essay, and sketches, with the author's life by his friend, D. M. Moir*. Edinburgh: Blackwood & Sons, 1838.

Mann, Phyllis G. *Collections for a life and background of James Manby Gully, M.D.* Bosbury, Herefordshire: executors of Phyllis G Mann, 1983.

Marshall, Peter. "Lord Hillsborough, Samuel Wharton and the Ohio Grant, 1769-1775," *English Historical Review*, Vol. 80, 1965. London: Longman's.

Masterman, Lucy. *C. F. G. Masterman*. London: Frank Cass & Co. Ltd., 1968.

Maynard, Frederick W. *Descriptive notice of the works of the Arundel Society, 1869-1873*. London: Nichols & Sons, 1873.

McAllister, Ethel M. *Amos Eaton*. Philadelphia: University of Pennsylvania Press, 1941.

McCalman, Iain. *Radical underworld: Prophets, revolutionaries and pornographers in London, 1795-1840*. Cambridge: Cambridge University Press, 1988.

McConnell, Anita. *R. B. Bate of the Poultry, 1782- 1847*. London: Scientific Instrument Society, 1993.

McJimsey, George. *Harry Hopkins: Ally of the poor, defender of democracy*. Cambridge, MA: Harvard University Press, 1987.

Millar, A. A. *Alexander Duff of India*. Edinburgh: Cannongate Press, 1992.

Miller, Karl. *Doubles: Studies in literary history*. Oxford: Oxford University Press, 1985.

Miller, Mary Ruth. *Thomas Campbell*. Boston: Twayne Publishers, 1978.

Morgan, Susan, and Noltie, Henry. *New work by Laura Owens, 1999-2000, and John Hutton Balfour's botanical teaching diagrams, 1840-1879*. London: Sadie Coles HQ, 2000.

Morris, A. D. *James Parkinson, his life and times*. Basel: Birkhauser, 1989.

Motion, Andrew. *Wainewright the poisoner*. Chicago: University of Chicago Press, 2000.

Nelson, Paul David. *Anthony Wayne, soldier of the early republic*. Bloomington, IN: Indiana University Press, 1985.

Nichols, Harold J. "The acting of Thomas Potter Cooke," *Nineteenth Century Theatre Research*, Vol. 5, No. 2, Autumn 1977. Alberta: University of Alberta.

Niven, John. *Gideon Welles: Lincoln's secretary of the navy*. Baton Rouge, LA: Louisiana State University Press, 1973.

Noll, Michael G. *Prince Maximilian's America: The narrated landscapes of a German explorer and naturalist*. (unpublished diss., University of Kansas, 2000).

Oettermann, Stephan. *The Panorama, history of a mass medium*. New York: Zone Books, 1997.

Palmer, Alan. *Bernadotte. Napoleon's marshal, Sweden's king*. London: John Murray, 1990.

Peachey, G. C. *John Heaviside*. London: St Martin's Press, 1931.

Pearce, Charles E. *The jolly duchess*. London: Stanley Paul & Co., 1915.

Pidgley, Michael. "Cornelius Varly, Cotman, and the graphic telescope," *"The Burlington Magazine*, Vol. 14, No. 836. London: The Burlington Magazine Publications Ltd., November 1972.

Pocock, Tom. *Captain Marryat, seaman, writer and adventurer*. London: Chatham Publishing, 2000.

Porter, Kenneth W. *John Jacob Astor: Businessman*. Cambridge, MA: Harvard Studies in Business History. Vol 1., 1931.

Presser, Stephen B. *The original misunderstanding: the English, the Americans and the dialectic of Federalist jurisprudence*. Durham, NC: Carolina Academic Press, 1991.

Quarles, Benjamin. "Lord Dunmore as liberator," *William and Mary Quarterly*, No. 15, 1958, pp. 494-507.

Randall, Willard Sterne. *Benedict Arnold: Patriot and traitor*. New York: Morrow, 1990.

Reeve, Henry. *Journal of a residence at Vienna and Berlin in the eventful winter 1805-6*. London: Longmans, Green & Co., 1877.

Reilly, Robin. *Josiah Wedgwood, 1730-1795*. London: Macmillan, 1992.

Reinikka, Merle A. *A history of the orchid*. Coral Gables, FL: University of Miami Press, 1972.

Richards, L. L., and Gill, A.T. "The Mayall story," *History of Photography*, Vol. 9, 1985. London: Taylor & Francis Ltd.

Ritchie, G. S. *The Admiralty Chart. British naval hydrography in the nineteenth century*. London: Hollis & Carter, 1967.

Robinson, Blackwell P. *William R. Davie*. Chapel Hill, NC: University of North Carolina Press, 1957.

Robson, Lloyd, updated by Roe, Michael. *A short history of Tasmania*. Melbourne: Oxford University Press, 1997.

Roche, John F. *Joseph Reed. A moderate in the American revolution*. New York: Columbia University Press, 1957.

Rolt, L.T.C. *The aeronauts: A history of ballooning, 1783-1903*. London: Longmans, 1966.

Rose, W. L. *Rehearsal for Reconstruction*. New York: Oxford University Press, 1964.

Roth, M. *The prevention and cure of many chronic diseases by movements*. London: John Churchill, 1851.

Sanders, M. L. and Taylor, Philip M. *British propaganda during the First World War*. London: The Macmillan Press Ltd., 1982.

Sargent, D. *Mitri: Or, the story of Prince Demetrius Augustine Gallitzin, etc*. New York: Longman's & Co., 1945.

Schaffer, Howard B. *Chester Bowles: New Dealer in the Cold War*. Cambridge, MA: Harvard University Press, 1993

Schull, Charles A., and Stanfield, J. F. "Thomas Andrew Knight, in memoriam," *Plant Physiology*, Vol. 14, No. 1, January 1939. London: Johnson Reprint Co. Ltd.

Schultz, Duane. *The Doolittle Raid*. New York: St. Martin's Press, 1988.

Sessions, William K., and Margaret E. *The Tukes of York*. London: Friends Home Service Committee, 1971.

Sim, Katharine. *David Roberts R.A*. London: Quartet Books, 1984.

Sinclair, David. *Sir Gregor MacGregor and the land that never was*. London: Headline Publishing, 2003.

Slagle, Judith Bailey. *Joanna Baillie: A literary life*. London: Associated University Press, 2002.

Smith, Adrian. *Mick Mannock, fighter pilot. Myth, life and politics*. London: Palgrave in association with King's College, London, 2001.

Smith, E. H. *The diary of Elihu Hubbard Smith (1771-1798)*. Edited by James E. Cronin. Philadelphia: American Philosophical Society, 1973.

Smith, W. D. A. *Henry Hill Hickman, MRCS, 1800-1830*. Leeds: University of Leeds, 1981.

Southey, Robert, and Southey, Charles. *The life of the Rev. Andrew Bell*. London: John Murray, 1844.

Standage, Tom. *The Neptune file*. London: Allen Lane, 2000.

Stansfield, Dorothy A. *Thomas Beddoes M.D., 1760-1808, chemist, physician, Democrat*. Dordrecht, Holland: D. Reidel Publishing Co., 1984.

Starkey, P. and J., eds. *Travellers in Egypt*. London: IB Tauris, 1998.

Steele, Joan. *Captain Mayne Reid*. Boston: Twayne Publishers, 1978.

Stewart, Joyce, and Stearn, William T. *The orchid paintings of Franz Bauer*. London: The Herbert Press, 1993.

Street, Roger. *The pedestrian hobby-horse at the dawn of cycling*. Christchurch: Artesius, 1998.

Sypher, F. J. *Letters by Letitia Elizabeth Landon*. Ann Arbor, MI: Scholars' Facsimilies & Reprints, 2001.

Taylor, Bernard, and Clarke, Kate. *Murder at the priory. The mysterious poisoning of Charles Bravo*. London: Grafton Books, 1988.

Taylor, Hilary. *James McNeill Whistler*. London: New Orchard Editions, 1978.

Tilley, N. *The R.J. Reynolds Tobacco Company*. Chapel Hill, NC: University of North Carolina Press, 1985.

Tisdall, John. *Joshua Cristall, 1768-1847: In search of Arcadia*. Hereford: Lapridge Publications, 1996.

Tod, Robert. *Caroline Fox, 1819-1871*. York: William Sessions Ltd., 1980.

Tree, Isabella. *The bird man. The extraordinary story of John Gould*. London: Ebury Press, 1991.

Treneer, Anne. *The mercurial chemist. A life of Sir Humphry Davy*. London: Methuen & Co., 1963.

Tuell, Anne Kimball. *John Sterling, a representative Victorian*. New York: The Macmillan Company, 1941.

Ullmann, Alec. *The Sebring story*. London: Bailey Bros & Swinfen Ltd., 1969.

Vickers, Hugo. *Private World*. London: Harrods Publishing, 1995.

Walcott, C. H. *Sir Archibald Campbell*. Boston: Beacon Press, 1898.

Wallace, E. M. *The first vaccinator*. Wareham: Anglebury-Barlett Ltd., 1981.

Walthew, Kenneth. *From rock and tempest: The life of Captain George William Manby*. London: Geoffrey Bles, 1971.

Watkin, David. *The life and work of C. R. Cockerell*. London: A. Zwemmer Ltd., 1974.

Webster, John Clarence. *The life of Joseph Frederick Wallet Des Barres*. Sheldiac, NB: privately printed, 1933.

Webster, Sally. *William Morris Hunt (1824-1879)*. Cambridge: Cambridge University Press, 1991.

Weekley, Montague. *Thomas Bewick*. London: Oxford University Press, 1953.

White, R. *The Count de Montalembert: His life and writings*. London: Washbourne, 1867.

Whittington, Keith E. *Constitutional construction: Divided powers and constitutional meaning*. Cambridge, MA: Harvard University Press, 1999.

Willey, Keith. *Strange seeker: The story of Ludwig Leichhardt*. New York: St. Martin's Press, 1966.

Woodhouse, C. M. *The battle of Navarino*. London: Hodder & Stoughton, 1965.

Woodress, James *A Yankee's odyssey: The life of Joel Barlow*. New York: Greenwood Press, 1968.

Wright, Thomas, ed. *The works of James Gillray, the caricaturist, with the story of his life and times*. London: Chatto & Windus, 1873.

Wroth, Warwick. *Cremorne and the later London Gardens*. London: Elliot Stock, 1907.

Ziegler, Philip. *King William IV*. London: Cassell Publishers Ltd., 1971.

American National Biography. Oxford: Oxford University Press, 1999.

Dictionary of Scientific Biography. New York: Charles Scribners Sons, 1981.

The Grove Dictionary of Art. Oxford: Oxford University Press, 1996.

The New Grove Dictionary of Music. Oxford: Oxford University Press, 2000.

Oxford Dictionary of National Biography. Oxford: Oxford University Press, 2004.

INDEX

JAMES BURKE

"ONE OF ... S IN THE
WESTER... *...GTON POST*

"JAMES B... OF MINE."
— BILL GATES

What are t... of Arc, and
waxed-cardb... e Suez Canal
related to Tesla coils, P. T. Barnum, and the opera *Aida*? How does
one technological innovation unexpectedly lead to the next? In his
witty and intelligent style, bestselling author James Burke proves
that ideas do not exist in a vacuum, the unlikeliest subjects may
be connected, and that the distance between two points can be
a fascinating and illuminating journey.

Available wherever books are sold or www.simonsays.com

SIMON & SCHUSTER PAPERBACKS
A CBS COMPANY